Health Inequality

In memory of Nan Sinclair Patterson

'my soul to keep'

Health Inequality

An Introduction to Theories, Concepts and Methods

Mel Bartley

polity

Copyright © Mel Bartley 2004

The right of Mel Bartley to be identified as Author of this Work has been asserted in accordance with the UK Copyright, Designs and Patents Act 1988.

First published in 2004 by Polity Press in association with Blackwell Publishing Ltd.

Editorial office:
Polity Press
65 Bridge Street
Cambridge CB2 1UR, UK

Marketing and production:
Blackwell Publishing Ltd
108 Cowley Road
Oxford OX4 1JF, UK

Distributed in the USA by
Blackwell Publishing Inc.
350 Main Street
Malden, MA 02148, USA

ISBN: 0-7456 2779-X
ISBN: 0-7456 2780-3 (pb)

A catalogue record for this book is available from the British Library.

Library of Congress Cataloging-in-Publication Data
Bartley, Mel.
Health inequality : an introduction to theories, concepts, and methods / Mel Bartley.
p. cm.
Includes bibliographical references and index.
ISBN 0-7456-2779-X (hb) – ISBN 0-7456-2780-3 (pb)   1. Social medicine.
  2. Social classes – Health aspects. 3. Health status indicators. I. Title.
RA418 .B366 2003
362.1 – dc21
2003006083

Typeset in 10 on 12 pt Times NR
by SNP Best-set Typesetter Ltd., Hong Kong
Printed and bound in Great Britain by TJ International, Padstow, Cornwall

For further information on Polity, visit our website: www.polity.co.uk

Contents

List of Tables and Figures   vi

Acknowledgements   ix

1   What Is Health Inequality?   1

2   Measuring Socio-Economic Position   22

3   Figuring Out Health Inequality   35

4   Models of Aetiological Pathways, I: Behavioural and 'Cultural'
Explanations   64

5   Models of Aetiological Pathways, II: The Psycho-Social Model   78

6   Models of Aetiological Pathways, III: The Materialist Model   90

7   Models of Aetiological Pathways, IV: The Life-Course Approach   103

8   Social Ecology   116

9   Gender Inequality in Health   135

10   Ethnic Inequalities in Health   149

11   Health Inequality and Social Policy   164

References   179

Index   200

List of Tables and Figures

Tables

1.1 Health inequality in England and Wales, 1931–1991:
Standardized Mortality Ratios by Registrar-General's
Social Class (RGSC) in men aged 15–64   3

1.2 Class differences in mortality by different diseases,
1949–1953: Standardized Mortality Ratios in men aged
20–64 in England and Wales   4

1.3 Class differences in mortality by different diseases,
1991–1993: Standardized Mortality Ratios in men aged
20–64 in England and Wales   4

1.4 Trends in health inequality, England and Wales,
1931–1991: annual deaths per 100,000 in each
Registrar-General's Social Class (RGSC) in men
aged 25–64   5

1.5 Explanations for the relationship of social inequality to
health   16

2.1 (a) Wright class schema for those who own assets in the
means of production   25

2.1 (b) Wright class schema for those who do not own assets
in the means of production   25

2.2 Classification of Registrar-General's Social Classes
(RGSCs)   31

3.1 Direct standardization   44

3.2 Odds Ratio: depression by gender   47

3.3 Exposure and disease   49

3.4 Social class differences in disease before adjustment for smoking 50

3.5 Social class differences after adjustment for smoking 51

3.6 Odds of poor health before and after adjustment for smoking 52

3.7 Example of indirect standardization: Standardized Mortality Ratio 63

4.1 Cigarette smoking by Registrar-General's Social Class (RGSC) in men and women aged 20–74, 1998 65

4.2 Hypothetical relationship between social position, locus of control and health risk behaviour if the 'direct behavioural model' is accurate 67

7.1 Health by social class in adult life 107

7.2 Social class difference in health in adult life, adjusting for childhood poverty 108

7.3 Adult health inequality, adjusting for childhood poverty and educational attainment by age 21 109

7.4 Accumulation of health risk over the life course 114

8.1 Coefficient of variation measuring degrees of inequality in income for a more and a less unequal population 119

8.2 Health inequality and social ecology studies: typology of explanations 123

9.1 Registrar-General's Social Class (RGSC) by marital status in men and women in England aged 35–55, 1998 138

9.2 Difference in mean GHQ scores by gender for men and women aged 20–60, in full-time work in Registrar-General's Social Classes (RGSCs) II or IIINM and married 138

9.3 Self-rated health by gender in married, full-time working men and women aged 20–60 in lower managerial or clerical and sales occupations 139

9.4 Gender differences in rates of illness: married full-time workers aged 20–60 in lower managerial or clerical and sales occupations 140

10.1 Racial/ethnic disparities in mortality by cause: USA, 2000 155

10.2 Mortality by country of origin: England and Wales, 1989–1992 156

10.3 Mortality by country of origin and Registrar-General's Social Class (RGSC): men, 1991–1993 158

Figures

1.1 Change in health inequality, 1931–1991   7
1.2 Indirect selection model   10
3.1 Relationship between weight and calories   53
8.1 Smoking by income inequality   127

Acknowledgements

This book owes a great deal to my colleagues at the International Centre for Health and Society, in particular to Amanda Sacker, Pekka Martikainen, Archana Singh-Manoux, Meena Kumari, Mai Stafford, Paul Clarke and Eric Brunner for their expert advice. The work was financially supported by a UK Economic and Social Research Council Fellowship, number R000 27 1112. Data from the Health Survey for England, 1993 and 1998, were provided by the UK Data Archive – depositor: National Centre for Social Research; principal investigators: Office of National Statistics (1993 Survey), National Centre for Social Research and University College London, Department of Epidemiology and Public Health (1998 Survey); sponsor: UK Department of Health. The original data creators, depositors or copyright holders, the funders of the Data Collections and the UK Data Archive bear no responsibility for their further analysis or interpretation.

1

What Is Health Inequality?

Health inequality was put firmly on the map of both public policy and academic study with the publication in the United Kingdom of the Black Report in 1980 (Department of Health and Social Security, 1980; Townsend, Davidson and Whitehead, 1986). This compilation of data on the relationship of ill health and mortality, in England and Wales between the 1950s and the 1970s, showed that the prospects of death at most ages, and thereby of a long life, were strongly related to a measure of social and economic position referred to as 'social class'. In the British context, the term 'social class' created such a powerful popular image that then, and for many years afterwards, the relationship to health seemed to require little further explanation. Formally, social class was defined in the official British government reports, going back to 1931 and from which the Black Report took its facts and figures, as 'general standing in the community based on occupational skill'. Many other European nations' official statistical organizations use rather similar measures. In the United States, Canada and Australia the notion of social class is less familiar and less widely used in research. However, interest in, and concern about, health differences between people with more and less favourable situations in respect of income, prestige ('standing in the community') and education has continued to grow in most industrialized and many developing nations.

The purpose of this book is to offer an introduction to the theories, concepts and methods used in research on health inequality, most of which are common to different countries. It is intended to inform readers whose intellectual backgrounds and interests lie in arts, humanities, social sciences, journalism and policy debate and formulation. Consequently, it does not concentrate too closely on enumerating the results of all possible studies, which in any case emerge far too quickly to be well summarized in a book. There are a number of papers that I think have made a particularly important contribution to the body of research that readers might like to consult for themselves: it will be obvious from the text which these are. In addition, each chapter is followed by a short list of the books I have found most useful myself ('Further Readings'). But the aim is to equip readers to make their own judgements of studies. However, the attempt to assemble a clear set of definitions of the concepts and methods used in health inequality research does in fact involve quite a lot of thinking that is useful for more experienced participants in these discussions. I have had to change some of my ideas about my own research agenda as a result of writing this book. This is in part because studies, carried out over a wide range of different countries and within different intellectual traditions, do not use terms in a consistent way. For example, in chapter 2, we will be looking in greater depth at what 'inequality' in general and 'social class' in particular might mean. We will see that the term 'inequality' is now defined and measured in a number of different ways, which are important to distinguish.

How Unequal is Health?

Subsequent chapters of this book present a basic introduction to some of the most common methods used in health inequality research; a discussion of different ways in which social inequality is defined and measured; and accounts of the different theoretical approaches to health inequality. This chapter gives some examples of what health inequality research in the past twenty years has told us about the size of social differences in health.

Table 1.1 shows the relationship of social class to mortality risk in the Black Report, and how this persisted in the following twenty years. The measure of social inequality used here is a traditional classification used in the UK: the Registrar-General's Social Classes or RGSC. (The Registrar-General is the official who presides over records of births and deaths.) The figures used to express class differences in the risk of death in tables 1.1–3 are called Standardized Mortality ratios or SMRs. The SMR takes account of the fact that there may be more older people in some classes than others (this might be the only reason for the higher death rates). This and other measures will be discussed more fully in chapter 3, but for the moment these can easily be understood as indicating how far above or below the average mortality for all men of working age any one

Table 1.1 Health inequality in England and Wales, 1931–1991: Standardized Mortality Ratios by Registrar-General's Social Class (RGSC) in men aged 15–64

RGSC	1931	1951	1961	1971	1981*	1991*
I professional	90	86	76	77	66	66
II managerial	94	92	81	81	76	72
1991 III routine non-manual						100
III routine non-manual and skilled manual	97	101	100	104	103	
1991 III skilled manual						117
IV semi-skilled manual	102	104	103	114	116	116
V unskilled manual	111	118	143	137	166	189

*ages 20–64
Source: Wilkinson (1986: 2, table 1.1); Drever, Bunting and Harding (1997: 98, table 8.2)

class falls. The figure of 100 is taken to represent the 'average' mortality for that particular population, so that 88 is considerably better than this, and 65 is much better, while 120 is distinctly worse than average.

At the time of its first publication, the Black Report produced considerable surprise. It was commonly held that in the late twentieth century 'diseases of affluence' were the main problem. Heart disease, linked to stress, a rich diet and a sedentary lifestyle, was widely regarded as a perfect example of such a disease. We can see from table 1.2 that at the very beginning of the National Health Service in Great Britain, in 1949–52, mortality from the type of heart disease regarded as due to an affluent lifestyle, 'coronary disease and angina', was indeed relatively higher in the professional and management classes I and II than in the other classes. Accountants and managers were thought to be subject to greater stress due to the responsibility of their jobs, and were known to have richer diets and to do sedentary work. In fact, doctors in the 1920s had recommended longer holidays and shorter working hours as the best way to prevent heart disease in their middle-class clients.

Table 1.3 shows social class differences in 1991 for the major causes of death. Comparing tables 1.2 and 1.3 shows that by 1991 the relative risk of death from heart disease was no longer higher in the professional and

Table 1.2   Class differences in mortality by different diseases, 1949–1953: Standardized Mortality Ratios in men aged 20–64 in England and Wales

RGSC	Coronary disease/angina	Diabetes	Cancers	TB	Influenza	Pneumonia	Bronchitis	Ulcers
I	147	134	94	58	58	53	34	68
II	110	100	86	63	70	64	53	76
IV	79	85	95	95	102	105	101	99
V	89	105	113	143	139	150	171	134

Source: Townsend and Davidson (1982: 62, table 5) [The Black Report]

Table 1.3   Class differences in mortality by different diseases, 1991–1993: Standardized Mortality Ratios in men aged 20–64 in England and Wales

RGSC	Ischaemic heart disease	Diabetes	Cancers	TB	Pneumonia	Bronchitis	Ulcers
I	63	54	78	32	58	44	54
II	73	70	79	47	69	43	50
IV	121	114	116	141	108	137	125
V	182	214	165	285	197	268	296

Source: based on Drever, Bunting and Harding (1997: 122, tables 10.2–4, 10.7, 10.8, 10.9)

management classes, and that class differences had also increased for the other diseases.

Over the period from 1931 to 1991, the 'absolute risk' of death at all ages below 75 (that is, the risk of death for everyone in the population of England and Wales) was falling constantly. At the same time, the risk for those in less privileged social circumstances (social classes IV and V) was tending to rise *relative to the average risk and to the risk for those in more favoured situations.*

An alternative way to look at the sort of data first presented by the Black Report, and follow these trends up to the present day, is to consider what happened to men in different age groups within each social class. Doing this allows us to understand a little more about the way health inequality has changed over time. This can be done using a simple rate per 100,000 in each age group, rather than the SMR. The advantage of looking at these 'age-specific rates' is that we can use them to compare one time-period to another. The SMR compares mortality risk in each social class to an 'average' for each particular time-period. So it is not possible to compare one time with another. By examining age-specific rates we can

Table 1.4 Trends in health inequality, England and Wales, 1931–1991: annual deaths per 100,000 in each Registrar-General's Social Class (RGSC) in men aged 25–64

		Registrar-General's Social Class			
Age	**Year**	**I**	**II**	**IV**	**V**
25–34	1931	288	283	360	374
	1951	147	112	172	224
	1961	82	81	119	202
	1971	65	73	114	197
	1981	54	62	106	204
	1991	39	57	96	187
35–44	1931	439	468	609	667
	1951	241	232	291	417
	1961	166	177	251	436
	1971	168	169	266	394
	1981	114	131	233	404
	1991	101	111	195	382
45–54	1931	984	1,021	1,158	1,302
	1951	792	706	725	1,041
	1961	535	545	734	1,119
	1971	506	564	818	1,069
	1981	398	462	728	1,099
	1991	306	314	545	916
55–64	1931	2,237	2,347	2,340	2,535
	1951	2,257	1,957	2,105	2,523
	1961	1,699	1,820	2,202	2,912
	1971	1,736	1,770	2,362	2,755
	1981	1,267	1,439	2,082	2,728
	1991	953	1,002	1,620	2,484

Source: Blane, Bartley and Davey Smith, 1998

see how risk in each social class changed over time. Unfortunately, it is not possible to investigate health inequality in women in the same way. This is because social class is defined in terms of occupation, and women's occupations are very badly recorded in official statistics. Health inequality in women is further discussed in chapter 9.

Table 1.4 shows the numbers of annual deaths per every 100,000 men in each social class and age group each year around the times of the censuses of 1931, 1951 (there was no census in 1941 because of the Second

World War), 1961, 1971, 1981 and 1991. We use deaths per 100,000 because in some age groups death is very rare, so that a percentage would be tiny: for example, only 0.0039 annual deaths of men aged 25–34 in social class I at the time of the 1991 census. This table shows how sharply death rates have fallen, especially in younger men and in RGSC I and II. We can see that in the youngest age group in RGSC I, aged 25–34, 299/100,000 men died in 1931 and only 39/100,000 in 1991, a decrease of 86 per cent. There was also a large decrease, of around 50 per cent, in RGSC V. This can be compared to what happened in age group 55–64. Here, in RGSC I, there were 2,237/100,000 deaths in 1931 and 953 in 1991, a 57 per cent decrease. But in RGSC V, 2,535/100,000 in 1931 fell minimally to 2,484/100,000 in 1991, a decrease of only 2 per cent. As a result of the much greater decline in the death rate in RGSC I than in RGSC V, the amount of inequality between the classes increased.

Figure 1.1 shows these trends in a graphical form. Here, it is easier to see what happened. Each small graph represents an age group. Because there are such large differences in mortality between younger and older age groups, each graph has a different left-hand axis. The top (maximum death rate) figure doubles in each one. In the graph for age group 25–34, the left-hand axis goes from zero to 400. In age group 35–44, the left-hand axis goes from zero to 800, then from zero to 1,600 in the next age group, and from zero to 3,200 in the oldest group. The graphs show how, on the whole, death rates were falling in all classes. However, in RGSC V among the 55–64 age group, this was not the case: here, there was actually an increase after 1931, and the rate did not fall below the 1931 level until 1991 (Blane, Bartley and Davey Smith, 1998). At each time, and for each age group, there were clear inequalities between the classes. Different nations have different traditions for measuring health inequality. In the United States attention has centred more on education and race or ethnicity, and the more widely used term is 'health disparity'. But the phenomenon is clearly to be seen. In 1999, the death rate for Americans with less than twelve years of education, at 585 deaths per 100,000 persons, was well over double that for those with thirteen years or more (219 per 100,000, after taking account of age). The death rate for Black Americans in this year, at 1,147 per 100,000 also exceeded that for White Americans (860 per 100,000) (USA, 2002). In the late 1990s, Americans with a high school education (those who stay until the end of secondary schooling) could expect to live nearly five years longer than those who left school before this, and White Americans to live over six years longer than Black American people (Wong et al., 2002).

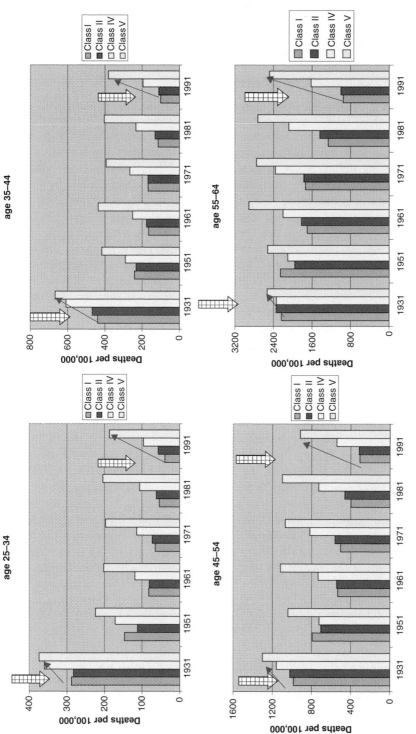

Figure 1.1 Change in health inequality, 1931–1991

Why Health Inequality?

The Black Report's explanations

In 1980, the Black Report assembled a lot of this kind of data from official public health reports and created an overview of links between health
and social class that had not previously been visible even to doctors
working with individual patients. It was, however, part of a far longer tradition of public health commentary which had been used in political
debates since the nineteenth century. Public health reformers had long used
differences in the risk of death due to infectious diseases to argue for and
against the need for public investment in sewage, water supply and sanitation. The emphasis in this work was on differences between poorer and
richer geographical areas, between the country and the town, between
market towns and industrial cities. Because these earlier 'Sanitary Reports'
were read as part of a highly political debate over large amounts of tax-
payers' money, their methods came under close examination. Did areas
with dirty water have higher mortality just because they contained different sorts of people? Were the inhabitants of these areas condemning themselves by their feckless drinking habits and lack of domestic cleanliness?

Facts and figures ('data') on health differences between groups of
people have always been debated, because they have led to politically significant conclusions. As a result of this, the degree, even the very existence,
of differences in health between more and less advantaged people have
been topics for strong argument. The findings of the Black Report in the
UK were no different. Sanitation was an accepted fact by the 1970s, of
course. There were two relevant political issues at the time the report was
compiled. One of these was the doubt that had been raised over the effectiveness of a National Health Service, to which all citizens have free access.
By 1980, British citizens had had access to health care paid for from
general taxation for over thirty years. It was a shock to find that health
inequality not only still existed but also seemed (as we have seen) to have
increased in a situation where everyone could get health care without
payment at the time of the illness (Morris and Heady, 1955). The second
political issue raised was that of income distribution. Income inequality
was still very much a fact of life in the welfare states of Great Britain and
other European nations in the 1970s, despite progressive taxation and the
provision of social services. However, income inequality had fallen from
pre-war levels, and was not thought to be large enough literally to affect
the length of life. In the eyes of some commentators, the fact that it did
so brought into question the usefulness of both the large amounts of
public money spent on health services and of what was regarded by some
as the very high taxes paid by the rich.

The Black Report and all the following studies during the 1980s put forward three different types of explanation for health inequality (Blane, 1985; Davey Smith, Bartley and Blane, 1990; Davey Smith, Blane and Bartley, 1994). One of these was based on a 'material' interpretation: that low income and its consequences could be the cause. The research relevant to this explanation will be discussed in more detail in chapter 6. The second explanation put forward was a 'cultural-behavioural' one, which laid emphasis on the possibility that different cultures might be prevalent in lower income groups or less privileged social classes (discussed more fully in chapter 4). People in manual occupations and lower income groups were believed, for reasons that were not widely discussed, to share a culture that promoted behaviours such as smoking, unhealthy diet and low levels of physical activity. Why there might be class differences in such cultural practices was seldom asked. At the time, however, it seemed that if health differences could be attributed to culture, the troublesome issue of income inequality could be avoided.

The third possible explanation for the persistence of health inequality in a welfare state was 'selection'. This idea was somewhat similar to Darwin's 'natural selection'. People were regarded as gaining access to high incomes and privileged occupations by means of a kind of struggle involving 'the survival of the fittest'. One version of this, the simplest, held that people with poor health in childhood and adolescence were more likely to find themselves in the less privileged social classes as adults. So the son of a wealthy businessman, lawyer or doctor, if he were a sickly child, would end up as a miner or bricklayer. The relationship of class to health was therefore nothing to do with conditions in the social classes themselves. Those in lower-paid, manual jobs were already more likely to be ill because they had always been. This version of the selection explanation is usually referred to as 'direct selection' (Fox, Goldblatt and Adelstein, 1982; Wadsworth, 1986). It may seem a bizarre idea that people in poor health from childhood or adolescence would be more likely to find their way into such occupations as mining, building or labouring (Fox, Goldblatt and Jones, 1985; Power et al., 1990). For this reason a more commonly held version of this explanation was that of 'indirect selection'. This was a more complex idea (Blane, Davey Smith and Bartley, 1993; Marmot et al., 1997; van de Mheen, 1998). Could it be that people with different amounts of 'potential' for good health found their way into the less privileged social classes? Did those with higher intelligence, better coping styles, or more stable personalities gravitate towards the social classes with higher levels of occupational skill? Given the definition of social class in official statistics, it seemed quite logical that people with greater intelligence and energy in early life would gain access to higher-paid, higher-status or more skilled jobs, and these in turn had a higher 'standing in the community'. These

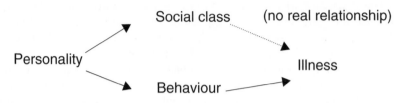

Figure 1.2   Indirect selection model

people would also have the ability to manage their consumption, leisure and use of health services in a more health-promoting manner. The implications for political debates of the selection explanations were similar to those of the cultural-behavioural explanation: inequalities in income, housing, stress or hazardous working conditions were not responsible (see figure 1.2). Various versions of selection explanations will arise throughout the discussions of theoretical frameworks in the following chapters.

Genetic explanations

The Black Report did not consider genetic explanations for health inequality, perhaps for two reasons. In the days before the sequencing of the human genome, there was far less interest in genetics than there is nowadays. Also, twenty-five years ago when the work was being done, memories of the Holocaust were perhaps fresher in people's minds, certainly in the minds of the report's authors who had fought in the Second World War. The idea that any important differences between human beings could be due to biological inheritance was linked in their minds to the policies of ethnic cleansing and to the slaughter of persons with disabilities carried out under Hitler. In the 1970s, few social scientists would have sympathized with the idea that illness was more prevalent in people who were socially or economically disadvantaged because of genetic inheritance. On the contrary, the defeat of Fascism had been accompanied by a commitment to provide better living and working conditions for less privileged people and by a widespread questioning of social inequality. The 'selection' arguments I have outlined above were the nearest to a genetic explanation for health inequality that were put forward. Even in this case, there was no claim that the illness that might cause people to be poorer and to live shorter lives was 'inherited'. Times have changed, however, which means that it is necessary at least to address the possibility that health inequality could be in some sense genetic in origin.

The best example of the difficulty in getting the facts to fit a genetic theory is to be seen in table 1.2, concentrating not on the differences between the social classes but on an important similarity. Here, we saw that over the seventy-year period from the 1920s to the 1990s death rates in young men of all social classes, and in older men in the more advantaged classes, fell dramatically. As any geneticist will tell you, genetic changes in a population of humans or animals take many generations to evolve. It is simply not possible for the kind of changes in mortality we see in table 1.2 to have taken place because of genetics. This kind of change can only happen when there are great changes in the environment.

A more sophisticated appreciation of the application of genetics to the understanding of health inequality would have to take account of what it is that genes actually do. This cannot be attempted here. Holtzman has written a clear but comprehensive account of the problems involved in claiming that health inequalities are genetic (Holtzman, 2002). To outline briefly one of its main points, let us take the idea that some characteristic that would fit a person to be a member of a privileged social group is 'caused by a gene'. A gene has several alleles; if it is the gene for eye colour, there will be an allele for blue eyes, one for brown eyes and so on. Each allele 'codes for', or influences, a protein, and it is this protein that in its turn influences the colour of a person's eyes. This 'influence' of the protein is itself complicated, and the form the 'influence' takes is very variable, depending on what characteristic we are talking about. It may be that the protein works as an enzyme (facilitating some other chemical reaction), or it may act as a hormone or a transporter of other molecules. Sometimes all that an allele will do is make another gene do something different from what it would otherwise have done. So that, even if you inherited an allele of one particular gene that meant you were not susceptible to a certain illness, you would only be less likely to contract this illness than other people who were exactly like you in all other respects. This is because what the allele does depends on all kinds of other genes and, in many cases, also on the environment. A striking example given by Holtzman is what happens to women who have the BRCA alleles that increase the risk of breast cancer. Of women with the high-risk allele born before 1940, 38 per cent got the disease, but as many as 69 per cent of those born after 1940 did so. Nobody knows why this is. But although the great difference between women with and without the relevant BRCA gene may be 'due to genetics', the difference in disease risk between women with the same gene but born at the earlier rather than the later time cannot be. The very size of the genetic difference itself seems to depend on some kind of change in the environment, or perhaps in lifestyles, that happened quite quickly.

The complexity of how genes actually work also makes it hard to argue that complex characteristics are more common in one social group than in another because of inheritance. If we look at a characteristic like 'leadership potential' or 'intelligence', this would involve so many genes and such complex relations between them that, even if a person's high income were due to some set of genetic influences, there would be very little chance of them passing all of this on to their offspring. The idea that health inequality is genetic needs not only 'favourable' psychological characteristics but also favourable health to be passed on from one generation to the next, which is even more unlikely.

However, the notion that health inequality exists because, somehow or other, people with more money, power and status are just 'superior' to other people and therefore bound to be healthier, is a very powerful one. It reappears in various different forms throughout the body of research on health inequality and therefore will keep reappearing in this book, mostly in the form of arguments about 'selection'. These are arguments about the effect on health inequality of characteristics that individuals have from early life or from birth. But in many cases similar arguments apply to thinking about genetic causes of health inequality.

Contemporary social and environmental explanations

There are three theories for the persistence of health inequality that have developed since 1980, as more studies were carried out and as the debate became more international in its scope, and these will be dealt with in detail in later chapters. Of these, the *'psycho-social' model* relates to the psychological effects of the experience either of stressful conditions at work or home or of low social status (Schnall, Landsbergis and Baker, 1994; Elstad, 1998; Theorell et al., 1998). Some researchers, whose studies have laid emphasis on 'materialist' issues (such as working conditions), were not convinced that chemicals, fumes and other hazards were enough to explain health differences between more and less privileged workers. Large differences in health and life expectancy were even found in people working in office-based organizations with none of the classical industrial hazards (Marmot et al., 1991). According to this model, whether we are looking at circumstances in the present or in the previous life course of the individual, we need to give at least as much attention to the causes of psychological stress as physical danger. Such stresses may include the social rather than the physical characteristics of the work environment. These include the amount of control and autonomy over the work a person has to do (Bosma et al., 1997), how routine the work is, how much support is available from co-workers (Johnson et al., 1996), and relationships to supervisors (Lynch et al., 1997a). The extent to which individuals feel adequately rewarded for the amount of work they do has also been a focus of enquiry (Siegrist et al., 1990, 1992; Bosma et al., 1998). This research will be further discussed in chapter 5.

Additional evidence for the importance of psycho-social factors has come from a different strand of research that has compared health in populations with greater and lesser degrees of income inequality. Wilkinson and others (Kaplan et al., 1996; Wilkinson, 1996; Kawachi et al., 1997) have presented evidence to show that where the differences in income between rich and poor are greater, health is better and life expectancy longer for the whole population. One explanation for why this might be is that social relationships are more favourable to good health in more economically equal societies. The research on income inequality and health will be more fully explored in chapter 8.

The psycho-social model of explanation has some promise to help us integrate the individual- and group-level studies with the income-distribution studies. Perhaps it is not the amount of money you earn, but how you feel about the status that this gives you in society, that influences your health. This might in turn be influenced by how many people earn a lot more than you do. Likewise, perhaps it is not how much you earn at work which is important for your health, nor the physical conditions under which you earn it, but how your work conditions and relationships make you feel day to day. These ideas seem plausible to many people, simply on the grounds of their personal experience: it certainly feels much worse to have to go in day after day to a workplace where things feel out of control and where people's relationships are unsupportive than one in which work is stimulating and a source of satisfaction. Likewise, perhaps being able to afford only a second-hand car and mass-produced, inexpensive clothes is a less potent source of stress in a society where most people are in the same situation, or where the main sources of prestige in the community arise from non-material values.

The *life-course explanation* for health inequality was not put forward in the original Black Report, but has developed in the 1990s. It only became possible because of studies that were not available to the authors of the Black Report. The British Birth Cohort studies and other longitudinal studies followed the lives of people over long periods of time, sometimes from birth. There are five major longitudinal studies in the UK: cohorts of people born in 1946, in 1958, in 1970, and in the millennium year 2000; and a large group of people of all ages in 1971. The 'life-course approach' was not only a new type of explanation, but also made possible new explorations of the older ones. One of the most important aspects of the life-course approach was the suspicion that the chances of good or poor health were influenced by what happened to people in very early childhood and even before they were born (Barker, 1992; Barker and Clark, 1997). For the first time, researchers could actually investigate whether sick children were more likely to find themselves in less skilled jobs as adults (Wadsworth, 1986, 1997; Power et al., 1990). It is possible to measure health in cohort members when they are children and to see if this predicts their social class membership, income and employment patterns as adults. It is also possible, though more difficult, to measure the factors which have been claimed as the basis for 'indirect selection'. We can see whether children who, although healthy, had more troublesome behaviour were more likely to end up in less advantaged social and economic circumstances later on, and to have less healthy behaviour (Caspi et al., 1998). Chapter 7 will examine life-course explanations in more detail.

The *'neo-materialist' explanation* for health inequality pays less attention to the individual. Like the studies of income inequality of Wilkinson and colleagues, it pays more attention to whole societies and how they differ. Neo-materialists look at differences between societies in social policies and institutions (Davey Smith, 1996; Lynch, 2000; Osler et al., 2002). On the whole, countries where income differences between richest and poorest are smaller provide more generous benefits to those unable to work. They also tend to have better public health, education and transport provision. In countries with these kinds of policies, individuals with lower incomes are not thereby excluded from reasonable levels of education, health and social participation. We can investigate how important factors such as the provision of high quality public services, generous welfare benefits and pensions might be in producing health inequality by comparing health differences in nations with different policies in these respects.

Provision of health services might be regarded as a 'neo-material' factor. Countries where there was more emphasis on equality might also be expected to provide better health care for people with lower incomes. Research up to the present does not support the idea that health services themselves are an important reason for health inequality, however. The work of McKeown (1966), while itself controversial (Colgrove, 2002; Link, 2002), revealed many years ago that the greatest decrease in the killer diseases of the nineteenth and early twentieth centuries, such as typhus and TB, took place before the development of effective treatments. The numbers of doctors or of hospital beds or high-tech machinery in a nation do not seem to be important reasons for health inequality. At the beginning of this chapter we saw that one reason why the Black Report was such a shock was that it showed that health inequality had widened since the coming of the UK's National Health Service. The availability of the best of medical care to people of all income groups free at the time of use had done nothing to reduce health inequality. As medical technology improves, this may be changing. However, the aetiology (causation) of the most common causes of mortality and disability in modern industrial societies almost always involves processes that take place over a very long period of the life course. By the time anything which looks like a recognisable disease appears (a heart attack, a visible tumour), it is often too late for cure. These diseases have to be combated by preventive measures extending over many years, such as protection from hazardous environments and lifestyles.

Perhaps potentially the most important 'neo-material' factor of all is the standard of publicly subsidized housing available to those with lower incomes. Unfortunately, there is relatively little research on the role played by housing quality in the causation of disease (Lloyd, 1991; Eng and Mercer, 1998). We will see later on that one of the great puzzles in the academic writing on this subject is why health inequality seems lower, at least in Europe, in the southern nations around the Mediterranean, such as Spain, Italy and Greece (Kunst, 1997; Mackenbach et al., 1997). These are not particularly rich or egalitarian countries. The most popular explanation for their lower levels of health inequality is the 'Mediterranean diet'. However, climate may have some relevance as well, in that cheaper housing will not expose its residents to cold and damp to the same extent as it does in more northern regions (Blane, Mitchell and Bartley, 2000; Mitchell, Blane and Bartley, 2002).

Provision of education of high quality to children from all income groups, good facilities for leisure exercise and public transport are all part of the 'neo-materialist' explanation as to why countries with less income inequality have better health. In particular, egalitarian countries seem to pay more attention to the well-being of parents and children. This may be particularly important in view of recent evidence on the significance of early life influences on health, even many years later in middle and older ages (Wadsworth, 1997; Kuh and Ben-Shlomo, 1997; Davey Smith et al., 1997). It may be that neo-material factors exert much of their influence over different phases of people's lives, in such a way that any single misfortune a person might experience is less likely to result in a vicious spiral (Bartley, Blane and Montgomery, 1997; Krieger, 2001). Marital breakdown is less likely to result in poverty, for example; and a spell of unemployment is less likely to result in having insufficient money to heat one's home. This kind of idea might be described as a *'life-course political economy'* of health inequality.

We have seen that, combining the Black Report's explanations originating in the 1970s with more modern explanations, we can distinguish four types of influences that may be responsible for health inequalities between socio-economic groups (see table 1.5). These may be classified as

Table 1.5 Explanations for the relationship of social inequality to health

	Explanation type				
	Material	**Cultural/ behavioural**	**Psycho-social**	**Life course**	**Political economy**
Influences	Individual income determines diet, housing quality, polluted environment, dangerous work.	Differences in beliefs, norms and values mean that individual members of less advantaged social groups are less likely to drink alcohol moderately, abstain from smoking and take exercise in leisure time.	Status, control, social support at work or at home, balance between effort and reward influence health through their impact on body functions.	Events and processes starting before birth and during childhood may influence both physical health and the ability to maintain health. Health and social circumstances influence each other over time.	Political processes and distribution of power affect provision of services, quality of physical environment and social relationships.

material, cultural-behavioural, psycho-social and life course. But these explanations do not have to be mutually exclusive. It is likely that they need to be understood in combination with each other, although this creates a very complex task. In the life-course accumulation model, exposure to any of these types of risk factor may build up across the whole of life, the amount of exposure being linked to a person's position in society. What is important about being in a certain social class or status or income group is the longer-term experience of being in this group. The life-course model of the social influences on health proposes that each additional 'advantage' in terms of material living standards or psychosocial conditions, either experienced by oneself in the present, in childhood, or by one's parents, may produce a higher chance of good health and long life. Likewise, each additional 'disadvantage' adds to the risk of poor health and a shorter life. A life-course political economy of health inequality would regard lifetime exposures, in turn, as structured by social and economic policies and institutions.

These different explanations form the basis for understanding health inequality at the present time, at least in the more economically developed nations. Although we can see that the explanatory models proposed for health inequality have changed and become more complex, there still remain many intellectual gaps. Concepts as central as that of 'inequality' itself are in fact not clear, and careful examination of existing studies shows that the term is used inconsistently. Closely linked to this problem is the question of how we define 'advantage and disadvantage'. The terms 'advantage' and 'privilege' are used throughout this account because of their connotation of the relative. Lack, or possession, of an object or an attribute (a car, high mathematical ability) are not in themselves advantages or disadvantages. All of this depends on the context within which the individual, their income and their material possessions are located. This context in turn may affect, or be affected by, norms and values in the wider society. And these norms and values may simultaneously give rise to economic and social policies, which make a major difference to the meaning to the individual of whatever they do or do not possess.

Chapter 2 will argue that there are three major forms taken by socioeconomic inequality: financial (income and wealth), employment relations and conditions, and prestige. These are distinct concepts and have different, even if related, effects on health. It is quite possible that an individual may be low on one while being medium or high on one or both of the others, and these effects need to be understood in combination. But even if we accept that income, wealth, prestige and employment relations may matter in different ways for health inequality, why should this be? Chapter 3 will outline some of the most commonly used methods in health inequality research. The purpose of this chapter is to make it easier for readers to evaluate the original research on health inequality for themselves. Chapters 4 to 7 consider in more detail each of the explanatory models that can be applied to understanding health inequality: behavioural, material, psycho-social and life course. Chapter 8 discusses a separate but very important aspect of research on health inequality: the work that examines relationships between the degree of income inequality in different countries or areas and the health and life expectancy of their populations. Chapters 9 and 10 extend the explanatory models to look at health differences between men and women, and at the effects on health of the discrimination suffered by ethnic, national and religious groups. Finally, chapter 11 looks at the ways in which the findings of research on health inequality are beginning to be used in the formulation of social and health policies in some countries.

Inequality and Identity

It is not the purpose of this book to set out a general theory of health inequality. Rather, it aims to provide readers with the wherewithal to understand and evaluate arguments and explanations put forward by other researchers (and possibly to think up their own explanations). However, the researcher should admit her own biases and prejudices, and of course I do have my own hunches about why health inequality exists and is so persistent in the face of rising living standards and improving general levels of health. These hunches centre around the problems involved in the negotiation of personal identity (Bunton and Burrows, 1995; Langman, 1998; Howard, 2000).

Identities are shifting and have highly variable sources, making generalization hazardous (Giddens, 1991). But it is possible that the 'psycho-social' and the 'behavioural' processes thought to be involved in health inequality, and even the importance of money, have their roots to some extent in problems of identity (Siegrist, n.d.). Where an individual's sense of identity is assured by the stable occupation of the 'central life roles' (Siegrist, 2000), such as worker, partner or parent, and/or by acceptance in a reasonably stable community, the cost of identity management is lower. But these sources of stability may have a high cost. Constraints on occupational choice or sexual behaviour or orientation are examples of such costs. Where there is no stable community of acceptance, or where restrictions on behaviour have been rejected by the individual, identity may depend more on outward symbolic display, which needs to be constantly repeated and updated. The individual gains little sense of inherent worth, just by 'being myself'. Large cities are places where the shackles of traditional role-performance may be gladly shaken off, but where making and retaining alternative sets of social ties may present other problems. Such circumstances may increase the importance of large numbers of material goods, and goods of the right culturally symbolic kind. Living in a fragmented society tends to be expensive.

Identity may be supported or threatened by any of the major forms of inequality. High prestige protects against adverse events of shorter duration. For example, living in a run-down student flat for a few years does not threaten someone from a secure middle-class family who knows they are sacrificing income at the present time in order to secure a satisfying, high-status long-term career. Security and autonomy at the workplace support a stable sense of self, even for people without high income or status. And income? As indicated above, this may act as much as a means to an end in terms of the prestige and security it can buy. Or in other cases, consumer goods bought with money may act as substitutes for other sources of stable identity. The implication of this is that money may be more important when autonomy, security, or other sources of support for identity are not present.

As societies modernize, institutional constraints exerted by religion, family, caste or clan loosen, and freedom for many (in particular, for everyone who is not an adult male of the 'majority' or dominant cultural and ethnic group) increases. But under these conditions the maintenance of stable identity may become more problematic. Social integration requires time and effort to be devoted to maintain identity-sustaining relationships. Identity-maintenance has traditionally depended on being able to exert superior power for those in dominant positions, and has been provided by women for everyone else. If traditional forms of dominance are breaking down and women's time is more occupied with paid employment and the 'public sphere', this changes. Along with greater individual freedom comes the necessity for every individual, male and female, and, increasingly, older children as well as adults, to do their own work in creating and maintaining the relationships that contribute to a sense of creditable identity. There is an ever-greater premium on the capacity for internal self-regulation and the management of one's own identity and the creation of one's own community.

Here again, a life-course approach offers useful sources of understanding. Those individuals whose experiences in their family of origin have given them an inner sense of security and the ability to form and maintain relationships may revel in the freedom of a less constrained community, even if social ties are looser (Beck, 1992). Those with fewer inner resources may adopt images from the mass media as a substitute source of identity. For these individuals, periods with *relatively* little money can be catastrophic for the sense of self. If self-esteem depends on possession of symbolic goods, these will be given priority over, for example, nutrition and warmth. And the cost of imitating cultural, mass-media images is what will determine in part how much health will suffer during financially insecure periods.

One way of understanding the dynamic that produces health inequality may be in terms of the vital importance of social participation to identity, and the effect of social inequality on the costs of social participation. But wider social inequality has another effect. This is the influence of the experience of inequality on the consumption of mood-altering substances. By this is not only meant drugs such as heroin and cocaine, or even alcohol. In the early 1980s, Cameron and Jones termed alcohol and tobacco 'Drugs of Solace' (Cameron and Jones, 1985). They argued that while doctors and health educators see alcohol and tobacco as 'a problem', for those who use them they are in fact a solution. To these, I would add a wide range of 'comfort foods', all of which are consumed to dull the experiences of uncertainty and isolation.

The importance of the struggle for a stable identity in the causation of health inequality is shown by the age-patterned nature of many of these influences. Very large numbers of adolescents become obsessed with expensive consumer items, and take up smoking and the use of recreational drugs. It is a period when the struggle for identity is at its most acute and the outcome is uncertain. As they grow older, adolescents from the more socially (and perhaps emotionally) favoured backgrounds tend to moderate their attachment to these – they find other sources of identity in work and in stable adult relationships. Difficulty in establishing adult identity can come from a number of different sources: disturbed relationships of the parents and inability to find work which is sufficiently well paid to make independent life possible are two of the most common. For those with very disturbed emotional backgrounds, even great riches may not be sufficient to feed an unsuccessful quest for identity, as is frequently seen in media 'stars' and in members of rich and aristocratic families who engage in self-destructive forms of behaviour.

In what follows we shall see whether existing research on health inequality can be understood with the help of a model of accumulated biological, psychological and social advantages and disadvantages, within the contexts of different national and local economies and cultures. There are a vast number of potential combinations of circumstances that individuals may pass through in their life course, all of which may contribute to healthy life expectancy many years in the future. The challenge for research is to arrive at adequate measures of these, and adequate methods for putting them together in causal models. We shall then be able to begin taking the causal nexus apart and reducing health inequality.

FURTHER READING

Still the classic study of health inequality in the United States
Kitagawa, E. M., and Hauser, P. M. S., *Differential Mortality in the United States: A Study in Socioeconomic Epidemiology*. Cambridge, Mass.: Harvard University Press, 1973.

The original British reports that started the debate on health inequality
Townsend, P., Davidson, N., and Whitehead, M., *The Black Report and the Health Divide*. Harmondsworth: Penguin, 1986.

A more recent and very useful compilation of work from the United States
Amick III, B. C., Levine, S., Tarlov, A. R., and Chapman Walsh, D., *Society and Health*. Oxford: Oxford University Press, 1995.

The most recent official British government report on health inequality
Drever, F., and Whitehead, M., *Health Inequality*. London: Office of National Statistics, HMSO, 1998.

A collection of papers that combines British and American thinking on both health inequality and the relationship of health to income distribution
Marmot, M., and Wilkinson, R., *Social Determinants of Health*. Oxford: Oxford University Press, 1999.

2

Measuring Socio-Economic Position

One of the most important messages of this book will be that we use oversimplified and poorly thought-out concepts and measures of social position and circumstances at our peril. When reading through research papers, it will be evident that the measures of social position used are many and various. With some honourable exceptions, they use terms such as 'social class', 'social status', 'socio-economic status' interchangeably. The measures used tend to be mainly (again, with honourable exceptions) based on convenience or on rather casually developed ideas about what might be important for health inequality. The convenience aspect of studies is often hard to avoid – some assemble data from massive national or international databases with no choice whatsoever as to the measures used. But studies specially designed to investigate health inequality have more opportunity to define their measures on the basis of clearly speci-fied hypotheses. What do we think is important for health inequality? And how should we best measure the important factors?

The most serious result of lack of attention to the definition and mea-surement of socio-economic position in studies of health inequality has been the difficulties this produces for understanding the mechanisms by which social circumstances may affect health. Without clear definitions of forms of inequality, we have little hope of tracing the pathways through which social inequality may affect health in individual people. As Breen and Rottman have pointed out: 'Even where class differences in outcomes are very stark – as in health – it is not obvious why they arise. And one consequence of our inability to tease out these linking mechanisms is that policy to address class inequalities is likely to be a very blunt instrument' (Breen and Rottman, 1995: 461). Literature on health inequality is cur-rently plagued by a plethora of terms that are intended as indications of a person's social position and circumstances, such as 'social class', 'social status' and 'socio-economic status'. There are just as many measures, any of which is likely to be attached to any of these terms: social class is measured in some studies according to education, for example, and social status is sometimes equated with either education or income. A first task, therefore, is to try and sort out the different concepts and measures, and establish a consistent set of links between them.

One way to begin to clarify our definitions and measures of social position and circumstances is to separate out 'social class', 'status (prestige)' and measures of material living standards, including income, and measures which are based on household and individual ownership of goods. The way to measure the last of these is relatively obvious: income can be used wherever possible, and in data sets, such as the UK censuses, which do not ask about income, alternatives, such as ownership of homes, cars and household amenities, are used. However, ways to measure both 'class' and 'status' are more problematic.

In this account I use two terms to refer to people's positions in the social and economic structure. I prefer to use the term 'socio-economic position' (SEP), to include class, status and material asset measures. I also use the term 'social position' to refer to class and status. These terms are proposed only as a tool for taking things forward, and are by no means a perfect expression of the underlying ideas. For example, income and assets are not really types of 'position' in society, although one's place on the income ladder (relative income) might be regarded in this way. Two people with the same economic circumstances in terms of monthly income, and whether or not they own their home and have a car, central heating, a computer and so on, may be in different socio-economic positions in terms of their social class, status or relative income. For this reason I also use the term 'socio-economic position and circumstances' to cover class, status, relative income ('positions') and absolute measures, such as income and ownership of assets.

It should also be noted that measures of social position are based, in one way or another, not on the characteristics of individuals but on the characteristics of their occupations. This raises a number of problems, the greatest of which is that of classifying the social position of people who are doing unpaid caring work, or who are retired, or who have either never had an occupation or only had one for a short time many years ago. These people can, of course, be classified according to their income, and can be given a 'socio-economic position' in terms of where that income places them in relation to others.

Measures of Social Position

There are two ways in which social position is usually represented: social class and social status or prestige. Although in many studies these two concepts have been used interchangeably, health inequality research now increasingly recognizes that these dimensions of inequality may not have the same relationships to health (or to different types of disease outcomes). When we understand what class and prestige are supposed to measure, we can see more clearly what kinds of effects they might be expected to have on health and how these effects may come about.

Social class

Within sociology, there is a long-standing debate on the nature and measurement of social class. Measures of social class are based on theories of social structure: people choose their measure according to the theory they prefer. The two most prominent theories of social structure used in studies that work with a concept of class are those of Marx and Weber. They divide occupations into groups according to typical employment conditions and relationships. These groups are the social classes. Both schools of thought agree on the importance of two things. The first is the ownership of assets, such as property, factories or firms. That is what determines whether a person needs to work at all or whether she or he is the owner of a business, land or other assets sufficient to make work for pay unnecessary. The second feature of social class which is of generally agreed significance is the relationship of all those who do have to work for a living to those who own and manage the establishments in which they work, and also to any others whose work they in turn may manage or supervise.

The American sociologist, Erik Olin Wright (1985, 1997), has devised a class schema that begins by distinguishing those who own property from those who do not. The second classificatory principle is the concept of 'organizational assets'. People with a certain occupation have more organizational assets if members of their occupational group are able to benefit from controlling the work of others by using their authority over them. For example, managers' control gives them access to much of the benefit that arises from the efforts of the workers they supervise, and requires very little, if anything, in return: this is their 'organizational asset'. Many people can think of managers who not only take the credit for their subordinates' increased productivity but also present their staff's new ideas as their own, to further their own careers. Wright's third classificatory principle is the idea of 'credentialled skill'. Skill certified by 'credentials' (qualifications) is, in

Table 2.1 (a) Wright class schema for those who own assets in the means of production

	Social class
Own enough capital to hire people and not work	Bourgeoisie
Own enough capital to hire workers but needing to work for themselves also	Small employers
Own enough capital to work for themselves but not to hire other workers	Petty bourgeoisie

Table 2.1 (b) Wright class schema for those who do not own assets in the means of production

Skill/credential assets	Organizational assets		
	High	**Some**	**None**
High	Expert managers	Semi-credentialled managers	Uncredentialled managers
Some	Expert supervisors	Semi-credentialled supervisors	Uncredentialled supervisors
None	Experts: non-managers	Semi-credentialled workers	Workers

his view, in a sense a form of 'property', which can be owned, and offered on the market, by those without any property assets such as land or factories. Those with credentials can use them in two main ways to influence their class position. They can offer them in exchange for a position where they will have a high level of 'organizational assets', that is, their claim to skill enables them to exploit the effort of subordinates to some degree. Or they can use their skills and credentials to establish themselves as independent or quasi-independent professionals. In this way, they avoid being exploited by others who have organizational assets. In his book *Classes*, Wright (1985) set out a twelve-class schema, as set out in tables 2.1 (a) and (b).

The definition of social class most widely used in British sociological and political research (though not in health research) is based rather more on the work of Weber than on the Wright schema, although there are considerable similarities between the work of the two classic theorists (Marshall et al., 1988). Goldthorpe originated this measure, and first used it in his work on social mobility in the UK (Goldthorpe, Llewellyn and Payne, 1980). It is described as combining occupations whose members would tend to have similar sources and levels of income, amounts of job security and chances of economic advancement, and who would have a similar location within systems of authority and control within businesses, and hence similar degrees of autonomy (Marshall et al., 1988). Erikson and Goldthorpe further developed the original Goldthorpe schema in order to conduct a large international comparative study of social mobility (Erikson and Goldthorpe, 1992). The most basic classificatory division in this schema is between those who are owners, either of a company or of property such as real estate or land, and those who are not. In this respect the Erikson-Goldthorpe schema resembles that of Wright. Within the group of 'owners' there are those who employ large numbers of others working for them, those with a few employees and those with none. Those who own no property or company may either be employees or self-employed workers. The much larger group of people who are employees has more sub-divisions. At the most basic level, they are divided according to the nature of their employment contract.

Erikson and Goldthorpe distinguish two basic forms of employment contract: the 'service contract' and the 'labour contract'. The service contract is what you find in managerial and professional work. Employees with this kind of contract of employment have to be trusted: their work cannot be supervised in any simple way by monitoring their time-keeping or how many nuts or bolts they have produced by the end of the day. In order to motivate performance, employees with this kind of job are offered more job security, salary increments and a progressive career as incentives to good and loyal service. In addition, this type of work entails a degree of command, either over the work of other people, or at least autonomy over one's own work. Workers with a service contract are usually paid monthly, may have share options or a similar stake in the profitability of the company, and seldom have to do things like clocking in and out. In contrast, employees with a labour contract perform work that is more easily monitored. They have little autonomy, and tend to be more closely supervised and restricted in their patterns of work. Payment is more closely tied to hours of work and, in many cases, to how much is produced in that time (piece rates and bonus rates). There is less likelihood of career progression, no annual salary increment, and job security is lower. As in the Wright schema, the Erikson-Goldthorpe (E-G) classification acknowledges that many occupations have a mix of these conditions, so that allocating them into classes is a matter of deciding which occupations more closely resemble each other in these respects (Evans, 1992).

The Erikson-Goldthorpe schema

1   Higher level professionals, administrators and officials; proprietors and managers in large firms

2 Lower level professionals, administrators and officials; higher level technicians; managers of small firms; non-manual supervisors
3 (a) Higher level routine non-manual workers
   (b) Lower level routine non-manual and service workers
4 (a) Small proprietors and self-employed with employees
   (b) Small employers and self-employed without employees
   (c) Farmers and self-employed workers in primary production
5 Lower level technicians and manual supervisors
6 Skilled manual workers
7 (a) Semi- and unskilled manual workers
   (b) Agricultural and primary production workers

The concept of skill is used to distinguish class groups in the E-G schema, as it is in the Wright schema, although not in the form of 'credentials'. Whereas Wright had concluded from his studies that the distinctions between 'white versus blue collar' or 'manual versus non-manual' divisions were not useful, the manual/non-manual divide does form part of the classificatory logic of the E-G schema.

The principles behind the E-G schema, of employment relations and conditions as the basis for defining social classes, have been further developed by the new class schema used in the 2001 censuses of England and Wales and of Scotland. This schema is known as the National Statistics Socio-Economic Classification or NS-SEC. The concepts underlying the E-G schema are further refined in the development of the NS-SEC. Most importantly, the notion of 'skill' and the manual/non-manual divide have disappeared from the classificatory principles. These principles have been made totally explicit. They are: the timing of payment for work (monthly versus weekly, daily or hourly); the presence of regular increments; job security (over or under one month); how much autonomy the worker has in deciding when to start and leave work; promotion opportunities; degree of influence over planning of work; level of influence over designing their own work tasks (Coxon and Fisher, 1999). Because it will be used for a wide range of official statistics as well as for research, the NS-SEC in its 'full' form has a large number of categories which can be combined in different ways according to the purpose at hand. A seven-category version is likely to be that most frequently used in reports and studies:

National Statistics Socio-Economic Classification
1 Higher managerial and professional occupations, including employers in large firms, higher managers, professionals whether they are employees or self-employed
2 Lower mangerial and professional occupations and higher technical occupations

3   Intermediate occupations (clerical, administrative, sales workers with no involvement in general planning or supervision but high levels of job security, some career prospects and some autonomy over their own work schedule)
4   Small employers and self-employed workers
5   Lower technical occupations (with little responsibility for planning own work), lower supervisory occupations (with supervisory responsibility but no overall planning role and less autonomy over own work schedule)
6   Semi-routine occupations (moderate levels of job security; little career prospects; no pay increments; some degree of autonomy over their own work)
7   Routine occupations (low job security; no career prospects; closely supervised routine work)

Extensive empirical work went into deciding which occupations to put in each social class. Questions covering each of the seven criteria were asked of some 60,000 citizens in the UK Labour Force Survey of 1997. Occupations could then be allocated into social classes according to the typical answers of members of each occupation to these questions. For example, among biological scientists 78.6 per cent had incremental pay and 76 per cent planned their own work; among kitchen porters the comparable percentages were 27 per cent and 3.8 per cent. As may be imagined, the amount of work involved in the construction of this measure was enormous, and it will be necessary to carry out regular updating of the classification as job conditions change over time, and altogether new occupations appear.

When we are asking 'is there a relationship of social class to heart disease?', therefore, we are asking what there might be about the relationships and conditions of employment in a certain type of occupation that could make people more at risk. The class measure that is chosen will determine which aspects of employment relations and conditions are being given more importance. So, for example, people may be in the same NS-SEC class but in different Wright classes because they have different 'credentials'.

Social status

The sociological definitions of social class described above are very different to what is often meant by it in lay terms. In everyday talk, people often use 'social class' to refer to what a sociologist would call 'status'. Unlike social class, the concept of status centrally involves the idea of a hierarchy or ranking 'from top to bottom' of society. The term 'status' is used often in everyday talk, and everyone thinks they know the meaning of the word. Sociologists and anthropologists use the synonymous term 'prestige' to refer to the differential ranking of respect and 'social honour' accorded to persons in a society. It may have many different sources: for example, the identity of one's parents, or one's ethnic origin. In Hindu cultures, fine gradations of prestige are represented by the caste system, based on the traditional occupations of extended kin groups (Beteille, 1992).

The clearest attempts to measure status in industrial societies have been by means of the development of so-called 'reputational measures'. These measures are worked out by giving people from the general population ('judges') a list of job titles and asking them to rank these in some kind of order (Duncan, 1961). Alternatively, the 'judges' may be asked to give judgement of status in terms of 'high', 'medium' and so on. Then either the job titles are given an average rank, or they are ordered according to how many people have voted them 'high'. These are obvious ways to make more objective the sorts of feelings that most people are thought to have about the degree of respectability or 'social honour' involved in various occupations.

There are, however, enormous problems in developing measures of prestige for very large numbers of occupations. How many 'judges' should be used? How many of the myriad occupations in a society is it fair or sensible to ask them to rank or to score? The original study of this kind was carried out by the National Opinion Research Center in the USA in 1947, and asked respondents to rank ninety occupations. But there are many hundreds of occupations in any society. One way around this, used in American research, was to find out the average income and education level of the jobs which had been given a score, and to use this to transfer a score to all other occupations (Duncan, 1961; Hollingshead, 1971; Nam and Terrie, 1982). Suppose, in other words, in the last big national study of prestige (using a panel of judges), a doctor had a rank of 2, and a bricklayer had a prestige rank of 9. Suppose also that doctors on average earned £50,000 a year and had twenty years of education while bricklayers earned £5,000 a year and had ten years of education. Then a new occupation arises, that of web page designers. On average, they have £25,000 a year and fifteen years of education, so their prestige score could be estimated at around 6 (because in terms of education and income they are about halfway between the doctor and the bricklayer).

In the USA, this process led increasingly to the practice of using combined income and education as the sole measure of social position, and calling this 'socio-economic status' (Featherman and Hauser, 1976). Income is obviously an 'economic' measure, and education is widely regarded as raising a person's status, more or less regardless of their income. For example, a highly educated scientist might be regarded as having a higher status than certain types of managers, or than stock-brokers who earn a great deal more than scientists. There are several different methods of using the information on education and income to derive socio-economic status scores, and some debate on what these might actually mean (Hauser and Warren, 1996). In recent work in the USA, as it has become clear that women and men with similar education do not obtain similarly paid jobs, some researchers have called for measures of social position to be independent of both education and income (Warren, Sheridan and Hauser, 1998). This is the position that I take in this book: if we want to measure status we need to use the results of studies that do in fact show how the prestige of different occupations is ranked in people's minds. If we want to measure other things, like income or education, then we can use other pretty obvious methods (such as asking people what their income is and how much education they had). If we want to look at these in combination, then we should use the separate measures in the same analysis, not bundle them all up into one measure. In this way we can explicitly examine whether, say, two groups of people with the same education but different income have different health.

An important measure of something very close to what we might think of as 'status', has been devised by a research group initially located at the University of Cambridge in the UK. In the early 1970s, a strikingly original paper on the nature of inequality was published in the prestigious scientific journal *Nature* (Stewart, Prandy and Blackburn, 1973). (It is not very common for sociological papers to be published in this journal.) The paper proposed a measure of social inequality that had been developed by direct observation of the ways in which people mixed together. The researchers found a set of clusters of occupations whose members tended to mix socially and to inter-marry. These clusters arranged themselves into a hierarchy, which the researchers describe as 'general social and material advantage'. The originators of the measure do not use the terms 'status' or 'prestige' to describe their scale. They describe the basis of the scale in these terms: 'Occupations are ranged in a hierarchy, without any clear boundaries between particular groupings of them, and this social hierarchy is associated with employment characteristics such that those at the higher levels tend to enjoy more favourable conditions than those lower down.' However, they do state that those who score similarly are more likely to 'mix together as equals' (Marsh and Blackburn, 1992). People in the occupations that cluster more closely together are those who regard each other as having equal standing in society; those in occupations which are more distant from each other regard each other as having more

Table 2.2 Classification of Registrar-General's Social Classes (RGSCs)

Class number	Description
I	Professional
II	Managerial
III non-manual (NM)	Skilled non-manual
III manual (M)	Skilled manual
IV	Semi-skilled manual
V	Unskilled manual

Source: Office of Population Censuses and Surveys, 1980

widely different standing. So, unlike the American status measures, the Cambridge scale does not depend on the judgements of people making decisions in the abstract about other people's occupations (Stewart, Prandy and Blackburn, 1980), but on observed patterns of how people actually appear to esteem each other as friends and potential spouses (Prandy, 1986; Prandy and Bottero, 1998).

Registrar-General's Social Class (RGSC): a noble relic

Although we have spent some time carefully thinking through concepts of class and status, we have not considered the most commonly used measure of social position in British research, the Registrar-General's social classification. This measure, or something regarded as very similar, is the most commonly used indicator of social inequality used in British studies of health inequality. Many other European nations have modelled their own classifications on it. Because it has been routinely used in British official statistics, I will in fact have to use it here for many of the examples given in the following chapters of the book. But we need to be very clear that the Registrar-General's class schema, like the term 'socio-economic status', creates intellectual pitfalls for the attempt to understand (as opposed merely to describe) health inequality.

The Registrar-General's classes are said to be based on either general standing in the community or occupational skill. The classification consists of six categories (see table 2.2). To those familiar with British research on health inequality, it may seem strange to reiterate yet again the names of the RGSCs. But now that we have discussed the concepts and measures of class and status that are widely used in social and political research, such as the E-G and Wright classifications, it is helpful to think a little more carefully about how these relate to the 'classes' distinguished by the Registrar-General's schema. The schema is in fact not a measure of class at all, in the sense used by Wright, Erikson and Goldthorpe or the NS-SEC. It is usually regarded as a hierarchy, that is, I is 'higher' than II, which is 'higher' than IIINM, and so on. There is an assumption that any form of non-manual work is 'higher' on this continuum than any form of manual work. There is the further assumption that any professional is 'higher' than any manager. This would mean that a junior doctor or a minister of religion, for example, would have a superior social position to that of a manager in a company regardless of their relative incomes or the amount of authority they exercise. Implicitly, it is clear that prestige is the underlying ordering principle which takes precedence over all other characteristics of occupations.

The Registrar-General's classification has at different times been officially described as a measure of 'general standing in the community', or of 'occupational skill'. Although this is never said in so many words, the assumption seems to be that occupations requiring more skill are held to be of higher 'standing in the community'. There is no evidence that the different Registrar-General's classes are actually widely regarded by the population as having different levels of general standing in the community, and no 'reputational' studies have been carried out equivalent to those in the USA to investigate perceptions of status among the general public. Nor have there been any studies to see whether the Registrar-General's classes are an accurate grouping of occupations with different levels of skill.

The Registrar-General's classification is a bit like aspirin: everyone knows that it works, but nobody knows why. So knowing that it works is of little help in further explanation, just as knowing about the effectiveness of aspirin has not helped to understand the causes of migraine. However, such is the power of the phenomenon of health inequality that even such a vague measure has produced large and consistent differences over a very long period of time, as we have seen in chapter 1. Problems have arisen when it is a matter of attempting to explain these differences. In order for explanatory models to be developed and tested, all terms need to be clearly defined and measures developed with reference to some explicit theory about what it is about social inequality that leads to effects on health.

Why Measurement Matters

The importance of knowing about these different measures for understanding health inequality is twofold. First, it alerts us to the necessity of defining what we mean by whatever concept of 'inequality' we are using, and of making sure we use valid measures of the concept. Secondly, it reminds us that we need to specify what we think it is about social position (the general term that I am using to refer to both class and status) that may relate to health. Is it money, status or the conditions in which people work? And if, as is likely, what matters is different combinations of these for different illnesses, which forms of inequality are the most important for which conditions? Both health and social policy makers need answers to these questions. Because if, for example, we try to reduce inequalities in a certain illness by giving people more income when it is actually work conditions which are significant for that illness, effort and resources are wasted.

In terms of understanding health inequality, we need to think carefully about what it might be about class position and prestige that might plausibly affect health. It is no longer sufficient to observe that a large variety of measures based on a large number of different concepts (or none at all) repeatedly appear to yield similar 'health gradients'. For one thing, this is not true for women nor for members of all ethnic groups. The theoretically based social class measures (E-G classes, Wright classes, NS-SEC) offer one kind of possibility. This is because some of the criteria used to classify occupations into E-G classes in their various forms, such as work autonomy and job security, have been found in other studies to be related to major diseases, such as heart disease (Schnall et al., 1990; Karasek, 1996; Bosma et al., 1997).

Prestige may be thought of as having a different kind of effect. Caste groups display their prestige by distancing themselves from forms of activity and people which are considered unclean or unworthy. They also mark their social status by bodily adornment, clothing and various other aspects of what sociologists of industrial societies might call 'lifestyle'. These include dietary practices and attitudes towards mood-altering substances such as alcohol. There are strong similarities between the display of prestige in both more and less traditional societies (Bourdieu, 1984). In both, individuals mark their actual prestige, and attempt to increase it, by confining themselves to what are considered worthy activities and attempting to associate only with others who are perceived as of appropriate rank. An essential part of the claim to prestige includes the adoption of certain forms of lifestyle. A 'cultural' theory of the relationship between prestige and lifestyle makes more sense of the social distribution of smoking and exercise, for example, than a theory based purely on income, as neither non-smoking nor vigorous exercise need cost any money. In contrast, being a non-smoker is more or less obligatory in certain high- and medium-status social circles, and being seen to go jogging certainly helps.

Or it may be that the subjective experience of low prestige creates feelings of strain increasing the lure of 'comfort behaviour' to compensate (this will be discussed more fully later). How about employment relations? Might it not be that those who are more in control at work are better able to control their risk behaviours? This is also a plausible idea, which can only be tested properly when we have distinct measures of the different dimensions of social inequality.

It is this possibility, of using measures of social position to construct 'causal narratives' (Marshall, 1997; Rose and O'Reilly, 1998), that makes it possible to take our attempts to understand health inequality forward more quickly. Not because any one of the measures is superior to the others, but because we can see that inequality can be of different kinds and may influence health in different ways. As the originators of the Cambridge score have observed 'it may be that policemen and skilled workers . . . interact with each other as equals, yet their relations to the productive system are different and this can have important behavioural consequences under certain conditions' (Stewart, Prandy and Blackburn, 1980: 28). So we can, for example, test out whether lower prestige may affect diet or smoking even within the same set of employment relations.

There are rich possibilities for developing more complex and sensitive causal models which, at the same time, are more likely to be useful for health policy. Before going any further, however, we need to look more closely, first at the kinds of methods used in studies, and then at the theoretical approaches to health inequality that are used most widely in the contemporary literature.

FURTHER READING

An excellent account of the social theories lying behind different social class measures, combined with an empirical study of class differences (not in health)
Marshall, G., Rose, D., Newby, H., and Vogler, C., *Social Class in Modern Britain.* London: Hutchinson, 1988.

The best summary of British work on social inequality: indispensable
Crompton, R., *Class and Stratification.* Second edition. Cambridge: Polity, 1998.

The theory and measurement principles behind the Wright schema and many useful examples of its use
Wright, E. O., *Class Counts.* Cambridge: Cambridge University Press, 1997.

Describes the development of the new British government class schema, and includes very useful discussion of the surrounding issues
Marshall, G., *Repositioning Class.* London: Sage, 1997.

3

Figuring out Health Inequality

In general, research on health inequality up to the present has not used very complicated methods, but there are a few basic ideas that are very helpful to understand. Chapters 1 and 2 have shown that studying health inequality involves constantly making comparisons between groups. When studies find that one group is less healthy than another, the next step is to try and single out what is different between the groups that might account for the differences in health. This chapter will go through some of the most frequently used methods used to compare health between social groups and try to arrive at the causes of health differences. Of course, it would be surprising if there were single explanations for such differences. Studies usually have to be prepared to consider more than one causal factor at a time. But it is not very difficult to reach a general understanding of how this is done. In order to make it possible for readers to approach the literature on health inequality with confidence and with a critical eye, this chapter will deal in some detail with the most common methods used for description and analysis. Examples will be used to show in a simple way some of the 'mechanics' of these methods, step by step – with the advantage that it is then possible to make one's own more critical appraisal of studies as they appear. No more advanced mathematics is needed to understand these methods than multiplication and division.

Preliminary Concepts

Other concepts that need to be understood from the outset include the notion of 'statistical explanation', and those of 'spuriousness' and 'confounding'.

Statistical explanation

The idea of 'statistical explanation' that underlies most accounts of health inequality might usefully be given some thought. In sociology, we often claim to have explained something if we can see how the motivations of all parties involved in some process or activity have led them to act as they did. This is Weber's notion of 'understanding' (*verstehen*), which is expressed in terms of being able to put oneself in the place of another social actor and see why they did what they did. However, 'taking the role of the other' very often does not go far in helping us to understand the actual outcome of several people's actions. We also need to understand the 'unintended consequences' of action. This allows us to see why the ultimate result of several different parties' actions can be something that none of them individually expected. In such cases, understanding in the sense of *verstehen* does not actually allow us to explain the outcome, only why each individual participant acted as they did.

Statistical explanations are different from both of these. They have nothing to do with understanding the motivations, intentions or feelings of the people involved. You have attained a degree of statistical explanation insofar as you have located a group of measures of some factors (variables), other than the outcome you are interested in, whose values can be used to predict that outcome. Imagine starting with no idea about who in a given population might have worse health, measured in terms of life expectancy, than anyone else. In statistical terms, you have no reason to expect anything other than that health is 'randomly distributed': any one person is as likely to be as ill or as healthy as any other. Then you observe that men and women have somewhat different levels of health: women have longer life expectancy. Gender then becomes part of a statistical explanation (although you may have no idea why). Then you observe, further, that people with higher income, higher education and higher-level managerial jobs, all seem to have longer life expectancy. All these variables – gender, income, education and job type – become part of the statistical explanation. Once again, there is no requirement to understand why any of these characteristics might lead to longer or shorter lives, only that if you know a person's 'score' for any of them, you will have a better idea of how old they will live to be. The next step is to try and find out whether your list of predictor variables are related to each other: do women live longer than men because they have higher incomes and are more likely to have higher managerial jobs? No, in fact women tend to have lower incomes and are less likely than men to have managerial jobs. So the explanations for gender differences in health will be different from the explanations for health differences between people with different incomes and types of work. Perhaps we then observe that people whose high incomes do not depend on their own work alone, but come partly from other people (in the form of inheritance, dividend and interest payments or the earnings of other family members), live longer than those who spend many years at work. In each of these steps, all we are doing is putting people into groups and seeing how similar the health of group members might be. Eventually, we would like to have a set of groups in which everyone's life expectancy was very similar. Then the characteristics of these groups would be a 'complete explanation' in statistical terms. The longest-living people might be *either* men *or* women who all had degrees and very high incomes, who had spent about 30 per cent of their working life doing advanced studies, 30 per cent looking after a comfortable family home with the help of several domestic servants, and 30 per cent in a powerful managerial job. Let us say members of this group lived on average to 90 years of age. If you, the researcher, knew how far any individual in your population departed from this 'perfectly healthy' paradigm, you would be able to predict with some confidence how much shorter that individual's life would be. This set of values, and the predictions they allow you to make, would be a 'statistical model explaining life expectancy'.

Having arrived at this very good statistical model, you would still quite possibly have no idea why this should be the case in terms of anyone's personal or biological experience. This type of understanding would need to be pursued by clinical and qualitative methods: taking biological measurements, life-histories and in-depth interviews, and making an ethnographic study of different social settings. At the present time, there are very few studies of health inequality that aim at this form of explanation (Ostergren et al., 1995; Cable et al., 1999; Fassin, 2000). Most research has aimed only at statistical explanation, so that is the form I will concentrate on here.

Spuriousness and confounding

I have emphasized the political nature of debates on the causes of health inequality. A frequent move in these debates has been to claim that an apparent relationship between a health measure and a measure of the social and economic environment is not real, but is due to something unconnected to social or economic inequality. Such a move may often be expressed in terms of 'spuriousness' or 'confounding'. These terms are often explained by telling stories about storks and babies. In a mythical society, it is observed that babies often arrive in the spring, at the same time as migrant birds such as storks. In this way the idea arose that the storks brought the babies – the arrival of storks was the 'cause' of the babies. But of course we all know this is not true, it is just a coincidence.

So the relationship between storks and babies may be described as 'spurious'. Or someone might say that the relationship between storks and babies is 'confounded by the season'. By this they would mean that there is a third factor, the season, which is the 'real' cause of the arrival of both storks and babies. In this tale, humans deliberately plan the arrival of their babies to coincide with the warmer seasons of the year. So the season is (in one sense or another) the 'real' cause of both the variables that it is 'confounding' (arrival of babies and storks). Throughout the rest of this book, there will be a number of examples in which some kind of personal characteristic such as 'intelligence' or 'coping abilities', is invoked as a type of confounder, and in which it is claimed that apparent relationships of social disadvantage and poor health are spurious. We might imagine quite plausibly that certain mental qualities could be the cause of a person attaining (or failing to attain) a certain social position or income, and also the cause of ill health. In these cases, it could be claimed that the relationship between social position or income and health was 'spurious with respect to', or 'confounded by', the personal characteristic.

Numerators and Denominators

Much of the information used in debates on health inequality comes from the national statistical services of various countries. Many nations keep a record of births, marriages and deaths – these are often called Vital Statistics. In order to trace what is happening to its death rate, a country needs two pieces of information. The first of these is a record of all deaths in a given time period. The second is a good estimate of the population. These two figures make up, respectively, the numerator and the denominator for the death rate in that period.

$$\frac{\text{numerator (number of deaths in population)}}{\text{denominator (number of people in population)}}$$

Death rates are usually not expressed as percentages, because luckily death is a fairly rare event, so these reports usually give 'rates per 10,000', 100,000 or even per million. Whatever is chosen as the basis for the rate, it is derived from this formula:

$$(\text{number of deaths (numerator)}/\text{number of people (denominator)}) \times [\text{e.g.}]10,000$$

So that if there were 500 people in the population and 2 of them died this would give a death rate per 10,000 for that year of

$$(2/500) \times 10,000 = 40 \text{ per } 10,000$$

If a death rate for a certain sub-group of the population is needed, it can only be arrived at if the relevant information has been included both at the time when the death was recorded and at the time when the population was recorded (usually at national censuses). So if we want to calculate death rates by gender, social class, ethnic group or whatever, social class, gender and ethnicity must be recorded both at each census and on the death record. National official statistics seldom include death rates according to income or ethnic group because many people might object to having these recorded at the time of the death of a family member. Social class, however, as we have seen, is based on occupation, which is a less sensitive piece of information. In order to obtain some idea of death rates in different ethnic groups or income groups, some countries carry out what are described as 'census-linked' studies. In this kind of study, some or all of the population's census information (which often does include all kinds of measures that it would be inappropriate to ask about at the time of a death) is linked to death records of the same people. In the simple 'rate method' (sometimes called the 'unlinked method') all that is needed is the numbers of people in a certain group who died, and the numbers of that group in the whole population. In the linked method, census information is linked to the death record for the same individual. In many Nordic nations, this can be done for the entire population, giving a very powerful data set for investigating health inequality. In the USA and Great Britain, there are special linked studies such as the Office of National Statistics' Longitudinal Study of England and Wales (Fox and Goldblatt, 1982; Goldblatt, 1990b; Drever and Whitehead, 1997) and the US Panel Study of Income Dynamics (Lillard and Panis, 1996; McDonough and Amick III, 2001; Duncan et al., 2002).

Absolute and Relative

Before trying to explain health differences between groups, it is a good idea to clarify one piece of terminology used to describe these differences. We have already met with the distinction between 'absolute' and 'relative'. But confusion often arises over this distinction, and it is worth further thought. The word 'relative' is used a great deal in work on health inequality. There are two common phrases in which it occurs: 'absolute versus relative difference' and 'absolute versus relative risk'.

Absolute versus relative difference

The distinction between absolute and relative *difference* is important, for example, when trying to decide how important a certain form of health inequality is for policy purposes. 'Absolute difference' means the difference between the numbers (not the percentages) of people who get a certain illness, or who die, in various groups (defined according to social position, gender, ethnicity, area of residence or whatever the study is concerned with). 'Relative difference' usually means the percentage difference in illness or mortality between groups. A large absolute difference can exist at the same time as a small relative difference; this depends on how common the disease is in the population. For example, there are very large *relative* social differences in lung cancer, even larger than the relative differences in heart disease. Take a population of 100,000 people with a heart disease rate of 2 per cent and a lung cancer rate of 0.4 per cent, and two social groups, the 'more favoured' and the 'less favoured'. Because heart disease is so common, there could be 900 deaths in a more favoured social group and 1,000 in a less favoured group, which would be a relative difference of 10 per cent between the social groups and an absolute difference of 100 deaths. Compare this to lung cancer, a much less common disease. Here, if there were 200 deaths in the favoured group and 250 in the less favoured, this would give a relative difference of 20 per cent but an absolute difference of only 50 actual lives saved. In public health planning terms, it may be regarded as more pressing to prevent an absolute difference of 100 deaths which is only 10 per cent rather than an absolute difference of 50 although it represents a 20 per cent reduction in inequality.

Absolute versus relative risk

Then there is 'absolute versus relative risk'. The term 'risk', or 'absolute risk', may be thought of just as the 'percentage' of people with a certain condition. This is not a very correct term in many ways and not all statistical experts would agree with its use. For one thing, the percentage of people with a certain condition today may not be a good predictor of who will get it in the future, and one thinks of a 'risk' as something that happens in the future. In contrast, the term 'relative risk' refers to the comparison between the percentage who have the condition and the percentage who do not. This figure is also often called the 'odds'. So that an absolute risk of 80 per cent is a relative risk (or odds) of (80/100)/(20/100), in other words, 4 to 1. Bookmakers on a racecourse would call this '*odds of 4 to 1 on*': if 80 per cent of a certain group have disease X, we could say the odds of getting the disease versus not getting it in this group were

4 to 1 in favour of getting it. Later in this chapter, we take a closer look at the 'odds ratio' (OR), which divides these 'odds' for one group by the odds for another group as a way of comparing their levels of risk.

Standardization: What Is It and Why Is It Needed?

In order to make valid comparisons between two or more social groups, and attribute the differences to a social factor such as class position or status, official statistical reports take steps to make sure that the difference is not simply due to different ages of the groups. Suppose that people tended to move up the income scale as they grew older. In this case, one might see worse health in the top income group than the bottom. More realistically, it sometimes happens that men doing manual work move from more strenuous jobs, such as mining, to jobs such as that of nightwatchman as they become older. The most commonly used illustration of this problem is in terms not of health inequalities between social groups but between geographical areas. If you found that the state of Florida in the USA, or the county of Hampshire in England, had higher mortality than other areas, would you suspect that there might be a lot of hazards in the environment? This would be a mistake unless you took account of the fact that many people retire to these areas, so that the average age of their citizens is higher than in most areas with heavy industry.

Standardized Mortality Ratio (SMR)

This correction for the possibility that a group that looks unhealthy is in fact just 'old' is called 'standardization'. The most common form, used in many of the older reports which contributed importantly to present understanding of health inequality, is the Standardized Mortality Ratio (SMR), which is also called 'indirect standardization'. Nowadays, most statisticians find this a rather strange measure and it is seldom used in research papers. But several tables from regular government reports on health inequality which show figures for SMRs are used in this book, and it is useful to have an idea of what this measure can tell us. It is called a 'ratio' because it compares the death rate in any social class to what that rate would have been if the social group had exactly the same age structure as the whole population (so it is the ratio between the two rates). The easiest way to think of it is as comparing the death rate in each of the social groups with the 'average' for the whole population. The 'average' is set by convention to be 100. If we find that the most advantaged social class has an SMR of 50, therefore, we can say that this group has only half the average death rate. If the most disadvantaged class has an SMR of 150 we can say that it has a death rate 50 per cent above the average, taking account of age differences between the groups. We need to be careful when thinking about what these can and cannot tell us, because the SMR only shows relative mortality, that is, the mortality in each class relative to the average for all persons in that year. So that if the SMR for heart disease in Registrar-General's Social Class (RGSC) V is 80 in one time-period and 160 in a later period, this certainly does not mean that heart disease in this social group has doubled! What it means is that in the earlier period a man in RGSC V was about 20 per cent less likely than average to die of heart disease whereas in the later period he was about 60 per cent more likely than average to do so. For example, in table 1.1, the SMRs tell us that in *c.*1931 a man in social class I was 10 per cent less likely than average to die before the age of 65 (SMR = 90), whereas by 1991 he would have been 34 per cent (SMR = 66) less likely to do so, taking account of age differences between the classes. It is not possible, using this measure, to compare one time-period with another, only to compare each social group to the average within each time-period. That is really all one needs to know about this measure. For those interested in exactly how it is calculated (a good party trick to impress your friends), I have given an example in the appendix to this chapter.

Direct standardization

A second form of standardization, called 'direct standardization' is now more commonly used, and is found in reports on health issued by the World Health Organization and by many national governments. The SMR, as we have seen, is a *ratio* between the death rate in a group and what we can think of as the 'average for the population'. (This is not exactly what it does, as can be seen from the appendix to this chapter, but there is no harm in thinking of it in this way.) Direct standardization gives us a standardized *percentage* (or rate per 10,000 or 100,000 and so on). It tells us what proportion of people would have fallen ill, died (or whatever other outcome we are interested in) in the whole population if that population had the same age structure as the social class in question. This method is useful for two main reasons. The first is that it can be read in just the same way as an ordinary percentage. When calculating SMRs for two or more different time points, at each time the 'average' death rate for the whole population for that time is 're-set' to equal 100 and all other groups are compared to this. If the SMRs for our rich and poor groups in 1981 were, let us say, 75 and 150, and in 1991 they were 65 and 170, this does not mean that mortality risk has fallen in the rich and risen in the poor. It only means that the risk for the rich has fallen relative to that for the whole population (the imaginary '100') and that for the poor has risen relative to the population. A directly standardized rate, on the other hand, does allow us to compare over time.

In order to carry out direct standardization, you need to have a 'standard population'. This can be taken from a number of sources. One common way to select the standard population is to take the population at one of the time points you want to compare. In the past, this used to be taken to be the whole population of, say, England and Wales, or Great Britain. Nowadays, many publications use a 'European standard population', or even a 'world standard population' in order to make international health comparisons ('Britain is healthier than France say experts'). It does not matter what country or what time-point is included in the standard population, as long as all other groups at all other times are compared to the same one. In the example used here, the standard population will be taken as the whole population made up of the 'rich' and 'poor' social classes that we want to compare to each other. Once again, the object of the exercise is to correct for the possibility that disease or death rates look different between times or between groups because the age structure varies between groups or at different times. Because direct standardized rates are so commonly used, I will show the way it can be calculated here in full. Table 3.1 shows a table giving an example of direct standardization. For those who might be interested in the comparison of the two methods, I have used the same imaginary population, with the same age structure and age-specific death rates as in table 3.2 (the SMR). This makes it possible to see the differences between the two methods. In this imaginary population there are two social groups, the 'rich' and the 'poor'. We want to see whether the poor group has higher death risk than the rich group, after taking account of the fact that there are more older people in the poor group.

How to do direct standardization:
1 Separate the population into age groups (10-year age groups for this example). In table 3.1 you can see that the two classes have different age profiles. Although there are the same numbers in each age group in the population as a whole (80), in the poor class there are 50 people aged 55–64 compared to only 30 people of this age in the rich class. Because older people have a higher risk of death, there is a chance here that differences between rich and poor could be due to their age profiles.
2 Get the rate of mortality in each age group for each social class.

Table 3.1 Direct standardization

'Class'		Age groups					Total population	Total 'standard' deaths	Directly standardized rate
		15–24	25–34	35–44	45–54	55–64			
1 'poor'	Number in age group % died	30 *13.3*	30 *16.7*	40 *15*	50 *16*	50 *20*			
	Number who would have died in whole age group if rate the same as in 'poor'	10.6 (13.3% of 80)	13.4 (16.7% of 80)	12 (15% of 80)	12.8 (16% of 80)	16 (20% of 80)		64.8	16.2 (64.8/400) * 100
2 'rich'	Number in age group % died	50 *8*	50 *6*	40 *10*	30 *13.3*	30 *20*			
	Number who would have died in whole age group if rate the same as in 'rich'	6.4 (8% of 80)	4.8 (6% of 80)	8 (10% of 80)	10.6 (13.3% of 80)	16 (20% of 80)		45.8	11.5 (45.8/400) * 100
	Total number in age group in all classes	80	80	80	80	80	400		

3 Calculate how many people would have died in the whole population of that age if everyone had the same risk as the people in each of the social classes.
4 This gives two numbers of deaths for each age group. In table 3.1 the death rate of 15–24-year-olds in the 'poor' group was 13.3 per cent, and in the 'rich' group it was 8 per cent. Because there are 80 people in that age group in the whole population, if the whole population in age group 15–24 had the same death rate as the 'poor' class there would have been 10.6 deaths, and if the whole population aged 15–24 had the death rate of the rich class there would have been 6.4 deaths. In age group 35–44, 15 per cent of the poor died, and 10 per cent of the rich. Because there are 80 people aged 35–44 in the whole population, there would have been 12 deaths in the age group if they had all had the same risk as the poor class. If the whole age group had the same death rate as the rich, there would have been 8 deaths. And so on. The estimated numbers of deaths that would have taken place in the population if it had the same age profile as each of the social classes are called 'standard deaths'.
5 Next, add up all the 'standard deaths' for each class.
6 Express the numbers of standard deaths in each class as a percentage of the whole population. The directly standardized rate for the 'poor' class may be thought of as what the death rate in the whole population would have been if each age group had the same rate as that for people in the poor class, and the directly standardized rate for the 'rich' class may be thought of as the death rate for the whole population if the risk in each age group were the same as that in the rich class.

To summarize the differences between SMR and directly standardized rate:
1 Indirect standardization gives the SMR, a ratio, not a rate.
2 SMR is the ratio that compares the risk of death in any social group to the 'average' risk for the whole population at that time.
3 Direct standardization shows what the rate for a whole 'standard' population would be if the age structure of the standard population were the same as that in each of the different social groups.
4 The standard population can be taken from a variety of sources, depending on the purpose of the research. It does not matter what the standard is as long as the same one is used to compute the standardized rate for all sub-groups.
5 You cannot compare two SMRs for different populations, or different years. You can only compare how far the SMR for any sub-group in the population is from 100 in that year.

6   Directly standardized rates at different time points can be compared, as long as the standard population used is the same.

Models of Health Inequality

The ways in which the SMR and direct standardization are calculated are shown here because these measures are widely used in national and international health reports (for example in those referred to in chapters 1 and 10). The important things to remember are: (1) that both of these methods try to take account of the fact that social classes may have different age structures, and this can effect differences in the risk of illness or mortality; and (2) it is not possible to compare two SMRs directly with each other, whereas it is possible to do this with two directly standardized rates.

However, in most academic papers (as opposed to official reports) on health inequality more use is made of statistical models. These models are the way in which researchers try to pinpoint the causes of health inequality. Are they really due to differences in people's inborn characteristics, for example, or to work hazards, or types of lifestyle? If you think you have cleverly discovered that illness and mortality in Brighton is higher than it is in Liverpool and someone points out that Brighton is full of retired elderly people, this would completely trivialize your 'discovery'. Finding evidence that health differences between groups could be due to genes or lifestyle might be regarded as really new knowledge. But it would still be a good idea to check whether groups of people with different genes or lifestyle might have other characteristics that could also be contributing to the health differences between the groups. Statistical models are really just an extension of the methods we have seen used in standardization. They look at the relationship between two variables (the one you think might be the 'cause' and your 'effect' or health outcome variable) with every other relevant variable held constant. Would the relationship between social class or income and blood pressure be the same if not just the ages of the different class or income groups were the same, but also their education, gender, coping styles, diet and so on?

The studies of health inequality that are discussed in the rest of this book address competing explanations or models of how this inequality might be caused. These hypothetical explanations contain several possible causal factors, and need to be tested by the use of statistical models. If we combine age and income in a model, we can think of the result as the relationship of income to health after taking account of differences in age between people with different income. This kind of exercise is often referred to as 'holding age constant'. If we combine social class with intel-

Table 3.2 Odds Ratio: depression by gender

	Depressed?		
	Yes %	No %	Odds
Women	28	72	0.39 : 1
Men	22	78	0.28 : 1
Odds ratio			1.38

Source: Health Survey for England 1993, author's analysis

ligence in a model, likewise we can think of the result as showing the level of health in each social class 'holding intelligence constant', that is, 'if everyone in each class had the same level of intelligence'. This is a very simple way to understand statistical models of health inequality and will not be enough to meet all cases. However, it is always worth bearing in mind when first considering any study. Introducing another variable into a model in this way is often referred to as 'adjustment'. But the principle is the same as 'standardization'.

The odds ratio (OR)

The outcome measure in most studies of health inequality is some kind of qualitative or categorical measure, such as the presence or absence of an illness, so that we have "the percentage of ill people" in richer and poorer groups combined, for example. This percentage is regarded as reflecting the risk or probability of illness in each individual member of the group. The conventional way to compare these probabilities in statistical models is to use a measure called an odds ratio (OR). Statistical models that present their results in terms of odds ratios are called 'logistic models'. This is the method used at any time when the result of a study can only be represented in terms of categories such as 'ill' and 'healthy', or 'large' and 'small'.

The OR is just what it says it is: the ratio of two sets of odds. Rather as in gambling, one might say that the odds of having good health are 10 to 1 in a rich class versus 2 to 1 in a poor class. Here the ratio of the two odds would be 5 to 1; you are five times more likely to have good health if you come from the rich than from the poor class. In table 3.2, 22 per cent of men as opposed to 28 per cent of women are depressed. The odds of being depressed in men are $22/78 = 0.28$ to 1, while the odds of being depressed in women are $28/72 = 0.39$ to 1. Dividing 0.39 by 0.28 gives 1.38. This is the OR and we can think of it as saying that women have 1.38 times the risk of depression in this population as men do. When calculating an odds ratio, one group has to be given the odds of '1'. It does not matter which group is chosen, but this will often be the group with the lowest risk, so that the ORs for all the other groups are greater than one. In research papers the most favoured, lowest-risk group is referred to as the 'baseline', with all the others having ORs greater than 1, to show how much greater their risk is. In table 3.2, men are the 'baseline category'.

This method was devised to help in finding the cause of outbreaks of infectious diseases. The epidemiologist would compare the rate of disease in people who had been exposed to whatever she thought was the relevant risk factor (a type of food, say) with the rate in those who had not been exposed. So another way to think of the data presented in the table is in terms of 'exposure' and 'disease' (see table 3.3). If the odds of illness are significantly higher in those who ate the suspect food than in those who did not, then the evidence against the food is increased.

Statistical adjustment

In most studies, odds ratios are not calculated in exactly the same way as in this illustration. The 'causes' of health inequality are nothing like food-poisoning bacteria: they are far more complex. As a result, we need to check whether any apparent relationship has been biased by factors other than the measure or measures of social inequality that are used in any study.

When it is proposed that some variable which is not a result of social disadvantage or privilege is the 'true cause' of an instance of health inequality, we have seen that this variable is often referred to in epidemiology as 'a confounder'. Although there is some confusion and debate around the question of confounding in studies of health inequality, for the moment we just need to be clear about what it is usually supposed to mean. In other disciplines the same idea is referred to by different terms, for example, 'spuriousness'. The way many studies check for confounding or spuriousness is by statistical adjustment. This is essentially the same thing as 'holding constant'. As we have seen, standardization 'holds age constant'. Just as in the more traditional SMR and directly standardized measures age is held constant, statistical adjustment is a way to 'standardize' or hold constant a range of other factors as well as age in more complex statistical models. Adjusting, standardizing and holding constant are basically the same exercise. We want to see if a relationship we think we have discovered (say between class and health) is still there when other factors are taken into account. And, roughly speaking, this is done by re-examining the relationship within groups whose members resemble

Table 3.3 Exposure and disease

Exposure	Disease		Odds
	Yes %	No %	
Yes, did eat suspicious food	A % of people who did eat the food and became ill	B % of people who ate the food but did not become ill A + B = 100% All who ate the food	A/B Odds of getting ill if you ate the suspected food
No, did not eat food	C % of people who did not eat the food but are ill	D % of people who did not eat the food who were not ill C + D = 100% All who did not eat the food	C/D Odds of getting ill if you did not eat the suspicious food
Odds ratio			(A/B)/(C/D) Odds ratio comparing the odds of getting ill in those exposed to the odds in those not exposed

Table 3.4 Social class differences in disease before adjustment for smoking

Social class	Disease		
	Yes	No	
Middle-class number	49	290	339
%	14.4	85.5	
Working-class number	83	310	393
%	21.1	78.9	
ALL	132	600	732
Odds Ratio		1.58	

Artificially constructed data

each other in terms of a third (fourth, fifth and so on) factor – that is, within groups where the value of the other factors is 'constant'. If the original relationship disappears within the sub-groups with 'constant' values of the other factors, the original relationship is regarded as having been 'explained'.

The classic example of a confounder in epidemiological studies is smoking. Once again we have to leave aside for the moment the question of whether smoking is not in itself an outcome of the experience of inequality. In most studies other than the most recent, the underlying idea is that smoking cannot be part of the reason why social disadvantage is associated with ill health. Therefore, if any relationship between an illness and, let us say, social class position can be shown to 'disappear when smoking is adjusted for', then it would be said that the apparent relationship with social disadvantage was not real but due to confounding. If we take the concrete example in table 3.4, we see that working-class men are more at risk of suffering our 'disease' (21.1 per cent have it) than middle-class men (only 14.4 per cent). In fact you can even work out the odds ratio, which is $(21.1/78.9)/(14.4/85.5) = 1.58$. So it looks as if working-class men have around half as much risk again of suffering the disease.

However, what happens if we 'adjust for smoking'? The way to see what happens when statistical adjustment is carried out on these kinds of data is by dividing the population up into smokers and non-smokers and looking at the disease rates within each social class group.

Table 3.5 Social class differences after adjustment for smoking

Social class	Smokers disease		Non-smokers disease		Total numbers in both classes
	Yes	No	Yes	No	
Middle-class:					
Number	25	70	24	220	339
%	26.3		73.7	9.8 90.2	
Working-class:					
Number	70	190	13	120	393
%	26.9	73.1	9.8	90.2	
Odds ratio	0.97		1.0		732

Artificially constructed data

We can see from table 3.5 that when you divide the sample into smokers and non-smokers, the odds of having the disease in working versus middle-class people are little different from 1 : 1, that is, there is no excess risk in the working class. This is the easiest way to think about statistical adjustment: it is what happens when the original relationship you thought you saw is re-examined in those who do and those who do not have the possible 'confounding' factor. In this case, we repeat the relationship of socio-economic position to ill health in those who do and those who do not smoke. What would be presented in a research paper on health inequality would not usually be the odds ratios for the two different groups, but a single 'adjusted odds ratio'. We can think of this as the extra risk to a working-class over a middle-class person if both classes were equally likely to smoke. The adjusted OR is more or less an average, that is, calculated by adding up the ORs from the two social groups and dividing by two. This is not quite what happens: in fact more weight is given to larger groups than to the smaller ones. But when you see an 'adjusted odds ratio', it does no harm to think of it in this way. In table 3.5 it is easy to see that the adjusted OR would be around 1.

Showing only a single 'adjusted odds ratio' would not have allowed us to see an important fact about the relationship of class and smoking to health in this example, however. Because I have shown the relationship separately for smokers and non-smokers in each social class, we can see how the appearance of an excess risk was due to the fact that more working-than middle-class people smoke, and the disease is more common in those

Table 3.6 Odds of poor health before and after adjustment for smoking

	Odds of poor health	Odds of poor health adjusted for smoking
Rich	1 (baseline)	1 (baseline)
Poor	2.2	1.7

who smoke. While about 26 per cent of both groups have the disease among the smokers, only around 10 per cent have it among the non-smokers. And while 95/339 = 28 per cent of the middle class are smokers, 260/393 = 66 per cent of the working class smoke. Such a clear case of confounding is in fact rather unusual, and the example given here is a contrived and artificial one, not using real data. But it serves to show in detail what people are thinking of when they say 'health differences between group A and group B were explained away by adjustment for smoking'.

In this example, once the social groups were divided according to smoking, the odds ratios were reduced to 1 : 1, that is, there was no remaining difference between the groups. In this case, we would say that the social difference was entirely due to smoking. But what more often happens is that the social difference is reduced, but only partly: it does not disappear altogether. It is useful to be able to have some idea of how much of the social difference can be explained in terms of smoking. In many papers you will find that the amount by which the relationship between two variables expressed as an odds ratio is reduced after adjustment for a third factor is calculated by this formula:

$$\text{(Unadjusted Odds Ratio} - \text{Odds Ratio for adjusted model)}/ \text{(Unadjusted OR-1)}$$

The result of this calculation is often called 'percentage (or "proportional") reduction in odds'.

In the artificial example given in table 3.6, if you want some idea of how much of the unadjusted excess risk of disease might be regarded as 'due to smoking' you can calculate this by

$$(2.2 - 1.7)/(2.2 - 1) = 0.42$$

This reveals that around 42 per cent of the relationship between social class and this disease was due to smoking.

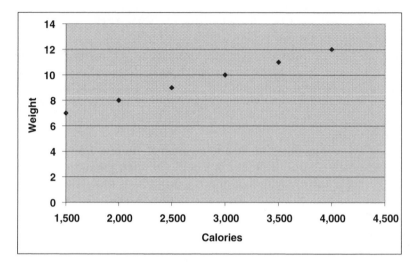

Figure 3.1 Relationship between weight and calories

Regression models, I: Linear regression

So far we have considered examples where the measure of health or illness has had only two values: dead versus alive; ill versus healthy. For these kinds of outcomes, it is necessary to use the odds ratio. But there are many interesting health measures that can be represented in terms of a continuous score or measure, such as blood pressure, height or weight. When this is the kind of health measure we are looking at, ordinary linear regression models can be used. In mathematical terms the equation for an ordinary regression is:

$$y = a + bx + e$$

In a linear regression model we are not looking at the percentages of people in different boxes in a table. Rather, we observe the 'average score' on an outcome variable y for people with a certain 'score' on a possible causal or independent variable x. These two amounts, the values of x and y, can be plotted as in figure 3.1. The regression equation describes the amount of change in the outcome measure y (weight, let us say) for a single unit change in the exposure measure x (such as the number of calories eaten per week, for example). In the equation above, 'a' represents the starting-point or 'intercept' (let us say, in this example, the minimum weight of all the sample of people we are analysing). The 'b' refers to the amount of change in weight per each unit change in the independent variable. This is referred to as the 'regression coefficient'. The equation tells us that weight in any one person will be equal to the minimum weight for everyone plus '*b*' times the exposure measure '*x*' ('*x*' could be calories eaten). The term '*e*' is an error term, which we do not need to think about in any detail, except to remember that in any real-world study, all the measures we take are subject to various types of error. These errors inevitably influence our conclusions about the effect each 100 calories will have on a person's weight.

How are real numbers filled in to replace '*y*', '*x*' and '*b*'? In this case, we would have studied the intake of calories of a large number of people and measured their weight, and drawn a diagram in which each individual's combination of weight and calories was plotted. The best way to think about the results is in terms of a plot on a graph, with weight up the side and calories along the bottom, as in figure 3.1 where we can see that weight goes up steadily as calories increase. The value of '*b*' (which may be referred to as the 'regression coefficient' or the 'parameter estimate') is discovered by measuring how much each extra 500 calories increases weight; in this case it is by 10 lb. The 'minimum' weight or starting-point for someone who eats only 1,500 calories a day is about 80 lb. So we can now rewrite the equation as

weight of individual 'i' = 80 + 10 × (number of 500-calorie meals) + allowance for mistakes

So that someone eating 2,500 calories would weigh about 100 lb.

Of course, all these figures are the result of averaging out the relationship between food intake and weight in a whole sample of people, maybe thousands. A graph like figure 3.1 taken from real research data would show lots of little dots representing each individual, scattered around the straight line. So if we try to use the equation to predict how much any individual weighs, it will not give exactly the right answer. The line that relates the points in the graph is only a 'best estimate', and for this reason researchers often talk about 'fitting a regression line (or curve)'. For the same reason, the '*b*' that gives us the relationship between calories and weight is known as an 'estimate' (or 'parameter estimate'). All we can say is that, on average, a person will weight 10 lbs more for each 500 extra calories they eat each day, but some will be far more than this and some far less (as many of us know to our regret). Also, because the relationships we can calculate from this kind of procedure are no more than estimates – although we try to get as close as possible to the observed data – this kind of exercise is known as 'modelling'. This means no more than that we are doing our best to arrive at a kind of sum or equation that reasonably closely describes all the individual scores on the variables that have been collected in the research.

Usually we want to take account of more than one possible causal factor. Perhaps the same amount of food has a different effect on weight in those who take more exercise? Say we want to predict weight from the number of cakes a person eats each day and how much time they spend jogging. Here the amount by which each factor (cakes and jogging) changes the outcome (a person's weight) will have its own separate regression coefficient ('*b*'), and these will be numbered, in other words, 'b_1' times cakes and 'b_2' times jogging. So if each cake per week added a quarter of a pound to the average person's weight, and each extra hour of jogging reduced weight by one-tenth of a pound, the results of the regression model would look like this:

Variable	Regression coefficient (*b*)
cakes	0.25
jogging	−0.1

If we imagine a population in which the weight of people who ate no cakes and did no jogging was 154 lb, a statistical model expressing the effects of cakes and jogging on the weight of each individual could look something like this:

weight of person i $= 154 + b_1$(number of cakes) $+ b_2$(hours of jogging)

which means, in this case,

weight of person i $= 154 + 0.25$ (cakes) $- 0.1$ (hours of jogging)

so that an individual who ate 10 cakes per week and jogged for 10 hours would expect their weight to be roughly

$154 + b_1$(number of cakes) $- b_2$(hours of jogging)
i.e. $154 + (0.25 \times 10) - (0.1 \times 10) = 154 + 2.5 - 1 = 155.5$ lb.

Once again, without going into great detail, it is important to realize that in this kind of model, the value of '*b*' for each individual variable has been adjusted for the other one: it is, in one sense, an 'amount of weight added per cake for a person who does the average amount of jogging'. Likewise the '*b*' value for the amount of weight deducted by an hour of jogging is that for a person who 'eats an average number of cakes'. In real research, we would also add age to any model like this, so that the values of '*b*' for both cakes and jogging would also be those for a person of the 'average age'. We might also add sex to the model, in which case all the '*b*' effects would represent an 'average' of their size in men and women.

This is relevant to health inequality because it enables us to begin to look at how, for example, differences in the amount of cakes and hours of jogging (or smoking, or alcohol and so on) among members of different classes or status groups may influence their risks of disease. These are very simplified and greatly exaggerated examples, but they serve to show the general shape of the sort of arguments for which statistical models are used in health inequality research.

Regression models, II: Logistic regression

This is not the place to go into detail about the mathematics of different kinds of regression models. But here I will try to give some idea of my own, greatly oversimplified, understanding of how statistical models with non-linear, categorical outcomes, are constructed. Many of the outcomes which interest us in health inequality research can only be measured in terms of 'ill' and 'healthy' (in one sense or another). So it is not possible to estimate literally how much change in some outcome measure or 'score' is produced by a 'one-point change' in the possible causal variable. Instead, it is possible to estimate how much difference in the *probability* of over-weight in group X relative to group Y might result from, for example, members of group X eating one more cake or doing one more mile of jogging. The interesting figures in tables such as tables 3.4 and 3.5 are the percentages. The percentage of people who have a disease is regarded, in statistical thinking, as representing the *probability* of any person in that group having the disease. Probabilities can only be somewhere between 0 and 1. So if 10 per cent of rich people and 32 per cent of poor people have disease X, this is the same as saying that the probability of disease X is 0.1 in the rich group and 0.32 in the poor group. This is quite different from saying that the average weight in the rich is 140 lb and the average weight in the poor group is 150 lb.

Why not have an equation that says: 'probability of overweight is equal to *b1* times number of cakes and *b2* times hours of jogging' in the same way as for linear regression? For various mathematical reasons, the relationship cannot be expressed in this way. The fact that probability can only vary between 0 and 1, while a variable such as weight, or blood pressure, or a mental health score (often called 'linear' measures), can vary from (in principle) 0 to infinity, sometimes creates peculiar results in statistical models. So instead of predicting the probability, the regression equation for categorical variables (like 'disease, yes or no') predicts the logarithm of the odds or log-odds. (In fact, it predicts the natural logarithm.) For example, instead of predicting the average weight in a group by knowing how many cakes they ate, you would be predicting the logarithm of the odds of overweight. The log-odds behave much better in mathematical terms, more like scores, and vary from zero to infinity in the same way as ordinary numbers do. So you can proceed just as for linear regression, adding variables to the model with the log-odds of overweight as the outcome you are trying to predict. At the end, the log-odds are 'anti-logged' and transformed back into odds. And then the odds of overweight in each group of cake-eaters is compared to the odds of overweight in the group that eats no cakes in the form of our old friend the OR. As we saw above, the odds ratio needs to be understood as how much greater or less the risk of overweight is in relation to a 'baseline' group. Instead of being able to say what was the average weight in a group who ate $b1$ cakes and jogged for b_2 hours a day, you would be able to give the odds of overweight in a group who ate b_1 cakes and jogged for b_2 hours per day relative to the odds in a 'baseline' group (say, who ate no cakes and did no jogging). Whenever you see these ORs given in research papers as the results of statistical models, you can understand them in just the same way as those shown in tables 3.2–.6.

Pathways from Inequality to Illness

Many studies of health inequality take the general form of 'social class' or 'socio-economic status' or some other measure of social position on the one hand, and a health or disease measure on the other. Having found that, let us say, those with a less privileged social position have more of the disease, the studies then proceed to carry out a number of statistical 'adjustments': for age, for psychological factors, for certain behaviours such as smoking and so on.

In many ways the term 'adjustment' is rather misleading. You will often see it used in research papers and reports on health inequality. But it is more helpful to think in terms of building up explanations by adding variables, according to whatever theory we may have as to the causes of a health difference between social groups. When we adjust for a categorical variable such as 'smoking, yes or no', we are sub-dividing the social groups according to the third variable to see if the relationship between social group and health outcome is the same regardless of the value of the third variable. An important example can be seen if we look back at smoking. If we want to claim that 'smoking is the reason that class X has worse health than class Y', we are expecting to see a certain kind of relationship. That is, we expect to see that smokers have more disease, regardless of what class they are in, and that there are just more smokers in class X. Smoking forms a 'pathway' between class and illness (Macintyre, 1997). Real life results will, of course, usually be less straightforward than this. But by using the 'percentage reduction in odds' method, we can even form some idea of how much of the original difference is 'explained' by each new variable we add to the model. When we add a linear variable such as the number of calories or miles of jogging to a model, we are looking once again at how far these can go in explaining a difference between social groups.

Thinking in terms of pathways does not entail anything radically different to this in technical terms. In order to see if an idea about health inequality is supported by data, models will be built up in more or less the same way. But it is a slightly different way of thinking about what we are doing. Instead of regarding all possible third, fourth or further variables as 'confounders', we have to decide how we really think each one is contributing. Smoking for example, is not very usefully thought of as a cause of being in a particular income group or social class. On the contrary, it looks very much as if smoking itself is in some sense 'caused' by socio-economic disadvantage. So we may have situations in which the effect of social disadvantage has two pathways of effect. The first of these is that socio-economic disadvantage (for some reason) makes it harder to give up smoking and therefore means that smoking-related diseases will be more common in disadvantaged people. The second pathway might have nothing to do with smoking, but act through the fact that the disadvantaged group experiences more damp housing, or hazardous work, for example. One way to look at this is, as I have done above, to divide the disadvantaged group into smokers and non-smokers to see if there is worse health even in the non-smokers. Then you could divide the non-smokers into those with better and those with worse housing to see if disadvantaged non-smokers with good housing had the same probability of ill health as the more advantaged group. And so on. As the number of factors that you think may be at work gets larger, it is necessary to use statistical models to carry out this kind of exercise and to check for potential problems of various kinds.

Simple linear or logistic regression models can go a long way in testing these kinds of ideas about the reasons for health inequality. But as our understanding becomes more detailed, it is sometimes an advantage to use more complex methods. This is particularly important for analysing pathways between social and economic circumstances and health over time. Some researchers are beginning to use methods such as path models and growth models. Readers with a special interest in these will have to consult the appropriate literature. But in these examples, I have tried to provide a straightforward account of the most common types of statistical method used in studies of, and arguments about, health inequality. It does not require advanced statistics to understand this logic, or to evaluate contributions to the debates in the literature. But reading about health inequality in an informed and critical way is made much easier by a grasp of these basic techniques. I have tried to emphasize the importance of the logic of each form of argument. Even the most sophisticated statistics can be wasted if hypotheses and the terms in which they are tested are not clearly thought out.

FURTHER READING

Basic statistics and data analysis:
Personally, I have found it far easier to learn about statistics through practical use in data analysis, which is the approach taken in these books
Bryman, A., *Social Research Methods*. Oxford: Oxford University Press, 2001.

Bryman, A., and Cramer, D., *Quantitative Data Analysis with SPSS Release 10 for Windows*. London: Routledge, 2001.

Field, A., *Discovering Statistics Using SPSS for Windows*. London: Sage, 2000.

More advanced but very clearly written:
For those who are interested in going into regression models in more depth, and in an introduction to some of the more advanced methods now coming into use

Plewis, I., *Statistics in Education*. London: Arnold, 1997.

APPENDIX: HOW TO CALCULATE A STANDARDIZED MORTALITY RATIO (SMR)

Say we have two social groups or classes, the 'rich' and the 'poor'. The groups are of equal size, 200, but in the rich group 25 deaths have been recorded in the past 10 years, while in the poor group 35 deaths have been recorded. Does this really mean that the poor are at a higher risk – that is, is there evidence here for health inequality? What if it is just a matter of poorer people being older? Calculating an SMR can check this.

1   Suppose we start with a population made up of 400 people, with two classes: there are 200 people in the 'rich' class and 200 in the 'poor' class. Over a period of time, 13.5% of all these people die (or become ill). This rate is made up of 16.5% of the poor class and only 10.5% of the rich class. But we know that the poor class contains rather more older people than the rich class. How far is this health inequality between rich and poor classes just a result of their different ages?

2   Separate the total population (rich and poor together) into age groups. (This is usually done by groups of 5 or 10 years: in this case, we take 10-year age groups.)

There are 2 classes: rich = 200 people and poor = 200 people
that is,
a total of 400 people: 80 each in age groups 15–24, 25–34, 35–44, 45–54 and 55–64

3   Calculate the death rate for each of these age groups – say 10% in age groups 15–24 and 25–34, 12.5% in age group 35–44, 15% in age group 45–54 and 20% in age group 55–64.

4   Now take each of the social classes and divide them into the same age groups. Suppose the 'poor' class has an older age profile:

30 people in ages 16–24
30 in 25–34
40 in 35–44
50 in 45–54 and
50 in 55–64

and imagine that the 'rich' group has a younger age profile, so that you have

50 people aged 16–24
50 people aged 25–34
40 people aged 35–44
30 people aged 45–54
30 people aged 55–64

(This is a far more extreme example of age differences between social groups than would ever be found in reality but it makes a vivid example.)

5   Work out how many people in each class would die in each of these age groups if the percentage dying was the same as in that particular age group in the whole population. This gives an 'expected number of deaths' in each age group in each class.

6   Add up all these deaths (some will be fractions). This gives a 'total expected number of deaths'.

The result would look like this:

For the 'poor' group:

Age group	Death rate	Deaths expected in age group
16–24	10% of 30 =	3
25–34	10% of 30 =	3
35–44	12.5% of 40 =	5
45–54	15% of 50 =	7.5
55–64	20% of 50 =	10
Total expected deaths		28.5

For the 'rich' group:

Age group	Death rate	Deaths expected in age group
16–24	10% of 50 =	5
25–34	10% of 50 =	5
35–44	12.5% of 40 =	5
45–54	15% of 30 =	4.5
55–64	20% of 30 =	6
Total expected deaths		25.5

6   This shows the way indirect standardization works. Even though the number of people in each of the social classes is identical in this example, there would be more 'expected' deaths in the poor than the rich. There is an 'expected' difference purely because the death rate in older people is higher and there are more older people in the poor group. In order to see if there is 'really' a higher risk in the poor group, we need to compare the actual numbers of deaths in each group with the numbers that are expected on the basis of age alone.

7   The next step in calculating the SMR is therefore to compare the number of deaths you would have expected to see in the two classes because of their age distributions with the number that has actually taken place.

8   Divide the number of people who actually died, i.e. the 'observed deaths' in the 'poor' social class (in this case that happened to be 33) by the expected number (28.5) and multiply this by 100.

9   This is the SMR for the poor groups:
Observed deaths = 33

SMR for 'poor' group = observed/expected × 100
i.e. $33/28.5 \times 100 = 115.8$

10   Do the same thing for the 'rich' group: we saw that 21 deaths took place in this group, resulting in

SMR for 'rich' group = observed/expected × 100
i.e. 21/25.5 × 100 = 82.4

If the number of observed deaths in each social group was exactly equal to the expected number, then all groups would have an SMR of 100. So one way to think of the SMR is that it tells us how much the death rate for a social group falls above or below the death rate for the whole population. In this case, the rate for the rich was about 18 per cent below that, and the rate for the poor was about 16 per cent above it. (Table 3.7. shows this example in the form of a table.)

Table 3.7 Example of indirect standardization: Standardized Mortality Ratio

Age	Number of people			Observed deaths		Death rate in each age group Both classes	Total number of deaths Both classes	Overall death rate	'Expected' death rate*	
	'Poor'	'Rich'	Total	'Poor'	'Rich'				'Poor'	'Rich'
15–	30	50	80	4	4	10	8		3	5
25–	30	50	80	5	3	10	8		3	5
35–	40	40	80	6	4	12.5	10		5	5
45–	50	30	80	8	4	15	12		7.5	4.5
55–	50	30	80	10	6	20	16		10	6
All	200	200	400	33	21	13.5	54	13.5	28.5	25.5

Note: SMR for each class is equal to 'Observed'/'Expected' $\times$ 100, i.e. for the 'poor' it is $33/28.5 \times 100 = 115.8$; for the 'rich' it is $21/25.5 \times 100 = 82.4$

*Number of deaths if rate for 'poor' and 'rich' were the same

4

Models of Aetiological Pathways, I: Behavioural and 'Cultural' Explanations

While many studies use a combination of aetiological (causal) approaches to health inequality, here, to begin with at least, the four types of model, behavioural, material, psycho-social and life course, will be dealt with separately. This is because I believe we need to take a step backwards and try to understand each individual model of explanation rather better before we can make sense of attempts at combination. It is also because some of the literature attempts to set some of the approaches against each other in a competitive manner that is unhelpful to anyone trying to understand them separately, or the possible ways in which they might be combined.

As discussed in chapter 1, one of the explanations put forward in the Black Report for the existence of health inequality, and perhaps the most popular in subsequent research, was what it called 'the behavioural/cultural explanation'. It was described in this way:

> emphasising unthinking, reckless or irresponsible behaviour or incautious life-style as the moving determinant of poor health status . . . Some would argue that such systematic behaviour within certain social groups is a consequence only of lack of education, or individual waywardness . . . Others see behaviour which is conducive to good or bad health as embedded more within social structure – as illustrative of socially distinguishable styles of life, associated with, and reinforced by, class. (Townsend, Davidson and Whitehead, 1986: 110, 114)

Since publication of the report, both individual research reports and official surveys have repeatedly documented persistent differences between social groups in various types of consumption and leisure activities that are related to health. Most prominent among these are smoking, leisure-time exercise, and the amount of fats, sugars and salt in the diet.

Table 4.1 Cigarette smoking by Registrar-General's Social Class (RGSC) in men and women aged 20–74, 1998

RGSC	Cigarette smokers %		Numbers = 100%	
	Men	Women	Men	Women
I	21.6	29.9	218	87
II	27.1	38.1	1,374	1,010
IIINM	42.0	41.8	462	1,563
IIIM	45.5	46.6	1,521	410
IV	48.3	55.3	714	985
V	55.4	56.4	233	413

Source: Health Survey for England, 1998, author's analysis

Table 4.1 shows the differences in the rates of cigarette smoking for men and women from the Health Survey for England, 1998. The measure of socio-economic position is that most frequently used in British official health reports at the time, the Registrar-General's social classification. Smoking displays a clear 'class gradient': the less advantaged the social class position, the more likely it is that a person, male or female, will smoke. (Note, however, that women are far more likely to smoke than men in the 'professional and managerial' classes I and II.) One could repeat this table for a large number of different 'risky behaviours', and for different measures of social position and circumstances such as income or status and find the same outcome. The lower the income or status, the more likely it is that a person will engage in the less health-promoting form of behaviours, such as consumption of refined white bread and high-fat meat, and the less likely it is that they will engage in health promoting behaviours, such as jogging or eating five portions of fruit and vegetables a day.

'Direct' Behavioural Explanations

The Black Report and a large number of subsequent studies use the term 'behavioural/cultural explanation' to refer to the role played by smoking, eating, alcohol and exercise in producing health inequality. In practice, most research using a behavioural model of health inequality focuses on 'behaviour' rather than 'culture' (see, for example, Woodward et al., 1992; Lynch, Kaplan and Salonen, 1997b; Osler et al., 2000). In general, most research also takes a rather less considered approach than that of the Black Report, in that it tends to leave undeveloped any theoretical perspective on why behaviour might vary systematically between social classes, income or status groups.

Underlying much research on health behaviour as an explanation for health inequality is what I will call a 'direct behavioural model'. It rests on an assumption, often not clearly spelt out, that people with less control over their employment circumstances, and with lower status and income, are less endowed with some types of personal characteristics (Bosma, van de Mheen and Mackenbach, 1999a). Implicitly, these can often be read as a version of 'intelligence', 'coping skills' or personal resilience. People with low levels of these attributes have not done well enough in school to acquire the better types of job that carry the other advantages with them. Why should such attributes be linked to risky health behaviours? Once again, the implicit assumption is that people with less money and status are not able to grasp the health education messages put out by governments and health professionals, or have not the 'self-discipline' to obey them. People with less social advantage may also be thought of as having less self-control ('external locus of control'), or may have a shorter time-perspective that makes them unable to grasp the longer-term health consequences of things that give them short-term pleasure. Although these ideas are seldom explicitly tested in research, they underlie some influential work.

The direct behavioural model, then, can be seen as a sub-type of the behavioural/cultural explanation. In this explanatory model the link between social position and behaviour is due to adverse personal characteristics of individuals, which are independent of their position in the social structure. The model can be expressed in terms of a testable hypothesis. If it were true, and if we had data on 'locus of control' (to take one of the potential underlying explanatory characteristics), social position and risky health behaviours, we would expect to end up with data similar to that presented in table 4.2.

Here, we can see that there are 100 people divided evenly into two social classes, one advantaged, the other disadvantaged. There are also 50 people with 'internal locus of control' and 50 with 'external locus of control'. No one with 'internal locus of control' engages in risky behaviours, while 50 per cent of people with 'external locus of control' do so (5/10 in the advantaged and 20/40 in the disadvantaged class). In the advantaged class, however, 40 people have 'internal locus of control' compared to only 10 people in the disadvantaged class. The fact that more people in the dis-

Table 4.2 Hypothetical relationship between social position, locus of control and health risk behaviour if the 'direct behavioural model' is accurate

Locus of control	Social position						Total
	Advantaged			Disadvantaged			
	Risky behaviour			Risky behaviour			
	No	Yes	All	No	Yes	All	
Internal	40	0	40	10	0	10	50
%	*100*	*0*		*100*	*0*		
External	5	5	10	20	20	40	50
%	*50*	*50*		*50*	*50*		
Totals	45	5	50	30	20	50	100

advantaged class (20/50 compared to 5/50) engage in risky behaviours is entirely due to there being more people with 'external locus of control' in that class (and vice versa). In percentage terms, the rate of risky behaviour in those with external (50 per cent) and internal (0 per cent) 'locus of control' is exactly the same in each class. So the difference between the classes depends solely on the different numbers of people with internal locus of control in each class. We could relabel the column for 'locus of control' with a range of other psychological characteristics – coping ability or fatalism or even 'intelligence'. The argument would take the same shape. If a direct behavioural explanation for social inequality in risk behaviours is true, then the differences between the social classes will be due entirely to the distribution into these classes of people with different psychological characteristics.

This example is so crude as to seem almost ridiculous. But it does have a purpose: it makes explicit the shape of the kind of argument that is used in research into behaviour as a cause of health inequality. Table 4.2 misses out a step, in fact. The next step in a classical argument of this type (also usually left unstated) is that people with favourable attributes such as internal locus of control have arrived in the more advantaged social positions as a result of their mental powers. In fact, this kind of explanation does not require there to be any 'effect' of social position or circumstances on health behaviours at all. The psychologically 'superior' people were always going to have better health, and they were always going to be in more favoured social circumstances. In this simplest and clearest version of the behavioural explanation, people with, shall we say, an external locus of control, are just more likely to be or become socially disadvantaged *and* more likely to smoke, drink a lot or take little exercise. The few unlucky ones with high locus of control who end up in a disadvantaged social position are still leading healthy lives, there are just not enough of them to influence the general level of behaviour in that social class as a whole.

There is obviously no role for 'culture' in the type of argument I have just outlined. It is in fact a form of the selection argument. In practice, of course, this 'direct behavioural' model has seldom been tested, and if it were, the result would be a great deal more mixed. Social advantage and disadvantage are usually found to be related to psychological characteristics, but not as strongly as in the imaginary table 4.2. Also, the relationship of psychological characteristics to health behaviours is far more mixed. One of the few studies to have tested the relative importance of psychological and social factors in social differences in health behaviours was carried out in the Netherlands. Although the psychological factors seemed to play some part, material factors played an even greater one. That is, although people with lower levels of education were likely to smoke and have a poor diet in part because they were psychologically different from those who were more successful, it was even more significant that they had lower incomes (Stronks et al., 1997). In terms of health policy, this implies that improving the income of people who did not do very well at school is more important for their health risks than trying to change psychological traits.

Behaviour as a Result of 'Culture'

The Black Report did not adopt the 'direct behavioural' type of explanation outlined in the last section. This is presumably why the authors used the hybrid term 'behavioural/cultural'. No social anthropologist or cultural psychologist could accept 'unthinking, reckless or irresponsible behaviour or incautious lifestyle' as a valid description of 'culture'. The authors of the report, and many who have followed them, seem to have regarded social differences in health-related behaviours as somehow being a consequence of their disadvantaged position in the social structure and of their low income. They do not seem to have viewed either the risky behaviour or the social disadvantage as a consequence of personal characteristics. A very few studies, such as that by Stronks and her colleagues referred to above, actually try to measure the degree to which the relationship between social class (based on occupation) and risky health behaviours can be explained in terms of psychological characteristics versus the life circumstances of people in different classes. They find that some of the differences in behaviour appear to be due to psychological differences, but, regardless of these personal characteristics, many are the result of differences in income. However, this does not solve the problem. In social policy terms, it might favour an argument for increasing minimum wages and benefit levels. But in intellectual terms, we are really no further forward. Why should it be that people with low incomes smoke more and take less exercise? Giving up smoking and walking more, or taking up jogging in leisure time, are not *prevented* by a low income. This is one of the reasons why the idea of 'culture' has crept into the explanation of social differences in risky health behaviours.

Experts in the study of culture have defined it in various ways. As long ago as 1871, the anthropologist E. B. Tylor defined it as 'that complex whole which includes knowledge, beliefs, art, morals, laws, customs and any other capabilities and habits acquired by man as a member of society' (Tylor, 1871 cited in Berry et al., 1992: 165). Under this very wide umbrella are often included shared rules (norms) governing the activities of a social group, and traditions. Some eighty years later Kroeber and Kluckhohn sum up their definition as 'traditional . . . ideas and especially their attached values' (Kroeber and Kluckhohn, 1952 cited in Berry et al., 1992: 166). This is an 'ideational' model of culture: culture seen as a system of meanings that exists in the heads of people within a community. The alternative 'behavioural' model of culture sees it as composed of behaviour which occurs regularly in institutional domains within a community such as religious, familial or political institutions (A. Singh-Manoux, personal communication). Under this heading could be included Bourdieu's concept of the 'habitus' as a collection of learned behaviours that are shaped by exposure to a certain social environment over the life course. Fassin has described the relation of life circumstances to behaviours and their outcomes vividly as 'l'inscription de l'ordre social dans les corps ou . . . l'incorporation de l'inégalité' (the inscription of the social order on the body, or . . . the incorporation of inequality) (Fassin, 2000: 135).

There is very little literature that relates social differences in health behaviours to anything that might be identified as 'cultural' differences between social classes, as understood in anthropology (Shatenstein and Ghadirian, 1998). But there are some studies that acknowledge that there may be more to the social differences in health behaviours than individual psychological variables alone. For one thing, the few studies that have investigated the question find that most people in all social classes understand perfectly well that smoking is not good for health (Blaxter, 1990; Shewry et al., 1992): differences in understanding do not explain the differences (as shown in table 4.1) in smoking itself. The most important example of an attempt to test the role of culture is Blaxter's analysis of the role of class differences in beliefs about healthy behaviour in her classic, *Health and Lifestyles* (Blaxter, 1990). She was able to show that class differences in attitudes toward 'healthy eating', for example, explained less than 1 per cent of the differences between manual workers and non-manual workers, the two class groups she investigated. In other words, the reasons why the non-manual workers had a healthier diet were not dominated by differences in beliefs between them and the manual workers about what a healthy diet was or how important it was. In this study, the strongest anti-smoking beliefs were in fact held by men who *did* smoke (who were also in less advantaged social classes). So in this case there was no chance whatever that 'cultural' differences in attitudes (culture in its 'ideational' sense in other words) could be responsible for social differences in smoking.

Education and Behaviour

On the other hand, both Blaxter's and every other study have found that measures of education have powerful relationships to health behaviours. Those with more years of schooling, and with more qualifications, are found to have healthier diets, to smoke less and to do more exercise in the great majority of studies (Gran, 1995; Hoeymans et al., 1996; Iribarren et al., 1997). This might lead us towards a version of the behavioural/cultural explanation more in line with Bourdieu's notion of habitus. Maybe in the culture of more advantaged social groups, both education and health are given more priority? So that as children grow up in these groups, they acquire a certain disposition towards a set of behaviours: they study harder, do better in school. We can posit that as a consequence, they are more likely to stay in the same advantaged social position as their parents, and that the habitus of this group includes 'healthier' lifestyles (Lynch, Kaplan and Salonen, 1997b). Any relationship between social position and smoking, for example, would not depend on attitudes, but rather on a set of habits acquired over time. This hypothesis would need to be tested by collecting data on the social position of people's parents. We would expect to see that parents' social position would be related to education, and education would be related to both the individual's own adult social position and circumstances and to health behaviours.

In general, when studies find the effect of education on health appears to be more powerful in statistical terms than a person's own socio-economic position and circumstances, this is regarded as giving support to the idea that health inequality is due to some kind of either psychological or 'cultural' superiority, a factor that results both in the achievement of social advantage and the ability to safeguard one's health. But even if we take what seems to be a reasonably plausible and simple version of the idea that somehow 'culture' causes social differences in health behaviour, it is necessary to be careful to specify just what we mean. There are different versions of the 'behavioural/cultural explanation', each of which needs to be stated clearly in order to pin it down and subject it to clear empirical tests.

Overall, it does not seem very likely that concepts of culture that define it in terms of beliefs about health and health-related behavioural risks are going to be enormously helpful. Blaxter's work, which comes closest to using a concept of culture as shared ideas, values or norms about healthy lifestyles, and makes a serious attempt to measure these, shows only a very small contribution of culture to differences between manual and non-manual social classes. But if we define 'culture' in terms of education, the influence appears to be far greater.

Health Behaviours, Self-Regulation and Psychological Reward

It is all very well to show the power of education to predict risky behaviour and states of health. But we still need to fill in the links between the two. One promising way to look at the relationship of social position to health behaviours has recently emerged from the psychological and neurological literature. It centres around the concept of 'self-regulation'. This work has begun to be assimilated into social epidemiology by Siegrist. He regards the fulfilment of central social roles (worker, family or intimate group member, active citizen) as supportive of what he calls personal self-regulation (Siegrist, 1998, 2000). The concept of self-regulation encompasses a notion of 'positive feedback' to the individual about their acceptance and esteem within their immediate social context, and by society more widely. Self-regulation thereby creates a stable contact between the individual and society which also gives signals about desirable behaviour, by rewarding actions that are valued. These positive signals appear actually to influence certain chemicals inside the brain. In their absence, tensions are experienced which can be, to some extent, alleviated by means of substances such as sweet and carbohydrate-rich foods, alcohol and nicotine, as well as certain 'hard' drugs.

Siegrist argues that when deprived of access to central social roles, as when a close relationship breaks down, or a job is lost, a source of self-regulation is removed from the individual. We could go on to see the ways in which socio-economic position and circumstances are related to the risk of such adverse events. Those in less advantaged classes according to the UK National Statistics Socio-Economic Classification (NS-SEC) schema are, by definition, in less secure jobs. Job security, as well as the availability of a career structure, are in fact part of the way in which membership of an SEC is defined. In this light it would not be surprising if members of SECs 6 and 7, in particular, were found to be more likely to smoke, or to have less healthy diets. Couples with low income, or living on state benefits, are known to be more likely to experience separation and divorce, putting them at high risk of this kind of 'role loss'. Social differences in active citizenship, in the form of participation in voluntary organizations, churches, political parties and similar activities, are less well researched and understood. However, there is some evidence that the 'social capital' of an area, defined in terms of how many people belong to local organizations, may be related to health.

Culture as Social Distinction

We might also look back at chapter 2 and be somewhat critical of the lack of evidence for a role for 'culture' in the *Health and Lifestyle* study. As the chosen measure of social position, Blaxter used the Registrar-General's schema of social classes. At the time, this was perfectly orthodox. But different measures of social position are now becoming more commonly used. For example, perhaps if we used the Cambridge scale, which is based on people's choices of who to mix with in their leisure time (see chapter 2), the relationship might look different. The research to test this idea has not been carried out. We would need to know if the measures of 'culture' (beliefs about health and health-related behaviours) were more closely related to position on the Cambridge scale than to Registrar-General's class, first of all. This is quite likely. But we might also think that the basis for the Cambridge scale (that is, friendship choices) might itself be a good measure of shared culture and 'habitus', over and above whatever people say about how important they believe diet or smoking to be for health, and how far they believe they can control their own health. Perhaps social differences in diet, smoking and the like are really more like choices of decorative style or fashion? It may be that people in certain social milieux simply do not think it is 'the done thing' to smoke, or not to go to the gym?

This version of the role of lifestyles is another that has been suggested by Pierre Bourdieu. He regards many forms of leisure activity, and choices of clothes, books, music and food, as ways in which social groups express and maintain their 'distinction' from other groups (Bourdieu, 1984). This is important in this context, as it means there may be powerful reasons for adhering to certain kinds of behaviours which have nothing whatever to do with people's beliefs about health. In Hindu culture, for example, vegetarianism is a sign of being a member of the highest, Brahmin caste. It is such an important symbol of social status, that social groups aspiring to higher-caste status adopt vegetarianism and give up wearing leather (Shatenstein and Ghadirian, 1998). This is a strategy called 'Sanskritisation'. In French society, Bourdieu (1984) points to the ways in which discussions of taste in food or music are subtle ways in which people seek to establish who is socially superior or inferior, and thus express relationships of dominance. The effects are so profound as to make it very hard for young people from less culturally advantaged backgrounds to fit into the social life, or even the intellectual life, of the elite Paris universities and technical colleges.

A few studies have found a strong relationship to health behaviours in a measure of socio-economic position that is based on friendship choices (the Cambridge scale). The findings of these studies give some support to the idea that shared culture or lifestyle may be an influence on social differences in health (Chandola, 1998; Bartley et al., 1999; Sacker et al., 2000a). Even if differences in expressed attitudes to health do not seem to have much effect on health risk behaviours, then, it may still be that other forms of cultural differences between people of different social status are important. Social differences in the adoption of a healthy lifestyle do not have to be a result of explicit beliefs about health itself. As we have seen in the context of education, they may simply be part of what is viewed as appropriate behaviour for 'people like us'.

There seems to be some support for the idea that culture in the sense of shared lifestyles, adopted as part of a process of social distinction, may influence health behaviours. This kind of cultural influence would also be less amenable to change as a result of health information (A. Singh-Manoux, personal communication). Although there are not many relevant studies, there is also support for persistent social disadvantage going back to childhood as another significant influence on health-related behaviours. There has as yet been no clarification of the extent to which childhood disadvantage is related to adult behaviours as a result of continuities in 'culture'. This relationship does not seem to be the result of psychological characteristics affected by childhood experiences to any great extent. But there are many separate studies that show both a strong relationship of educational attainment to health behaviours, and of childhood disadvantage to educational attainment. So this may add up to a degree of support for the idea that the 'culture' of the family may play a role in terms of the value placed on education. Once a young person begins to achieve status through their educational and subsequent occupational attainments, they may then enter a social milieu in which at least some aspects of the lifestyles adopted to express and display 'superior' status accord with advice on healthy behaviour. The evidence, such as it is, therefore, seems to support a pathway linking social status (prestige), and associated lifestyle 'cultures', rather than employment relations to health behaviours.

'Cultural Shift'

There is a recent and sophisticated version of the behavioural/cultural theory that has emerged from a major comparative study of health inequality in the European nations (Kunst, 1997; Mackenbach et al., 1997). I will call this the 'cultural shift' explanation. It focuses on the differences between countries in the overall prevalence of certain kinds of health risk behaviours.

To the great surprise of many (and still very controversially), this international comparative study found similar or greater inequalities (depending on age) between social classes in mortality in wealthy and egalitarian Nordic nations such as Norway and Sweden than it found in Italy, Ireland and Portugal. Even more surprisingly perhaps, inequalities in mortality during the 1980s were found to be larger in Sweden than in the United States in men aged 30–44 and no different in men aged 45–59 (Kunst, 1997). Kunst reflected that:

> There were good reasons to expect that egalitarian socio-economic . . . policies resulted in a substantial and lasting reduction in inequalities in health. However, comparative studies do not provide support for this expectation. Socio-economic differences in mortality in countries with more egalitarian policies are not small from an international perspective . . . The potential role of some circumstances, for example cultural factors, has been ignored too long in health inequalities research. (1997: 142)

One possible aspect of culture that might throw light on the puzzle was diet. In those Southern European nations with relatively large income inequalities but good health, the diet followed by the majority of people was a healthier one (Kunst, 1997: 206). 'Having a healthy diet' was not some special kind of lifestyle in these societies. So eating fruit, salads and olive oil was not seen as any kind of lifestyle choice and therefore was not associated with social advantage or disadvantage. Similarly, in nations where there was generally a low level of alcohol use (or at least of 'binge drinking') inequalities in alcohol-related deaths were low. It seems as if there may be a kind of 'national sin' that differs from country to country. Citizens who find themselves in difficulties are most likely to fall into whatever this particular 'sin' may be, with a resultant impact on the causes of disease responsible for health inequality. These vary from heavy alcohol consumption with resultant deaths from acute poisoning and accidents in Finland; high-fat, low-vegetable diet leading to heart disease in the USA; and smoking and lung disease in Great Britain to chronic high-alcohol consumption with resultant cirrhosis in France. The wide availability of guns in the USA may also be thought of as one reason for the very high mortality from homicide of young men in the poor inner-city areas which makes a major contribution to overall health inequality in that nation. The comparative study also found, to some extent, that social class differences in health behaviours differ between nations as one might expect from the observed differences in health inequality. A lot more middle-class people smoke in France or Spain than in Sweden for example. The middle-class obsession with healthy lifestyle was not as yet as widely adopted in France, Spain, Italy, Greece or Switzerland as it had been in Sweden, Norway or Britain.

There are therefore two elements to the cultural shift theory. One might be regarded as 'cultural': the idea of adopting no smoking, low-fat food and leisure exercise as a way of expressing social distinction has simply not yet penetrated Spanish or Greek society. If everyone eats olive oil, it is useless as a way of displaying one's high status. The second element has to do simply with the material realities of local existence. In countries where fruit and vegetables (and perhaps wine in moderate quantities) are cheap and plentiful, they form part of everyone's diet and are affordable to all. One does not need to have intelligence, coping skills, self-control and so on to decide to eat tomatoes, garlic and olive oil in Spain or Italy. Nor is such a lifestyle a signal of wealth. The role in national life played by heavy bouts of alcohol drinking (or the consumption of other kinds of drugs) is a more complex phenomenon, and harder to explain. In all Southern European nations, smoking is at a high level in all social classes, and there was far less social inequality in heart disease. Because heart disease is the most common single cause of mortality in men of later working age in most European nations, this meant that overall health inequality was low or absent in these nations. And it was in the Southern European nations where a 'healthy' diet and moderate alcohol consumption were seen more or less equally in all social classes. Health inequality would therefore only emerge in the Southern European nations, according to this theory, if their less socially advantaged populations developed a fondness for foods with a high fat and sugar content, and began to drink alcohol in the more Northern 'binge' pattern.

This is at present no more than a theory, it cannot be stressed too carefully. We do not at the present time have any data that follows representative samples of the populations of even a few of these countries through time to see if citizens of Greece or Spain in less advantaged social positions are less likely to suffer heart attacks even if they do 'binge' drink and eat burgers. We do not know if a salad-eating Swedish stockbroker has the same life expectancy as a steak-and-chips-eating Greek one.

The one exception to this is a study of health behaviours in British and Japanese men of different occupational grade (a measure of their social position) (Martikainen et al., 2001). Japanese men in less privileged socio-economic positions, as indicated both by employment grade and education, were more likely to smoke, and had higher fibrinogen (a substance that makes blood more likely to clot) and blood pressure. This was similar to the gradients seen in a comparable sample of British men. However, social differences in other risk factors for heart disease were quite different to those found in Britain. In Japan, the more privileged men in the higher occupational grades were more likely to have high body mass and an unhealthy 'pear-shape' than their lower-grade peers were. And this was all the more true for the younger men.

The authors of this paper surmise that in the younger men a Northern-Western lifestyle or cultural pattern was emerging, taking the form of a liking for meat and other high-fat foods that are not found in the traditional Japanese diet. Whether this could be regarded as a 'cultural shift' is an interesting question: the paper is an epidemiological study which does not include information on values or beliefs. Did these younger Japanese executives pick up signals about the status implications of lifestyle as they had more contact with Western colleagues? And have they adopted these behaviours as their own expressions of being both high status and 'modern'? Certainly, beef is a very expensive commodity in Japan, and consuming large amounts would operate as a signal of wealth. If so, and if the 'cultural shift' theory has some truth in it, the next thing we would expect to see would be the diffusion of high-fat food eating from the more to the less privileged social layers in Japan (although the price of beef would possibly have to fall before this could happen). As this happens, the high-status lifestyle can be expected to shift again towards jogging and salad, accompanied by a worsening of social inequality in heart disease among Japanese men. Whichever interpretation be closer to the truth in this case, it illustrates the need for better understanding of the links between social forces and lifestyle.

FURTHER READING

The classic study of the relationship of lifestyles to health
Blaxter, M., *Health and Lifestyles.* London: Tavistock, 1990.

Contains useful chapters on this topic from a US perspective
Amick III, B. C., Levine, S., Tarlov, A. R., and Chapman Walsh, D., *Society and Health.* Oxford: Oxford University Press, 1995.

The best recent study in this area
Stronks, K., *Socio-economic Inequalities in Health: Individual Choice or Social Circumstances?* Rotterdam: Erasmus University Rotterdam, 1997.

5

Models of Aetiological Pathways, II: The Psycho-Social Model

Most studies of health inequality that have investigated possible causes have included measures of behaviours similar to those discussed in the last chapter. In most such studies, health behaviours have not been found to explain all of the social differences (although some do so more than others) (Pocock et al., 1987; Bucher and Ragland, 1995). The 'Whitehall studies' in the UK compare the health and mortality risk of London civil servants in different employment grades. The British civil service being a rather hierarchical organization, grade of employment is a relatively accurate measure of prestige, income and employment relations (Marmot et al., 1978; Marmot et al., 1991; Marmot, 1993). The observed patterns of health-related behaviour did differ between grades, but this only explained about a quarter of the fourfold difference in the risk of death over a seven-year period (Marmot, 1989).

These and other studies have indicated that we need to look beyond smoking, diet and exercise for explanations of the existence of differences in health between more and less advantaged social groups. The health differences between people in more and less advantaged social positions also seem to be too great to be explained, at least in modern industrialized societies, by 'purely material' factors. Members of unskilled manual occupations (Registrar-General's Social Class (RGSC) V in terms of the most commonly used British classification) earn very much less than lawyers, doctors and managers. But it is not generally thought that the wages of a labourer are so low as to mean that he or she will be unable to buy enough food to avoid undernutrition. Working people with very low incomes usually receive various kinds of state help, for example in paying their rent, their children receive free school meals and so on. These issues will be more closely examined in the next chapter. For the moment let us accept that literal starvation or exposure are unlikely to be fully responsible for the approximate six to seven years' difference in life expectancy between the most and the least advantaged social classes in the UK (Harding et al., 1999). One of the most widely researched alternatives is the 'psycho-social model', which argued that we may need to include what are described as 'psycho-social risk factors'. These include social support, control and autonomy at work, the balance between home and work, the balance between efforts and rewards.

Another reason why many people think that an explanation for health inequality in terms of simple material scarcity is insufficient is that in country after country, study after study, what we see is not a group of very poor people at the bottom of the income distribution who have poor health while everyone else is fine. Instead, what we see is a steady gradation from the very top to the very bottom. Not only do men in the UK RGSC I have better health than those in RGSC V, but those in RGSC I with a car and a mortgage have a higher life expectancy than those in social class I with only one of these (Wannamethee and Shaper, 1997), while those in RGSC I owning 2 cars have better health than those with only one car (Goldblatt, 1990a). However many fine gradations of socioeconomic advantage anyone has been able to measure, these have so far all tended to show similar gradation in health, a phenomenon that has been called 'the fine grain' of health inequality (Davey Smith, Bartley and Blane, 1990b; Davey Smith, Blane and Bartley, 1994).

In perhaps the most comprehensive study on this topic undertaken to date, Lynch and colleagues studied the associations between income and mortality in a population-based sample of 2,272 Finnish men over ten years (1984–93). Compared with the highest income quintile, those in the bottom quintile were more than three times as likely to die from any cause during the period of the project. But by including in their models, as possible explanations of the income-health relationship, risk factors such as smoking, obesity and other behaviours as well as other psychological and social risk factors, they could fully explain this difference. This study showed two important things. One was that the link between income and mortality could be understood in terms that did not relate to starvation and exposure – persons on lower incomes were at higher risk of heart disease (in part) because they had higher weight, not lower, and because they smoked. In a modern welfare state, lower income seems to be a health hazard because it encourages certain patterns of consumption. The other important finding was that the researchers needed to include psycho-social variables such as social support and relationships at work to achieve this 'total explanation'. Behavioural variables such as smoking alone were not found to be sufficient (Lynch et al., 1996).

Although health-damaging behaviours are more common in people who are less socio-economically privileged, there is no logical link between having little money and many of these behaviours. Up to the present time, an additional 'cultural' rather than 'psycho-social' component has more commonly supplemented the behavioural explanation, but there has always needed to be some kind of a social rather than a purely economic explanation. The 'self-regulation/social reward' theory put forward by Siegrist (see chapter 4) has taken a step towards combining behavioural with psycho-social approaches. As we have seen, it proposes that under circumstances where the rewards derived from occupancy of central social roles are under threat, systems within the brain may become more vulnerable to cravings and addiction. The sorts of unhealthy substances (legal or illegal) which put people at risk of addiction become more attractive under certain psychological conditions. This might be regarded as a psycho-social explanation for behavioural differences between social groups.

Siegrist's version of the behavioural explanation for health inequality therefore relates feelings of low reward to changes in brain chemistry that may promote addictive cravings. But this is not a classic psycho-social model. In most of the psycho-social literature, the focus is on how feelings that arise because of inequality, domination or subordination may directly affect biological processes. In this chapter, I will describe such a 'direct' psycho-social explanation. In various guises, this kind of explanation for social inequality in health is one of the most pervasive at the present time. Rather than laying emphasis on physical hazards, or on behaviour alone, the 'direct' psycho-social model focuses on the way social inequality makes people feel, and how these feelings may themselves alter body chemistry.

Fight, Flight and Defeat

The original ideas behind this line of research were based on the existence of two types of response to external threats shared by both humans and other animals (Brunner, 1997). The most well known of these is the so called 'fight or flight' response. The body receives alarm messages from the brain that can be thought of as activating one or other of two 'response circuits': the sympathetic-adrenomedullary and the hypothalamic-pituitary-adrenocortical. Both of these circuits involve the adrenal gland (hence 'adrenaline'), which sits close to the kidney. The 'adrenomedullary' circuit involves a structure within the adrenal medulla, one of the inner layers of the gland, whereas the 'cortical' circuit involves the outer layer or cortex.

It is the sympathetic-adrenomedullary circuit that is perhaps nearer to popular ideas of the fight or flight response. This reaction involves the sympathetic nervous system, which, in balance with the parasympathetic nervous system, is responsible for much of what goes on in a routine way in the body without conscious awareness. They govern how fast the heart is beating, responses to changes in outside temperature (shivering, sweating) and the pH (acidity) level of the blood, for example. Sympathetic nervous stimulation releases adrenaline from the adrenal medulla, and at the same time the ends of the sympathetic nerves themselves release noradrenaline. This prompts the release into the bloodstream of fibrinogen, a substance that helps blood to clot more easily. At the same time, the heart rate and blood pressure rise, and the small blood vessels (capillaries) nearest to the skin narrow sharply. This would prevent excessive blood loss from a wound, but it also has the effect of raising the blood pressure.

In the human evolutionary past, the argument goes, violent activity would follow the arousal of the fight or flight response (Brunner, 2000; Steptoe and Willemsen, 2002). Adrenaline remains in the blood for only a few minutes. Then vigorous physical activity (fighting or running away) would burn off the excess. Once this was over, if the person survived, the parasympathetic nervous system would quickly return the body to a more normal state. However, under modern conditions, feelings of fear or anger must often be subdued. The examples often given are those of being caught in a traffic jam, or bullied by a superior at work. There is no prospect of actually being able to make any physical response to these events. Even when escape is made, this is done without physical effort. And endurance of prolonged stress over long periods of time is thought by some to eventually 're-set' the blood pressure to a chronically higher level.

The second stress circuit is the hypothalamic-pituitary-adrenocortical ('the HPA axis'). One of the most important links in this chain of effects is the release of cortisol. Hormonal messages travel from the hypothalamus to the pituitary gland (which are more or less next to each other at the base of the brain). The pituitary gland in turn secretes into the blood a hormone that stimulates the adrenal cortex, which then proceeds to release cortisol into the blood. Cortisol and other related hormones called 'glucocorticoids' regulate several aspects of human metabolism under normal circumstances. For our present purposes the most important of their actions is to increase the amount of energy we can expend by mobilizing reserves of sugars and fats into the bloodstream. If the stressful situation does result in violent activity, these will be burned off, as they would have been in our evolutionary past. But in the traffic jam, this does not happen. As a consequence, in susceptible people, the fats and sugars build up in the blood, and a porridgy substance ('atheroma', derived from the Greek word for porridge) is deposited, which begins to narrow the blood vessels. Fibrinogen (which, as we have seen, will have been increased by the fight or flight response to the same stress factor) then encourages the formation of small blood clots that may become stuck in these narrowed vessels. If this happens in one of the blood vessels that feed the heart muscle, the muscle becomes starved of its blood supply. The heart may then beat irregularly, accompanied by severe chest pain – a heart attack.

The glucocorticoids are also thought to affect mood directly. There is a rare disease called Cushing's syndrome, in which the body produces far too much cortisol, whose sufferers experience profound feelings of threat and depression regardless of their social environment. This has led some researchers to look for, and to find, links between depression and later heart disease (Kauhanen et al., 1996; Ford et al., 1998). Cortisol also has the effect of damping down inflammation. In general, the glucocorticoids may be thought of as 'diverting' some of the body's 'energies' from routine tasks, such as watching out for infections and abnormal cell growth and repairing damage to body tissues, towards mobilizing energies for short-term reactions. Once again, this is a useful process for meeting short-term extreme threats. The problems arise when people are constantly under threat with no obvious way to fight or run away. The ability to fight infections and even some early cancers may then be reduced.

Stress-induced damage to the metabolism and the immune system has been described as a result of excessive 'allostatic load' (McEwen, 1998). The term 'allostasis' means, literally, 'the ability of the body to keep itself stable' during changes in the external environment, such as changes in temperature and diet. The 'allostatic load' model of psycho-social causes of ill health focuses on what may happen when there are too many changes in too short a period of time, so that the body's attempts to respond produce overload and exhaustion. The idea would lead us to expect, for example, that an objectionable boss would be harder to bear in an environment that was also too hot, cold, or noisy, or when the individual also had a poor diet.

Failures of these processes of allostasis have been associated in one way or another with the aetiology of heart disease. It is known that people with high blood pressure are more likely to have heart attacks. The same is true of people with high levels of fibrinogen in their blood (Tunstall Pedoe et al., 1997). In several studies, blood pressure has appeared to react to situations of stress: people challenged with a difficult task, or anticipating a stressful event, experience rises in blood pressure, and in the amount of fibrinogen and/or dangerous fats in their blood (Friedman, Rosenman and Carrol, 1958; Moan, Eide and Kjeldsen, 1996). Some evidence can also be found that allostatic overload is more common amongst less socio-economically privileged people. Several studies have shown that people in less advantaged social positions have higher blood pressure and higher fibrinogen (Tyroler, 1989; Moller, Kristensen and Hollnagel, 1991; Wilson et al., 1993; Brunner et al., 1993; Myllykangas et al., 1995). It has also been observed that men who report feeling insufficiently rewarded for their effort at work have high fibrinogen levels (Siegrist, 1995) and those with an 'over-committed' work style have an impaired capacity for fibrinolysis (breaking down blood clots once they have formed) (Vrijkotte et al., 1999). These observations have led to the hypothesis that stressful experiences associated with lower levels of power and advantage in both the workplace and society at large may result in a tendency of the blood to clot too easily and thereby to an increased risk of heart attacks.

Cortisol released under stress conditions, as we have seen, also increases the levels of certain fats in the blood. The most common types of 'dangerous' blood fats commonly measured in studies are triglycerides and low density lipoprotein cholesterol (LDL). Studies have shown that stressful situations can also produce an increase of these fats in the blood (Friedman et al., 1958; Moan et al., 1996). Other studies have shown that indicators of more chronic anxiety, such as a high heart rate, are related to raised blood pressure and also to higher levels of triglycerides in the blood (Wannamethee and Shaper, 1994). Social epidemiologists have concluded that there might be a causal pathway by which stressful social circumstances produce emotional responses, which in turn bring about biological changes that increase the risk of heart disease. The people participating in the experiments that showed these biological effects were not poor. Studies of this kind have been carried out among accountants (Friedman, Rosenman and Carrol, 1958) and civil servants (Ferrie et al., 1995; Carroll et al., 1997), neither of whom are at the bottom of the income distribution.

Stress and Social Structure

These studies support a model that seeks to link adverse experiences and events of many kinds to health outcomes. Disadvantaged social class, low income or low status are only examples of such adverse experiences, although this is where the psycho-social literature meets the literature on health inequality. How, according to this model, would health be affected by one's position in the social structure? This question is seldom asked in a general way. Rather, individual studies tend to select a certain condition as their independent or hypothetically causal variable and then look for correlations. The health outcomes used in studies are also widely variable. Mortality from cardiovascular disease is frequently examined. But merely showing a relation of social position to mortality does not test the model – it does not prove that this association exists *because* people in more advantaged classes or status groups have lower levels of blood pressure or lower levels of dangerous blood fats (Wamala et al., 1999). Better tests of the psycho-social model would need to include measures of these. Ideally, we would need a study in which a group of healthy people (with normal blood pressure, blood fats, fibrinogen and so on) in different socio-economic positions were followed up over a period of time. Those in the less advantaged socio-economic positions and circumstances should experience more adverse events, their blood pressure and blood fats should rise, and ultimately more of the less advantaged than of the more advantaged should have developed heart disease (Steptoe and Willemsen, 2002). Outlined like this, it may sound a simple matter to test the psycho-social model of health inequality.

In practice, there are a number of reasons why it is a lot less simple than it seems to test the psycho-social model of health inequality. Not least important of these is cost. Collecting blood samples from large numbers of people is expensive, and this kind of exercise now needs to be approved by formally constituted ethical committees in many nations. Many of the sorts of social changes that would reduce stress caused by social inequality would be regarded as desirable regardless of whether they improved health. There is therefore some real doubt as to whether it is ethical to carry out invasive tests to prove the link of poverty or low social status with health. Processing the blood to establish the levels of fats, fibrinogen and so on then involves further substantial additional costs. The second major difficulty for this kind of study is that it is in fact rather difficult to find reasonable numbers of people in different social positions who all have equally good health to begin with. Some of the reasons for this may be obvious, and they will be considered further in the context of how social inequality affects the whole of the life course in chapter 7. A sufficiently healthy group of people in all social classes would tend to be rather young. Nowadays, it is becoming increasingly unusual to develop heart disease before the age of 60. This leads to the third problem, which is that, in order to observe a large enough number of heart attacks (let alone deaths from heart disease), the study would need to sample a lot of people, most of whom would remain perfectly healthy and not provide any 'outcome data' at all.

Types of Psycho-Social Factor

Social support

I have outlined the biological justification for using a psycho-social explanation to understand health inequality because it is easier to evaluate the plausibility of different kinds of psycho-social factors as explanations for health inequality with this in mind. Research until the present time has tended to concentrate on three spheres of life: the home, the workplace and the community.

Social support was perhaps the original psycho-social factor to be examined in the literature on the social causation of ill health. As a possible reason for health inequality it is less widely studied on its own. Social support has more often been coupled with other kinds of stresses and regarded as a 'buffering factor'. That is, when other stresses take place (such as an increase in stress at work or even the loss of a job), social support is thought of as a defence against the ill effects of the event (Steptoe, 2000; Vahtera et al., 2000). In the case of stressors such as the traffic jam or the bullying boss, there is a reasonably plausible sequence of social, psychological and biological events hypothetically linking the event to a disease outcome. The fight or flight response raises blood pressure and fibrinogen, then, if the threat does not recede, cortisol raises blood fats and sugars. If threats are very prolonged or repetitive, these high levels of blood fats and fibrinogen increase the risk of blocking the coronary arteries, and the effect of cortisol on immunity may weaken other aspects of the body's defences. An inclusive theory of psycho-social causation would need to look in a similar way at the different types of psycho-social stressors and ask what kinds of processes were likely to be at work. In practice this is not very easy to do.

Studies on this question relate various possible stressful events to health outcomes, and if any of these relationships looks strong (in statistical terms) a report is written. Because of the problems already mentioned, there are almost no studies of, for example, fibrinogen in people with low social support. Biologically speaking, we might expect that people with few supporting friends or relatives who experienced a threatening event might have a larger increase in the levels of blood fats and sugars (that is, a 'worse' response in terms of the HPA circuit) than those with greater support. If social support helps them by making the resolution of the stressful situation easier, the initial 'fight or flight' response is less likely to progress to 'defeat' with activation of the HPA axis. There is evidence from studies relating social circumstances to later illness and mortality that social support may be protective (Rosengren et al., 1993; Greenwood et al., 1996). But this kind of study, which relates a psycho-social factor to a later health event, does not necessarily guarantee the operation of what we have been thinking of here as a psycho-social pathway. We do not know if later disease was the outcome of the biological processes set out in the theory of psycho-social causation. The findings from studies of animals isolated from their fellows have been more positive. The blood vessels of isolated monkeys have been shown in one experiment to have become more thickened by fatty deposits (Shively, Clarkson and Kaplan, 1989). But some studies of humans have reported no relationship of social support to biological cardiovascular risk factors, such as blood fats and blood pressure (Jonsson et al., 1999).

In most long-term studies it is observed that people with good relationships to family and friends, and who participate in the community (for example, by going regularly to church), have longer life expectancies than those who are more isolated. This is impressive evidence: it is not just that cheerful, sociable people *say* they feel better. However, that is not proof of the existence of a psycho-social pathway in the sense discussed here. People who have good supportive relationships to others may differ in many health-relevant ways from those who do not. And there may be a number of mundane reasons why supportive relationships act to avert health disasters, by making it more likely that a person receives timely treatment, for example, or is nagged more persistently to 'look after themselves'. Be that as it may, social support is one psycho-social factor that has been most consistently found to be related to health. Other research also shows that those in more advantaged social positions tend to receive more social support, especially from outside of their immediate family (Marmot et al., 1991; Power and Matthews, 1997; Matthews, Stansfeld and Power, 1999).

Psycho-social work hazards, I: Job demands, work control and job strain

A number of studies have addressed the question of whether a combination of high demands on the worker with little control over the tasks undertaken, the skills used, or the pace of work might be related to the risk of heart disease. Demands and control are usually measured according to a set of questions based on the work of Robert Karasek, an architect who initiated this idea in the early 1980s. The combination of high demands and little control over the work situation is also called 'job strain'. One could imagine that reactions to job strain might well include some variety of the 'fight, flight and defeat' sequence as described above. Consistent with the earlier discussion of the 'fight or flight' response, studies in the 1950s showed that one of the occupations most at risk of heart disease at a young age was that of bus driver (bus drivers being constantly stuck in traffic jams). The early studies, however, merely looked to see if people who scored highly on an index of demands and low on a measure of control were more likely to develop or die of heart disease. They did not on the whole investigate the degree of physiological reaction to job strain.

The results of the studies to date are somewhat inconsistent. Many do show a relationship between the psycho-social risk and disease. Others do not. Theorell (2000) has reflected that the negative studies tend to be those with a very long follow-up, using outdated measures of demand and control, studying older people or populations with little variation in work conditions, or studying people who already had heart disease. Most well-designed studies do show a higher risk of heart disease over a period of up to around five years when demands are high and control is low. In the Whitehall II study for example, objectively measured low job control (no measure of demand was included in this analysis) made it around 50 per cent more likely that a person would develop heart disease in the following four to seven years (Bosma et al., 1998). The relationship between job control and heart disease in fact explained the occurrence of more heart disease in the lower employment grades (the 'social gradient'). Disease was more common in low grades because so many more people in these grades had low control. Men and women in lower grades who had high control were not at high risk of heart disease; men and women in higher grades with low control were at higher risk. This does not yet prove that there is a psycho-neuro-immunological (PNI) pathway. For that, we would have to see that people with high work demands and/or low work control also showed signs that the psycho-biological processes were operating, such as high fibrinogen and triglycerides in their blood and high blood pressure.

In many (Landsbergis et al., 1994; Pickering et al., 1996; Schnall et al., 1998; Netterstrom et al., 1998) but not all (Steptoe et al., 1995) studies, high job strain is related to high blood pressure. As with social support, there are in fact very few studies that follow the whole process through (Siegrist, Klein and Voigt, 1997). What we would need to see would be that men and women with high job strain (high demands and low control) showed a tendency to have high blood pressure, a 'risky' lipid profile, higher than ideal levels of clot-making fibrinogen (perhaps with lower than ideal levels of clot-busting fibrinolytic factors). Then we would need to see that it was the people with high job strain *and* the suspect physiological changes who developed disease. For this pathway to be 'the reason' for health inequality, we would have to see that people in less privileged class, status or income groups were more likely to develop heart disease both *because* they had low job control and *because* people with low job control had higher physiological risk factors.

In theoretical terms, the concept of job strain, involving as it does control and autonomy at work, creates a link between sociological theories of class (as discussed in chapter 2) and health inequality. Measures of social class, such as the Wright measure, the Erikson-Goldthorpe schema and the NS-SEC, use the degree of autonomy at work and the amount of control over one's own or other people's work activities as criteria for deciding which occupations fall in which classes. The theory of psychosocial causation therefore helps us to make sense of the observation that some social classes have better health than others. And, exactly as would be expected from the literature on job strain, it is found that the classes with greater autonomy and control, on the whole, experience better health (Dollamore, 1999; Sacker et al., 2000b). Once again, however, there is far less evidence that this is *because* members of more autonomous classes have lower blood pressure and fibrinogen or a less risky combination of fats in their blood. Although some tendency in this direction has been observed, the relationships could mostly be explained by the fact that men and women in less autonomous social classes also had lower status and incomes (Bartley et al., 1999). It has not been shown that people in occupations with greater autonomy have lower levels of stress hormones in their blood, or better health, regardless of their status in the wider community, their income or their health behaviours.

Psycho-social work hazards, II: Effort-reward imbalance (ERI)

Johannes Siegrist and colleagues in Germany have developed the concept of effort-reward imbalance (ERI) in relation to health. A number of studies have shown that workers who experience high effort combined with low rewards in the form of pay, security, approval of superiors and chances of promotion do tend to have higher blood pressure and fibrinogen, and a more adverse blood fat profile (Siegrist, 1995; Siegrist and Peter, 1996; Peter and Siegrist, 1997; Peter et al., 1998). These workers also have an increased risk of developing heart disease and strokes (Siegrist et al., 1992; Bosma et al., 1998; Kivimaki et al., 2002). In part because of the determination of Siegrist (a sociologist) to carry out studies that follow through the full PNI pathway, the 'full' psycho-social model is perhaps better tested in relation to ERI than in relation to job strain. This does not necessarily mean that ERI will turn out to be a 'superior' or stronger factor in the aetiology of heart disease, or a better explanation for health inequality more widely conceived. That remains to be studied.

Theoretically, ERI can be related to the concepts of prestige and status as well as to that of social class. Job security is one of the major forms of 'reward' whose lack acts as a risk factor in Siegrist's model. It is also a criterion for social class membership according to the Erikson-Goldthorpe schema and the NS-SEC. However, the notion of a mismatch between the amount or intensity of work and its rewards does not enter into class theory. It is explicit in the studies of ERI that one of the most stressful things about this imbalance is the feeling that progression in one's job does not match the amount of effort one has put into it. It is not so much control over what is going on in the work environment that matters in this approach, but the feeling of lack of recognition of one's efforts. Thus, ERI may be regarded as taking us beyond the 'fight or flight' model into the territory of status. Rewards for work done, either in the form of increased income or in the form of promotion, may be significant to the individual because of what they allow him or her to feel about their place in a social hierarchy. The question of which is more important, material goods, relationships and conditions of employment, or status in a social hierarchy, is an important but as yet unanswered question in health inequality research (Sacker et al., 2000a). Even if we had an answer to this question, much work would remain to be done to investigate the extent to which the link between social circumstances and health involves the psycho-biological pathways described in this chapter.

FURTHER READING

Essential readings included in this collection
Marmot, M., and Wilkinson, R. (eds), *Social Determinants of Health*. Oxford: Oxford University Press, 1999.

Sets out the basis for the 'work strain' hypothesis by its originators
Karasek, R. A., and Theorell, T., *Healthy Work: Stress, Productivity and the Reconstruction of Working Life*. New York: Basic Books, 1990.

Recent useful readings from members of the Whitehall II study group
Stansfeld, S., and Marmot, M., *Stress and the Heart*. London: BMJ Books, 2002.

More useful American readings on this topic
Amick III, B. C., Levine, S., Tarlov, A. R., and Chapman Walsh, D., *Society and Health*. Oxford: Oxford University Press, 1995.

6

Models of Aetiological Pathways, III:
The Materialist Model

The 'materialist' model was the one accepted by the authors of the UK Black Report, at the end of their extensive analysis of the evidence existing at the time. They identified the importance of 'the . . . diffuse consequences of the class structure: poverty, work conditions . . . and deprivation in its various forms in the home and immediate environment, at work, in education and the upbringing of children and more generally in family and social life' (Black, Morris and Townsend, 1982: 134). Yet despite the importance given to it by this pioneering document, there is less research using the materialist model than any of the others. Much of the evidence for the existence of material causes of health inequality comes from studies which show that health is worse and life expectancy lower in people who have, or may reasonably be assumed to have, relatively low incomes. In the British Whitehall II study of health in employees of the British civil service, for example, average pay in the lowest civil service employment grade in 1985, when the second Whitehall study began, was around £3,061 compared to around £62,100 in the highest grade (Marmot et al., 1991). Household income predicted mortality in the province of Manitoba (Mustard et al., 1997), and individual income showed a graded relationship to life expectancy in members of the Canada Pension Plan (Wolfson et al., 1993). Differences in mortality risk between those with higher and lower incomes in the United States have been demonstrated (Kitagawa and Hauser, 1973; Kaufman et al., 1998), and are thought to be increasing (Pappas et al., 1993). Wealth, as well as current income, is strongly linked to health in American citizens (Robert and House, 1996). Studies with information on individual income are not very common, but the observation of the link between income and health is made in the vast majority. Other studies have made similar links between measures of health (usually mortality) and average income in small areas such as neighbourhoods of the Canadian province of Winnipeg (Roos and Mustard, 1997), US census tracts (Stockwell et al., 1994; Stockwell, Goza and Roach, 1995; Anderson et al., 1997) and postal areas (Davey Smith et al., 1998), parishes in European nations (Osler et al., 2002), and boroughs in European cities (Reijneveld, 1995). Even AIDS, not for a long time regarded as a disease of poverty in industrialized nations, has been shown to have an 'income gradient', with highest rates in the poorest postal zones of Los Angeles, medium rates in the middle-income zones and lowest rates in the zones with highest average income (Simon et al., 1995), and a similar pattern has been seen in Ohio (Stockwell, Goza and Luse, 1997).

An impressive feature of many of these studies is that illness and mortality are not just high in 'the poor' and average in everyone else. Rather, the risk of illness and premature death shows 'the gradient': a stepwise increase with each step down the income ladder (whether this is individual income or an average for the area of residence) (Davey Smith et al., 1996a; Davey Smith et al., 1996b). The existence of the gradient offers one of the greatest puzzles to researchers trying to understand health inequality. When trying to explain an income gradient, the challenge is to look for convincing reasons why income should be related in this graded way to health and life expectancy. Townsend and his colleagues who wrote the Black Report and originated the idea of a 'materialist explanation for health inequality' did not equate a materialist explanation with one that concentrated on income or wealth. One reason for this was that the Black Report authors did not have access to information on income, as this was seldom asked in British surveys and never in the census. The Black Report was possible because of a unique series of official British reports on health inequality, using census data, which allowed changes to be traced over the whole of the period from 1921 to 1971 as shown in chapter 1. No other nation has data of this kind, which allow us to see what has happened to health differences between similarly defined social groups from the 1920s and throughout the affluent period that followed the end of the Second World War. The series was put together using data from the censuses that take place every ten years in England and Wales. Because there were no questions on income, the 'material' factors identified by the Black Report were expressed in terms of housing, car ownership and social class.

The second reason why the authors of the Black Report may not have concentrated on income is that we would not have explained health differences between classes or status groups very well, even if we could show that 'it is all due to income'. Obviously, a certain number of dollars, pounds or euros in wages or salary cannot literally affect the body. Income and ownership of goods, in most cases, do not give us a directly plausible causal pathway. One way to approach this puzzle from a 'materialist' perspective is to look at the ways in which income serves as both a cause and an indicator of exposure to physical hazards. In what ways might income cause people to be more at risk of exposure to danger in their everyday lives? Even if income is not a 'cause' of such exposure, what might it tell us about a person's life that is relevant to understanding the ways in which it may involve risks to their health?

Measuring Material Risk

Poor health and high mortality are found in almost all studies of geographical areas characterized by poverty (Gorey and Vena, 1995; Anderson et al., 1997), unemployment (Sloggett and Joshi, 1998; Malmstrom et al., 1999) or pollution (Mackenbach, Looman and Kunst, 1993). However, there has been little effort to improve the measurement of individual exposure to these kinds of 'material' risk factors. One reason for this may be that, taken one at a time, factors that can be clearly identified as 'material' do not seem to have much effect on health. There is a clear paradox here. When we look at income, social class or area of residence, those in the poorest circumstances have between 40 per cent and 150 per cent greater chances of illness and death in most studies. But when we look at hazards such as cold and damp housing, work hazards and inadequate (as opposed to 'unhealthy') diet, the effects are nowhere near this great.

In chapter 1 we saw that death rates have fallen steadily over the period from 1931 to 1991: what produces the level of health inequality we see in the UK today is the fact that this fall has been greater in the more privileged social classes. This raw fact is perhaps the most important reason for continuing to pay attention to material factors. Few people would argue that life in these social classes was more stressful, or that levels of social support were lower, in 1931 than 1991. If anything, an anecdotal impression of trends in 'stressfulness' in the different types of occupations that make up social classes would lead one to believe that professional and managerial jobs in the 1980s and 1990s were less leisurely and more stressful than in the 1930s. There are no particular grounds here to anticipate a widening of the health gap between professionals and managers, on the one hand, and workers in more routine occupations, on the other, if this were to have been produced by differences in levels of stress. As far as social support is concerned, both academic and popular commentary on social and family trends regrets the decline in the stability of marriages and of community relationships. The falls in mortality we observe are not therefore likely to result from improvements in community or family solidarity.

In contrast to these trends in 'stress' and social support, some commentators argue that changes in the social distribution of smoking are more consistent with the large-scale trends in mortality (Doll and Peto, 1981), although not all agree (Williams and Lloyd, 1991; Vartiainen et al., 1998). Here we need to discriminate between changes in the differences between social classes and changes overall. During the increase in smoking in all social classes between 1931 and 1951, overall mortality in men in Registrar-General's Social Classes (RGSC) I and II continued to decrease (as we saw in table 1.2). The generation who took up smoking in the First World War would have been around 18–25 in 1914, reaching the 48–55 age group thirty years later in 1958. By this time many of them would have been affected by the carcinogenic substances in their cigarettes. But mortality in RGSC I and II men of this age in 1961 was actually 32 per cent lower than in 1951 (792 per 100,000 in 1951 versus 535 in 1961), and mortality in RGSC II men was 23 per cent lower (706/100,000 versus 545/100,000). In contrast, mortality in RGSC V men rose by almost 7 per cent, from 1,041/100,000 to 1,119/100,000 (Blane, Bartley and Davey Smith, 1997). Although smoking became relatively less common in middle-class men than in working-class men between the 1950s and the 1990s, death rates did also fall in working-class men during this time, just not as quickly. The cause of death most definitely linked to smoking, lung cancer, did not fall at all. It is argued that tobacco takes a long time to produce tumours in the lung, so that we will only see the effects of lower levels of smoking on lung cancer rates around twenty years after smoking habits have changed. In contrast, the physiological effects of smoking mean that it may have a shorter-term effect on heart disease. For example, the carbon dioxide in cigarette smoke makes the blood less efficient in carrying oxygen around the body from the lungs, which can place strain on the heart. The main reason to attribute changes in health inequality to smoking is because of these effects on heart disease, although it does not play as great a role as it does in lung cancer and other serious lung diseases. Moreover, during the 1970s and 1980s mortality from many causes unrelated to smoking fell at a similar rate to mortality from heart disease.

The main impact on the overall improvement in life expectancy since 1921 has in fact been the decrease in deaths from infectious diseases. Although the advent of effective antibiotic treatment was part of this change, the most important change was the decrease in the numbers of people who developed serious infections, or complications resulting from less serious ones, in the first place. In fact, until the arrival of HIV/AIDS, the disappearance of infectious disease as a dreaded cause of death was so total that it was more or less forgotten. This is perhaps one reason why at present we find it difficult to understand why life expectancy improved so much more for people in more privileged social circumstances. Access to foods that are free from contamination, and homes that are sufficiently warm, dry and hygienic to protect people from serious infection are now taken for granted. But this is a relatively recent phenomenon. Even as late as the 1950s in the UK, many families shared kitchens and bathrooms, and had lavatories outside the home. By the 1970s this was very unusual (Wadsworth, 1991).

Hygiene and infection are probably a small part of the causation of the diseases that produced health inequality in the last quarter of the twentieth century and that will contribute to its continuation in the twenty-first. I say 'probably' here because it may transpire that infections suffered during childhood have more to do with chronic diseases later in life than we believe at present. To understand the material influences on health inequality in the early twenty-first century we need to look for factors other than infections. However, these factors must be linked to disease risk in the same way as biological hazards such as bacteria and viruses; they must be 'biologically plausible' factors in the chain of causation. Income and wealth may be related to illness in part because they are linked to both the type of job a person does and the type of home in which they live.

Evidence on the relationship of individual work and environmental hazards to actual diseases is rather difficult to gather. Cancer-causing chemicals in the workplace (occupational carcinogens), for example, are estimated by some studies to be the cause of 40 per cent of cases of lung cancer, and by other studies to cause less than 1 per cent. The 'average' amount, as far as one can tell from scattered studies, seems to be around 5–6 per cent (Blane, Bartley and Davey Smith, 1997). Fumes and dust might be estimated to cause around 10 per cent of deaths from lung diseases such as chronic bronchitis and chronic obstructive airway disease. Industrial accidents are easier to identify: in 1985, for example, work accidents caused 4 per cent of all accidental deaths in England and Wales.

Living environment and housing are other places where the body comes into contact with health hazards (Doniach, Swettenham and Hawthorn, 1975; Gardner, Winter and Acheson, 1982), and where the extent to which this happens is partly determined by the amount of money available to the individual. Accidental injuries to children in the home are far more common in socio-economically disadvantaged families, for example: twelve times more likely than in the most advantaged homes in the UK (Office of Population Censuses and Surveys, 1978). Damp and mould in the home have been linked to infections in children (Martin, Platt and

Hunt, 1987; Platt et al., 1989) with knock-on effects on their health as adults (Colley, Douglas and Reid, 1973; Mann, Wadsworth and Colley, 1992). Low temperatures where residents are unable to afford sufficient heating are one reason why the death rates in older people are very much higher in winter than in summer (Eng and Mercer, 2000). Cold raises the blood pressure and cholesterol level: this means that low temperature is a biologically plausible hazard for heart attacks (Lloyd, 1991). Area of residence will also influence how much people are exposed to fumes and dusts from factories in their neighbourhood (Lloyd, 1978), and to the noise and pollution of passing traffic (Gardner, Winter and Acheson, 1982). Air pollution is estimated by one study to be responsible for perhaps 2 per cent of all cancer deaths (Doll and Peto, 1981). There is no study that tries to put a figure on how much air pollution affects the rate of mortality from other lung diseases such as bronchitis, emphysema or asthma.

Adding up the results of the few studies that can be used to try and estimate the size of the effect of this type of material factor on health, it would appear that they are not responsible for more than 25 per cent of all deaths, at the most. Moreover this estimate includes aspects of work relationships, such as control at work, which we have included under the psycho-social rather than the material explanatory framework. Warmer, drier, cleaner homes and workplaces, fewer hours of work and more holidays resulting in less exposure to what hazards there are, seem to be plausible explanations for trends in mortality over time, but they do not seem very important for present-day health inequality. One reaction to this has been to pay more attention to the other types of explanation, such as behavioural and psycho-social, set out in chapters 4 and 5.

However, some caution is needed when considering the nature of the evidence in studies of material factors. Many of the causes of death most obviously linked to industrial hazards, such as certain kinds of lung disease and some cancers, make their victims eligible for compensation from owners of their workplaces. Death certificates are legal documents that may be used in court cases. Studies comparing what is written on death certificates to what can be seen at an autopsy have shown, for example, that between half and three-quarters of deaths due to diseases such as pneumoconiosis (caused by coal dust), asbestosis and mesothelioma (another disease that is caused by asbestos) were misclassified under other headings (Newhouse and Wagner, 1969; Hammond, Selikoff and Seidmann, 1979; Cochrane and Moore, 1981). Deaths and injuries caused by cars, vans and trucks being used to transport goods and workers are not recorded as industrial accidents. For these and other reasons, it is reasonable to think that quite a few of the deaths that result from workplace hazards are not classified as such in official statistics.

A 'purely material' model of health inequality is not, in fact, that easy to sketch out. What would such a model look like? It would mean that we could account statistically for most of the difference in illness and death between social class or status groups in terms of greater or lesser exposure to physical hazards. Someone with more advantaged class or status position would only be at greater health risk *if* they were more exposed to direct material risk factors: if they were not, they would not experience this risk. In the home these could include cold, damp, infestation, overcrowding and insufficient calories and nutrients in meals. Low income can also lead to direct hazards when it results in a person only being able to afford to live in an area with high levels of pollution, traffic and other accident dangers. Blane, Berney and Montgomery have commented that 'social class . . . in relation to health, is manifest in crucial ways through differential exposure to environmental hazards; such exposure resulting from class differences in money and power' (2001).

People who work in jobs where they are exposed to accident hazards and to dangerous substances, as well as extremes of temperature, also tend to be paid low wages. This link between income and employment conditions will produce a correlation between low income and hazard exposure. However, we cannot say in exactly the same way that low income 'causes' the hazard exposure in the same direct way that low income may 'cause' people to have poor housing. The relationship of income to housing takes place in the sphere of consumption (what we buy with our money once we have earned or otherwise obtained it). The relationship of employment conditions to income takes place in the sphere of production (how we obtain our income). One does not 'buy' a job (generally speaking) in the same way as a house. If we want to understand how the relationship of income to work hazards might be part of a materialist explanation of health inequality, we need to adopt a more complex definition of 'materialist'. Blane, Bartley and Davey Smith have defined materialist explanations as those which refer to experiences arising as a consequence of social structure and organization, over which the individual has no control (1997). This definition has obvious links to Weber's concept of 'life chances', which are distributed according to one's bargaining power in the labour market, as the concept is used by Olin Wright, Goldthorpe and Marshall. The person with a humble background, no influential contacts, and few qualifications or credentials is less able to claim a safer, cleaner, better-paid job. In this model, 'good' jobs are things that people compete for, and the ability to win one of them is related to qualities of the individual which have been acquired over their lifetime. It follows that a person well placed to compete successfully for a good job is also likely to have experienced other benefits earlier in their life course.

The Puzzle of the Gradient

One of the issues facing a materialist model of health inequality is that studies show that there are differences in health and life expectancy between the most advantaged groups and those just beneath them as well as between those who are poor and those who are 'getting by' (Davey Smith et al., 1996a, 1998; Marmot et al., 1997). A man born between 1987 and 1991 in England and Wales could expect to live for almost 75 years if he was born into RGSC I or II and 69.7 years if he was born into RGSC IV or V – but a man born into RGSC III non-manual would expect to live 1.4 years less than his contemporaries in I and II, and 1.1 years more than a man in RGSC III manual (Drever and Whitehead, 1997: 76, table 6.1). A similar gradient can be seen in women. This is clearly not just a difference between richest and poorest or between highest and lowest status.

We need to remember that we are thinking about life expectancy, that is, about being healthy enough to keep going over a long period of time. Research shows not only that, at the beginning of the 1990s, the least socially advantaged men lived on average to 69.7 years, while the most advantaged lived to 75. It also shows that men and women in the middle of this particular ranking of social advantage live to 73.6. So we have to ask ourselves, what is it about having a little more that makes you a little more healthy? One possibility is to go back to the definitions of social class in terms of power and life chances as well as money. The amount of money a person earns at any one time may be regarded in two ways. It buys things, some of which may be important for their health. But money also acts as an indicator of where that person is in the structure of power, and thereby of opportunities and life chances in their own society. It may be the power to influence what happens to you from day to day that we need to examine more closely. There are major differences in the ability of people in different positions in the social structure to avoid a wide variety of potential hazards. These range from having to take a dangerous job to having to live in a polluted area. And the ability to protect oneself from them may arise in a number of ways, from having parents who are comfortably off during youth and early adulthood to having a reasonable income during retirement. The answer to the puzzle of the gradient may lie in understanding how different combinations of these sorts of advantages combine across the entire life course. In the next chapter the implications of this life-course approach will be further discussed.

One example of the ways in which shorter-term differences in power may help to explain the gradient can be given using Wright's concept of 'organizational resources'. Imagine a very senior manager earning

£200,000 a year and a senior manager earning £70,000 a year. Both of these women live in good housing, can afford healthy diets, and have office jobs without problems of damp, dust or chemicals. But the very senior manager, by having many people working under her, may avoid even the very occasional hazardous task more easily than the senior manager. For example, an old cupboard needs to be moved out of an office. Imagine that the manager earning £70,000 is present to supervise the task, while the one earning £200,000 has a delegate to do this, and blue asbestos dust flies off the cupboard. Given what we know about the causation of asbestos-related lung cancer, this single exposure will be enough to shorten the life of the senior manager. Because there are few early deaths among those earning either £200,000 or £70,000 per year, a few extra, produced in this way, will considerably increase the *relative risk* of the senior managers (the difference between 1 and 2 deaths is 100 per cent whereas the difference between 50 and 51 deaths is only 2 per cent). So differences in power may give rise to differences in exposure to fairly unusual events and yet produce significant differences in health outcomes between groups of people who would all be thought of as 'privileged' in financial and occupational terms.

The Cost of a Healthy Life

It is obvious, then, that the amount of 'purely material' health advantages an income will buy is not determined by the amount of money alone. Many processes enter into determining what money will buy, and most of these processes take place at the level of whole communities, political and economic units, or even globally (Coburn, 2000). Communities differ in the degree to which social inclusion, recognition as a member of the community, depends on money. In any situation that could be characterized as 'social' (apart from some kind of catastrophic situation in which the only relations between people were those in which money was exchanged for food and shelter), relationships are an inherent part of survival. The money left over for material survival to some extent therefore depends on the 'costs' of maintaining relationships. At the very lowest level, people usually need clothes or some form of bodily adornment in order to be allowed to interact with other people. Even where it is warm, and clothing is not a material necessity for avoiding hypothermia, these adornments will have a cost. This cost will affect what is available for food and shelter. Of course, in the vast majority of situations, what is necessary for social acceptance and participation is far more complex (and expensive) than in my extreme example.

Morris and his colleagues have investigated the minimum cost of a healthy lifestyle for a young man in the year 2000, taking into account the costs of social participation (Morris et al., 2002). This research group did not just look for the cost of survival, but for the cost of a lifestyle that would, on current best evidence, enable a person to live to a ripe old age. In a society where it is common to live to 75, health research cannot rest at finding out how much income a person needs to live to 40. In any case, everyone doing health inequality research knows that they need to explain the gradient in life expectancy. Morris and colleagues devised an 'evidence based healthy lifestyle' using available research in the same way as a hospital doctor would (ideally) decide on the best treatment for a patient. The budget therefore included the cost of five portions of fruit or vegetables a day and two portions of fish a week. Because exercise was also included in the healthy lifestyle, the diet had to include 221 calories more than the minimum for a person in a sedentary job (2,771 calories a day), to provide enough calories for swimming and cycling. The healthy foods cost £14.05. Because the researchers recognized the importance of avoiding social exclusion, they also costed in TV rental, a small amount for books, telephone, some musical entertainment and the costs of participating in work-based social events, altogether costing £13.78 per week, and they also included £11.42 for meals outside the home. Then there was £33.70 for things like clothing, shoes, toiletries and fares (including £3.22 a week saved for a holiday trip) and pension contributions. Housing costs were assessed for a dwelling clean enough to avoid respiratory diseases caused by mould and digestive disease caused by dirty food preparation conditions. But Morris and colleagues admit that at present there is hardly any research that makes it possible for us to put a price on a healthy home. So they adopted the average expenditure on housing for young men in national surveys, admitting that this is probably too cheap, as many homes people who spend the average amount on rent live in will be damp or dirty: this comes to £46.80 per week.

We can see from this that the 'bare minimum for physical survival' is difficult to separate out from the costs of social participation. It is also hard to know how to evaluate housing costs in terms of 'survival', since rents depend on market forces. So if we add up the 'purely material' elements of the budget, the food eaten in the home, at £14.05 plus heating at £5.41, is really a fairly small proportion of the total costs. And these are the only items we can really regard as bottom-line 'material' necessities for physical survival. Even if we added the costs of clothes (£8.51 per week) and shoes, this only increases the price of survival to around £27.97. Compare this with the cost of the socially, rather than biologically, necessary costs of £11.42 for meals out and £26.97 for other necessities of social participation. And of course one could argue over how 'necessary' new clothes and shoes are: it would be possible to survive by patching up old ones or relying on second-hand shops. The single item that takes up the highest proportion of the total is the cost of rent. This shows why it is necessary to look at the wider economy and society even in order to gain the simplest or most 'materialist' understanding of how individual circumstances affect health. These questions will arise in chapter 8 when we look at the relationship of health to the economic structures in different societies.

Morris and colleagues' work has been criticized for its allowance of money for such items as meals out, holidays, books and a telephone. There are two answers to this criticism. The first relates back to the previous chapter: it is that there is quite a lot of evidence (though this has its critics as well) that social integration and social participation are necessary for good health. The second answer is that people will in fact sacrifice food and heat in order to pay for things like social occasions, holidays, hairdos and presents for their families. In the real social world, it would take the most draconian dictatorial policies to force people to spend money only on 'absolute necessities'. In fact, there is very little research on this subject. We do not know in any detail what people on low incomes do go without in order to maintain levels of social participation. In one study, food and clothing of other family members was sacrificed so that fathers could run their cars. In another, low-income families with children had money to spare where the father did not demand the conventional 'meat and two vegetables' for his meals, although the alternative meals were at least as healthy in nutritional terms. But everyone's personal experience tells him or her of many ways in which 'we cannot live by bread alone'. The economist Amartya Sen has put it this way:

> Relative deprivation in the space of incomes can yield absolute deprivation in the space of capabilities. In a country that is generally rich, more income may be needed to buy enough commodities to achieve the same social functioning such as 'appearing in public without shame'. . . . [T]he deflection of resources involved in pursuing these social functionings also drains the financial means that are potentially usable for health and nutrition. (Sen, 1992: 115–16)

Recognizing this fact may give us the strongest version of the 'materialist' explanation for health inequality. Quite simply, 'direct material deprivation' comes about when people do not have enough money to pay for social participation as well as food and heat. Not because there is not enough money in an absolute sense, but because psychological and social survival compete with biological needs.

Neo-Materialist Explanations

The advent of the 'neo-materialist' explanation for health inequality is a relatively recent development. It emerged from a debate around the significance of the relationship between population health and income inequality, which will be discussed in more detail in chapter 8. The basic idea underlying this model of explanation is that some countries provide more publicly funded subsidies to their citizens' living standards than others, and that this may have an effect on health.

It is important to realize that the neo-materialist explanation is very different from the type of materialist explanation put forward by the Black Report for health inequalities within a single country. Within countries, materialist explanations concentrate on the relationship of income, and what it can buy, to health of individuals. Neo-materialist explanations concentrate on the relationship of public provision such as schools and transport to health of everyone in a country. There is not, in fact, a great deal of evidence in favour of the idea that nations with more public provision have lower health inequalities between social classes. In one large study of health inequalities in European nations, Sweden, which provides generous benefits to pensioners and the unemployed and which has well-funded public health, education and transport systems, showed one of the highest degrees of health inequality (Mackenbach et al., 1997). Generally, there was no sign that the well-provided Nordic nations had less health inequality than countries like France or Britain, and they appeared to do worse than Italy, Switzerland and Greece. However, citizens of the Nordic nations do enjoy a long average life expectancy (regardless of their social class). So although the study by Mackenbach and colleagues does not support a neo-material explanation for health inequality, it does support such an explanation for average life expectancy (regardless of socio-economic position).

There are important points in common between neo-materialist and old-style material explanations. The first of these concerns what happens to people without work. If unemployment benefits are generous, so that the income of unemployed people is nearer to the average income of those who do have jobs, there is less pressure on people to take any job regardless of how hazardous it is. As a result, in countries with higher unemployment benefits, employers are motivated to improve working conditions in order to attract workers. This can also happen in any country during times of very low unemployment. When people have plenty of choices as to possible employment, employers must make jobs more attractive. And most things that make jobs unattractive, from dirty workplaces to bullying managers, can be found in the research papers as possible health risk factors.

The second point that links traditional and neo-material explanations is to do with housing costs. We have seen that in Morris's study of the cost of a healthy life, housing costs massively outweighed any of the other individual items. Yet housing costs are enormously variable, and subject to social and economic policies. The field of housing policy is a very complex one. Here we only need to note that income distribution (the gap in pay between rich and poor) and public provision will both have a major effect on how much of the money available to an individual on a moderate or low income will have to be devoted to housing costs. Economic and social policies also determine how likely it is that people will buy up homes as speculative investments, which can also drive up costs. The impact of such policies on health will be further discussed in chapter 8. But the example of housing costs gives us an example of the complexities of a 'material' explanation for health inequality. Asking 'do people in social class X or Y have enough money for a healthy life?' is in fact a question that involves wide-ranging issues of economic and social policy.

FURTHER READING

Few books contain very much in this area. These are recent studies using geographical data to show the relationship of poverty and deprivation to health

Mitchell, R., Dorling, D., and Shaw, M., *Inequalities in Life and Death: What if Britain Were More Equal?* London: Joseph Rowntree Foundation, 2000.

Shaw, M., Dorling, D., Gordon, D., and Davey Smith, G., *The Widening Gap.* Bristol: Policy Press, 1999.

Another excellent study of poverty and health

Graham, H., *Hardship and Health in Women's Lives*, London: Harvester Wheatsheaf, 1993.

7

Models of Aetiological Pathways, IV: The Life-Course Approach

This chapter will look more closely at an explanation for health inequality that began to emerge in the 1980s, as new ideas developed and new information became available from long-term studies. This is the 'life-course approach'. The chapter will discuss the ways in which this new departure may be seen as overcoming several of the problems arising from the older perspectives. As we have seen, studies repeatedly found, not just a difference in health between very rich and very poor, but rather a 'fine-grained' health gradient. This led to the idea that health in later adult life may be a result of complex combinations of circumstances taking place over time (Davey Smith, Ben-Shlomo and Lynch, 2002). Instead of thinking about selection, researchers began to talk of an accumulation of disadvantage (Mann, Wadsworth and Colley, 1992; Blane, Davey Smith and Bartley, 1993; Power and Hertzman, 1997). If people from less privileged social backgrounds do less well in education, and are less equipped for later social success, should this be regarded purely as a result of 'personal characteristics' that they were born with? It is just as plausible to regard this kind of process as a tendency for disadvantage, including the disadvantage involved in having developed certain kinds of psychological responses, to accumulate over time. Psychologists might see this as regarding psychological responses as 'outcomes' rather than as 'stable characteristics' (or indeed as nurture rather than nature).

Another strength of a life-course approach is that it does not require there to be just one set of causes for social differences in all diseases. The vast majority of serious diseases have a social gradient. But a life-course approach allows this to happen according to different processes, which will be specific to each disease outcome. For example, there are very similar social gradients in mortality from lung cancer and from accidents (Drever,

Bunting and Harding, 1997, tables 10.3, 10.13), yet no one would claim that the causal factors are the same.

The life-course approach is fairly new, and in one short chapter there is only space to set out a very simplified introduction to this fascinating area of research. Interested readers will find more detail and complexity in the growing number of studies and books (for example, Elder, 1985; Kuh and Ben-Shlomo, 1997). Within the broad category of 'life-course explanations', there are several theories which are to some extent seen as competing. In its earliest form, life-course research tried to see whether a health difference between people in different social groups at the present time might 'really' be due to something that happened earlier in life. So, for example, if the most advantaged status group in a certain society lived five years longer than the least advantaged, could this 'really' be due to the fact that the two groups had different levels of educational attainment? This version of the life-course explanation is in fact more or less the same as the 'indirect selection' explanation that has already been discussed. It can, however, be taken a step further and we can ask, were these different levels of educational attainment 'really' due to the fact that the more privileged group's parents were themselves better off financially? In this way, a life-course approach is used to break down a contemporary or present-day social difference, and analyse it in terms of things that happened in the past.

Some researchers look for 'critical periods', that is, they think that if a hazard or adverse experience takes place at a certain age its effect on later health will be far greater. This idea is taken from biology, for example, there are certain things that have to happen at a certain time in the development of a baby, and certain hazards (such as exposure to German measles) that are only dangerous at a certain time during gestation. Others have concentrated on 'accumulation', that is, on looking for the effects of the ways in which one hazard or advantage adds to the effects of others. In this version of the life-course theory, it does not matter when a hazard or advantage is experienced, but it does matter whether other hazards or advantages precede it or follow it. A third version looks for interactions between experiences. In some cases, it seems that an experience is only damaging to health in certain groups of people, namely, those who are vulnerable due to previous exposures or experiences. A biomedical example here that may be familiar is mumps: it can cause serious disease in adults who have not been exposed to the virus in childhood and developed immunity. Yet another version of life-course theory looks at 'pathways'. Sometimes a certain hazard (or advantage) may increase (or decrease) the risk of a disease *only because* it increases the probability of some other aetiological (causal) factor. For example, in some studies (Heck and Pamuk, 1997) women who have been highly successful in education have a higher risk of breast cancer. It is unlikely that educational study itself causes cancer, and more likely that these women's subsequent careers have resulted in later childbearing (or none at all) which has been linked to breast cancer for biological (hormonal) reasons. The exact definitions of these different forms of life-course theory are the focus of considerable debate. Of course, in many cases we do not have to choose one or another exclusively: the best explanations may lie in various mixtures of the different processes.

Sources of Information on the Life Course

The important studies taking a life-course approach have used various kinds of data. The simplest way to do this kind of investigation is to ask questions in a survey about people's past lives. In a series of important studies carried out in the Netherlands, this was the main source of information about people's life courses: they were asked the occupation (and hence the social class and status) of their parents, and in some cases whether they remembered economic hardship in childhood (Van de Mheen et al., 1997, 1998). In a series of studies of older people in the UK, a special kind of questionnaire called a 'life-grid' has been used to help people remember more accurately (Berney and Blane, 1997; Blane et al., 1999). The type of study that is needed to investigate more fully the ways in which social and economic advantage and disadvantage build up over the lifetime to affect health inequality is a birth cohort study. Although other countries are beginning to set up this kind of study, Great Britain is unique in having four of them (Wadsworth, 1991; Power, Manor and Fox, 1991; Bynner, Ferri and Shepherd, 1997). The study samples are made up of people born in 1946, 1958, 1970 and the millennium year of 2000. By the year 2001, the 1946 cohort contained around 3,000 men and women, the 1958 and 1970 cohorts around 11,000 each, and the millennium cohort 18,000. In addition, there is a smaller Scottish study in which information could be put together about childhood health and social circumstances and health in old age, the Boyd-Orr cohort study (Gunnell et al., 1996; Blane et al., 1999).

A type of study similar to a cohort study is possible in the Nordic nations by using the fact that citizens of these countries have 'unique identification numbers'. These numbers can be used to link information from different sources, such as birth records, school qualification records, health checks at the time of military services, hospital episodes and use of other medical services (Martikainen, 1995a; Kaprio et al., 1996; Lithell et al., 1996; Vagero et al., 1999). When a citizen participates in a social or health survey of a population sample, this information can also be linked to other official records. Great precautions are taken to make sure that the ability to link personal information in this way is not abused, and linked data sets are carefully protected and must be destroyed after completion of the project for which they are approved. A lot of the longitudinal research on health inequality carried out in the United States has in fact used this kind of data set (often called a 'register') from a Nordic country. Although there are several large longitudinal studies in the United States, such as the Panel Study of Income Dynamics (McDonough and Amick III, 2001) these tend not to contain information from early childhood, although they are very useful for studying relationships between health and socio-economic circumstances in adulthood and later life (Giele and Elder, 1998; Lantz et al., 2001).

As we have seen in other chapters, a group in the Netherlands has made a major contribution to health inequality research in the 1990s, and some of their studies have also taken a longitudinal approach. These researchers did not, however, have access to truly longitudinal data. Initial information in their longitudinal study was collected from adults, and people were asked to remember past events and circumstances. When people are asked to remember things about the distant or even the recent past, their memories are known to be affected by what has happened since. So there are real risks of seeming to discover links between anxiety and poverty in childhood, for example, because people who are feeling happy are less likely to remember unpleasant past events. The advantage of the register-type studies is that they can use every member of the population of a country. The advantage of the birth cohorts is that information on earlier circumstances is collected at the time, does not rely on memory and cannot be influenced by later events. The British birth cohorts were designed to look at life-course influences (on health and other outcomes, such as education, family building and careers). This has meant that they have collected more specialized information, including people's attitudes and feelings. The data on use of medical services (and its long-term effects) in the birth cohorts is patchy, and depends on someone having had the energy (and the funding) to try and find every relevant medical record for every cohort member from every hospital and medical practitioner they have had contact with. It is easier in the Nordic registers to link information from different sets of official records, say birth certificates, censuses and hospital records. For this reason, Nordic life-course research may be more reliable (although there are no studies that have evaluated this aspect).

Table 7.1 Health by social class in adult life

	'Disease'		
Adult class	**Yes**	**No**	**Total**
Working (+)	223	617	840
%	*26.5*	*73.4*	
Middle (−)	113	647	760
%	*14.9*	*85.1*	
Odds ratio		2.07	

Note: the symbol '+' indicates a 'positive hazard exposure' and '−' the absence of hazard exposure

Analysing the life course

Most life-course studies have used methods such as linear and logistic regression, similar to those already discussed in chapter 3. First, the researcher shows a social gradient in some form of ill health, or in mortality. Then other variables are introduced into statistical models, and success in explaining the social gradient is judged by how far the initial social differences are reduced as each possible explanatory variable is added. The difference between this method and those set out in chapter 3 is that possible 'causes' are included in the analysis, according to the time in a person's life when they might be expected to happen. So we do not have to agonise over whether health or educational success comes first. We can look to see how much worse children with poor health do in school, and how much this helps us to explain the relationship between less education, lower levels of social and economic advantage and poor health in adulthood. Of course, it is not really as simple as that, but this is the general approach and it demonstrates what a big step forward life-course studies can be for investigating health inequality. This work needs to be clearly understood, in order to evaluate subsequent progress in this area.

To make it easier to understand this kind of explanation, we will take a simple invented example, which is basically the same as the one we used to understand an 'adjusted odds ratio' in chapter 3, and apply the same ideas to understanding the search for life-course influences on adult health inequality. In table 7.1 the class difference is to be found in a 'disease' of some kind or other, which affects 14.9 per cent of people in the 'middle

Table 7.2   Social class difference in health in adult life, adjusting for childhood poverty

	Child circumstances			
	Poor (+)		Rich (−)	
	Disease		Disease	
Adult class	Yes	No	Yes	No
Working (+)	197	463	26	154
%	29.9	70.2	16.9	85.6
Middle (−)	27	113	86	534
%	19.3	80.7	13.9	86.1
Odds ratios		1.78		1.23
Common odds ratio			1.50	

Note: the symbol '+' indicates a 'positive hazard exposure' and '−' the absence of hazard exposure

class' compared to 26.5 per cent in the 'working class'. Looking back to table 3.4 in chapter 3, we can calculate an OR by comparing the odds of getting the disease for those subject to this 'hazard exposure' to the odds of getting the disease for those who are not subject to it. We can treat the working class as the 'exposure +' group, obtaining an OR of 2.07. The OR here will be (26.5/73.4)/(14.9/85.1), dividing the odds of having the health problem in those 'exposed to the risk factor' – by virtue of being in the working class – by the odds in those 'not exposed' – being in the middle class.

Suppose we think that part of the reason for the higher risk of this health problem in the working-class adults is that they were more likely to have been poor as children. Once again, we can think of this 'adjustment for childhood class' in terms of two tables like the one above, one for people who had been poor in childhood and one for people who had been affluent. The two resulting odds ratios for the two groups can be 'averaged', allowing for the larger group to have a bigger weight, to give the common or adjusted OR. In this example, the results might be as in table 7.2, where the group has been split up into those with poorer and those with more affluent childhoods. Within these two groups, the working-class adults are still considerably more likely to have poor health than the middle-class adults, although the excess risk has gone down. The common

Table 7.3 Adult health inequality, adjusting for childhood poverty and educational attainment by age 21

Adult class	Educational attainment: high (−)			
	Child circumstances: poor (+)		Child circumstances: rich (−)	
	Disease		Disease	
	Yes	No	Yes	No
Working (+)	45	235	6	74
%	*16.0*	*84.0*	*8.0*	*92.0*
Middle (−)	19	101	26	294
%	*16.0*	*84.0*	*8.0*	*92.0*
Odds Ratios	1.00		1.00	

Adult class	Educational attainment: low (+)			
	Child circumstances: poor (+)		Child circumstances: rich (−)	
	Disease		Disease	
	Yes	No	Yes	No
Working (+)	152	228	20	80
%	*40.0*	*60.0*	*20.0*	*80.0*
Middle (−)	8	12	60	240
%	*40.0*	*60.0*	*20.0*	*80.0*
Odds Ratios	1.0		1.0	

Note: the symbol '+' indicates a 'positive hazard exposure' and '−' the absence of hazard exposure

OR, which (as we saw) can be thought of as the rough average of the two ORs for the 'poor' and 'rich' groups, is 1.5. To obtain an approximate idea of 'how important' for the health inequality between the adult classes each life-course influence might be, we can use the formula for percentage reduction in odds given in chapter 3 as:

(OR for unadjusted model – OR for adjusted model)/
(OR for unadjusted model – 1)

Here it would be calculated as follows:

OR for the first model of inequality between adult classes = 2.07
OR after adjustment for childhood circumstances = 1.5

therefore adjustment for childhood circumstances has reduced the inequality in adults by the formula:

$$(2.07 - 1.50)/(2.07 - 1)$$
which gives $0.57/1.07 = 0.53$

In other words, around 53 per cent of the difference in health between adult classes might be regarded as having been explained by the fact that 'poor' and 'rich' adults also had different childhood experiences.

What if we want to do something a little more complicated and look at events or hazards at more than one stage in life? Suppose we introduce another possible life-course factor, namely the educational attainments of each individual? We can think of this as breaking down the social classes, first according to childhood poverty, and then these groups in turn according to their educational results. This might produce something like table 7.3.

This example is highly artificial. Real data would not all fit into such a simple sequence. But I have tried to create the semblance of a situation in which *all* of the social class difference in adult life is explained by taking account of both childhood poverty and educational attainment. I deliberately made the risk of illness the same for all combinations of childhood class and educational attainment regardless of what their adult social class was (8 per cent if they had a rich childhood and did well at school, up to 40 per cent if they had a poor childhood and did badly at school). So the ORs comparing the middle-class and working-class children within each sub-group defined according to their childhood circumstances and their education have all gone down to 1. This means that if we took our 'mean' OR for all four comparisons, this would also be 1 : 1 – no difference any more between the classes. The way in which the difference between working- and middle-class adults has occurred is by many more people with a rich childhood and high educational attainment being found in the middle class. For example, there are only 20 people with poor childhood and low educational attainment in the adult middle class, so that although 40 per cent of these people are ill, the rate of illness in the whole of the middle class is only around 15 per cent as we saw in table 7.1. Such an extreme distribution would be most unlikely in reality. But it does give you an idea of the ways in which movement between social circumstances over the life course can produce health inequality, even when there is no great impact from any single 'hazard' in adulthood.

'Selection' in the Life Course

We have seen that in many studies education has been shown to have a powerful relationship to health, and that well-educated people in North America, Australia and Northern European countries tend to engage in 'healthier lifestyles'. This is often taken to mean that health inequality may be no more than an expression of 'natural' inequalities in intelligence or other psychological characteristics (see chapter 4). If we found a pattern where children who did well in school were no more likely to have a health problem regardless of poverty or affluence in childhood, this would provide evidence for a process of selection. Some researchers believe that favourable psychological characteristics, perhaps genetic in origin, may help the individual to pass exams, and otherwise to increase her or his 'human capital', which is defined by economists in terms of education, skills and work experience (Caspi et al., 1998). These characteristics may include locus of control, coping skills and similar constructs. Those with these higher levels of 'human capital' then get better jobs, and therefore find themselves better placed in terms of income, status, work autonomy and power in the workplace (Bond and Saunders, 1999). The link that we see in studies and in official statistical reports between social position and circumstances and health is therefore regarded as a by-product of individual characteristics.

The idea that health and adult social position are both determined by individual psychological characteristics is referred to as 'indirect selection', as we have seen. It is not 'direct health selection', since people are not thought of as being in disadvantaged circumstances because of any specific disease, but because of other characteristics which make them more prone to disease. It is rather difficult to test the indirect selection theory in a rigorous way, because logically it is not possible to 'prove a negative'. One can never say there is absolutely no chance that item 'x' does not exist (aliens from other galaxies, for example). The idea that an observed relationship between *a* and *b* might actually be due to some other factor, *x*, is, as we have seen, referred to as 'confounding' or 'spuriousness'. Here we are talking about another form of confounding, but one in which the confounding factor has not been observed or measured properly, so that it cannot be tested directly. This is often referred to as 'unobserved heterogeneity'. This problem is always one that has to be considered in research. Rather than a statement about reality, the need to beware of 'unobserved heterogeneity' can be thought of as a principle: always to be self-critical of one's own apparent discoveries.

Because of the importance of selection-type explanations in the body of research on health inequality over the life course, we need to return to this question before drawing any general lessons from the evidence from longitudinal studies.

Evidence on Indirect Selection

Indirect selection is the idea that health differences between social groups in adulthood are due to psychological characteristics in childhood which tend to favour both more advantaged social position *and* better health. Van de Mheen and her colleagues in the Netherlands asked whether health-related behaviour in early adult life might be the link between childhood social background and later health (Van de Mheen et al., 1998). Do children with less privileged backgrounds have poorer health as adults because they smoke more, eat worse diets, binge drink and take less exercise? As the authors remark, there has been surprisingly little research to test this idea. In a recent Finnish study, it was found that a major cause of higher mortality in young adults from less advantaged social backgrounds was alcohol-related disease and accidents. The daughters and (particularly) sons of manual workers were more at risk of dying from alcohol-related accidents and violence, and from alcoholic liver and pancreatic disease (Pensola and Valkonen, 2000). Might these kinds of differences in risky behaviours be due to psychological characteristics? That is, if we see that people who were less advantaged as children feel worse as adults, does this appear to be because they have different sorts of personality?

Another study by the research team from Erasmus University in the Netherlands addressed the question of whether people with disadvantaged childhood had different psychological characteristics. They did find that childhood disadvantage was related to locus of control, neuroticism, weaker coping skills and other unfavourable adult personality attributes. Around half of the relationship between childhood social position and self-rated health in adulthood could be explained by the fact that people with less advantaged childhoods were not as good at coping, were more 'neurotic' and were more likely to feel out of control of events (external locus of control). This study is more or less unique in having attempted to define and measure psychological differences between people with different childhood circumstances to see how important they were for adult health (Bosma, van de Mheen and Mackenbach, 1999). Social and economic disadvantage in childhood were found to be associated with lower levels of the kinds of psychological resources needed to deal with life later on. It is possible that these links were genetic. We do not know how far this kind of complex characteristic can be regarded as heritable, and it is likely that the genetic component is not great (Holtzman, 2002).

However, many researchers would regard 'selection' as an unsatisfactory way to sum up the results of this kind of study. After all, if half of the excess of poor health in those with poor childhood may have been due to their 'personalities', the other half was due to the fact that this group subsequently encountered more hazards in adult life. So a more complete way to look at it is to see the study as supporting the idea that risk accumulates over the life course. Children are not only directly disadvantaged by a poor background in terms of physical health risks. There can also be an 'accumulation of psycho-social hazards'. Those with greater early adversity may develop fewer resources for dealing with later adversity. Unfortunately, the study does not present any information on medically defined disease, or even on self-reported serious conditions. So we do not know how far this link between childhood social circumstances and adult psychological attributes might contribute to observed social differences in serious disease and mortality.

Another important example comes from Lynch and colleagues (Lynch et al., 1994), an American team who used Nordic register data. They took income as their definition of socio-economic position and circumstances in the adult life of around 2,600 Finnish men. Income was related to death from heart disease and from all other causes. Men who had suffered poverty both in childhood *and* in their adult lives were worse off than those who had moved from being poor in childhood to a more affluent adulthood. Being poor in earlier life only made a difference to those who were also less well off as adults. The more affluent adults with poorer childhoods had the same risk of mortality as those who had never experienced low income. In another paper these researchers showed that men who had experienced worse childhood conditions were more likely to partake of 'risky' behaviours (Lynch, Kaplan and Salonen, 1997b). But if we put these two reports together, it is clear that these risk-taking proclivities acquired during a disadvantaged childhood only did any harm to the men who remained affected by low income as adults.

Table 7.4   Accumulation of health risk over the life course

Parents' social position	Own social position	
	More advantaged	Less advantaged
More advantaged	C	D
% ill	10	8
Less advantaged	A	B
% ill	8	4

Accumulation over the Life Course

The discovery of these patterns has encouraged many researchers to think that health inequality is the result of 'adding together' the amount of time different people have spent in more and less advantaged situations – an 'accumulative' process. Table 7.4 illustrates what the rates of 'illness' would look like in four groups of people with different childhood and adulthood socio-economic circumstances if their health had been affected over time in an 'accumulative' manner. This can be summarised as follows:

1   Group A comes from a disadvantaged background and has ended up in an advantaged social position;
2   Group B comes from a disadvantaged background and has stayed there;
3   Group C comes from an advantaged background and has stayed there;
4   Group D comes from an advantaged background and has ended up in a disadvantaged social position.

We can see that it makes no difference to the percentage of people who are 'ill' whether they moved from a less advantaged to a more advantaged social group (8 per cent are ill), or the other way round (8 per cent are also ill). It is as if time spent in a disadvantaged position gives people a 'risk score': they score more highly on risk the more time they have spent in disadvantage. There is now evidence from quite a few studies to show that this 'accumulative' pattern lies behind the social inequality in several forms of health risk. For example, Hilary Graham found that while 22 per cent of women were smokers, this rose to 46 per cent of those with no educational qualification, 50 per cent of those with no qualification and a low-skilled job, 67 per cent for women who also lived in social housing and 73 per cent for women who were also having to claim social assistance benefits (Graham, 1998). George Davey Smith, David Blane and their colleagues have shown accumulative patterns in health risk over the lives of the Boyd-Orr cohort of people born in the 1930s in Great Britain (Davey Smith et al., 1997; Hart, Davey Smith and Blane, 1998a, 1998b; Holland et al., 2000). Similar patterns have been seen in other large-scale longitudinal studies in the UK (Power, Matthews and Manor, 1998; Bartley and Plewis, 2002).

Summary: The Life-Course Explanation of Health Inequality

A life-course theory regards health as reflecting the patterns of social, psychological and biological advantages and disadvantages experienced by the individual over time. A life-course theory of health *inequality* regards these patterns as being profoundly affected by the position of individuals and families in social and economic structures and hierarchies of status. However, these links themselves depend on the political and cultural environment, which means that there is a need for a 'life-course political economy' of health, which examines the ways in which economic and social policies influence the accumulation of material and psycho-social risk. The ways in which advantages and disadvantages combine over the life course influence both how long each individual may spend in good health, and also what form of illness they may acquire.

FURTHER READING

This has become the standard reference text on life-course epidemiology
Kuh, D., and Ben-Shlomo, Y., *A Life-Course Approach to Chronic Disease Epidemiology*. Oxford: Oxford University Press, 1997.

This is a report of the work done by the Erasmus group on the life course, which was led by van de Mheen
van de Mheen, D., *Inequalities in Health: To Be Continued?* Rotterdam: Erasmus University, 1998.

An excellent account of the longest running of the British birth cohort studies
Wadsworth, M., *The Imprint of Time*. Oxford: Oxford University Press, 1991.

An important book including North American work
Keating, D. P., and Hertzman, C., *Developmental Health and the Wealth of Nations*. New York: The Guilford Press, 1999.

8

Social Ecology

Some readers may be surprised that up to now the work on health and income inequality (Wilkinson, 1996; Lynch et al., 1998; Wolfson et al., 1999) has hardly been mentioned. In the United States, this work (which I will call 'social ecology') has probably had more impact than research relating individual income or social position to health. The reason for this is that Wilkinson and his colleagues are not talking about health inequality. Health inequality exists between groups of individuals in a single society. The work on health and income inequality looks at the 'health', usually defined as life expectancy, of whole populations in different countries or areas. So while health inequality studies analyse differences in health between social classes, status or income groups, social ecology studies examine differences in health between nations (Wilkinson, 1992a; McIsaac and Wilkinson, 1997), US states (Wolfson et al., 1999), Canadian provinces (Ross et al., 2000), districts or regions in the UK (Ben-Shlomo, White and Marmot, 1996), or other geopolitical units. The environment in these areas is defined in terms of the degree of inequality in income, measured in various different ways. But all the measures attempt to describe the differences in income between the richer and poorer people in the area. Where there is less difference in income between the richest and the poorest residents in an area, many studies (though not all) find higher life expectancy. Even if you compare two regions with similarly low income, such as the Indian state of Kerala and the Philippine Islands, for example, you find that where differences between rich and poor are lower (as they are in Kerala) life expectancy is higher.

What, then, is the connection between these social ecology studies and 'health inequality' as we have been discussing it? How can our ability to build conceptual models linking dimensions of inequality to health outcomes be used to understand the ecological studies of health and income distribution? So far, the chapters of this book have unpacked some ideas about how to understand studies relating class, income or prestige in a single country to health differences between individuals and groups. We have considered the strengths and weaknesses of arguments based on health-related behaviour, on stress and its physiological effects, and on 'direct material' or 'neo-material' theories. A case can be made for each of these, and for different combinations according to what form of inequality is being examined, and what health outcome is being investigated. In addition, we have considered how such influences may be understood as operating over longer time-periods in the life course of the individual.

This chapter will attempt to integrate the influential 'social ecology' programme of research and argument into the framework that has been built up. It will argue that this might be done in two ways. A psycho-social model would regard health differences between more and less unequal nations as due to the different levels of stress experienced. A neo-material model would regard the key as residing in the different levels of provision of social goods, such as education, health services, public housing and welfare benefits.

The main reason for trying to find a common framework of understanding is that it will be easier to make sense of, and evaluate, health inequality studies (as well as to design future ones) if we can use such a framework. But there is another reason, which is that considerable controversy has surrounded the 'social ecology' work, and assessing this requires a degree of perspective. The controversy takes three major forms. The first source of disagreement is whether or not the relationship between income distribution and health actually exists. The second disagreement is over what might be regarded as causing the relationship (if it does exist). The third disagreement is over the policy implications of different possible causal explanations.

Is Income Distribution Related to Population Health?

The early research on the social ecology of health, as well as his own contribution to it, is very well summarized in Wilkinson's book, *Unhealthy Societies*. Readers are strongly advised to consult this very well-expressed and persuasive account (Wilkinson, 1996). The key idea is that after a certain level of average income per person is reached in a society, additions to this average do not seem to improve that society's health any further. This is not the same as the effects seen in the studies we have been considering of the social and economic position and circumstances (such as income, social class based on occupation, or prestige) of individuals. As far as studies are able to tell us, health of individuals within a country seems to be better the more money or prestige they have acquired, and the more favourable the conditions under which they are employed. 'Average' levels of health within social classes, income or status groups within a country, similarly, are better the higher the average income in the group. There is no 'limit' above which no further improvement in health takes place. By contrast, when you compare countries (as opposed to comparing groups of people within countries), it seems from many (if not all) studies that population health, as measured by life expectancy, does not go on getting better the higher the total amount of money earned by everyone in the country. Above a certain level of average income per head, countries (and other geopolitical units, such as states of the USA) have higher life expectancy if their total amount of income (sometimes called the Gross Domestic Product or GDP) is *more evenly distributed*. These differences in income distribution are measured in studies in several different ways. One of the ways most often used to summarize the relationship between individual incomes is the so-called 'Gini coefficient'. Without going into various complications to do with the construction of this measure, we can look at a similar measure, the coefficient of variation, which just divides the mean (average) income in a population by its standard deviation. The standard deviation gives the average amount by which each individual's income deviates from the average for everyone (this is not exactly how statisticians would calculate a standard deviation in a study, but it explains the general idea.).

Table 8.1 gives an imaginary example of two populations with the same average income, but with very different amounts of difference between each individual income and the average. It shows how these two different populations have different coefficients of variation. Each population has five members, and the average income in both populations is $5,800 per year. The large difference between the two 'coefficients of variation' is produced by the fact that in population 1 there is a far greater difference between individuals in how much they earn. This produces larger differences between the incomes of each individual person and the mean for them all (whether the difference between the mean and each individual's income is plus or minus can be disregarded in this kind of calculation). There are a number of other ways in which studies have measured income inequality, often by comparing the size of the top and bottom sections of the population (the highest-earning 10 per cent versus the lowest for example), such as the nicely named 'Robin Hood Index'. But the idea is

Table 8.1 Coefficient of variation measuring degrees of inequality in income for a more and a less unequal population

	Income	Variation of individual from mean		Coefficient of variation
Large inequality				
Person 1	9,900	4,100		
Person 2	9,300	3,500		
Person 3	5,700	100		
Person 4	2,100	3,700		
Person 5	2,000	3,800		
Mean income	5,800			
Sum of individual variations			15,200	
				2.62
Small inequality				
Person 1	6,600	800		
Person 2	5,500	300		
Person 3	5,700	100		
Person 4	6,300	500		
Person 5	4,900	900		
Mean income	5,800			
Sum of individual variations			2,600	
				0.45

always the same, somehow to capture the degree to which earnings differ between members of a population.

Some Controversies about Income Distribution and Health

Because the ideas about the economic ecology of health appeal strongly to many people and have obvious political implications, the debate around this question is lively and fast moving. It is not possible to cover every aspect in a single chapter, but the main points of controversy will be considered. For example, many participants in the debate on income inequality and health have agreed that it is important to see whether income distribution is still related to health after taking account of individual income. If countries with large differences in income between richest and poorest simply contain more people, then it is not surprising that health is less good. But at least in its original form, most people understood the social ecology studies to be saying that the same income was 'healthier' if the person receiving it lived in a less unequal country or area. However, this idea is recently beginning to be debated. Does it really matter whether people in less economically unequal places are healthier regardless of their own income? This remains an open question.

A second point of controversy is the extent to which the relation between income distribution and health is simply the result of the way the numbers operate: a person can have an income of several million dollars, euros or pounds a year, but no one can live for much longer than 110 years. If we consider the real income differences that are found in many nations, we find that in some cases the wealthiest people are as much as fifty or a hundred times better off than the least well off. This makes it impossible that a certain amount more money (say, US $1) 'buys' the same amount of health in everyone, no matter how much money they had to begin with. If an income of $1 per year bought 0.01 (one-hundredth) of a year of life, we would have to expect that people earning $3,000 per year would live to be around 30 years old, while people earning $300,000 would live to be 3,000 years old! We could look at this the other way round, at the average life expectancy of people earning $1 million a year (not an enormous amount in today's higher-earning professional and management jobs in the USA). If we found this to be 90 years, so that such a person had 'bought' a year of life with every $11,000 they earned, we would have to deduce from this that the child of a three-person family earning $33,000 ($11,000 for each person) would only live a single year. But this is not what actually happens. Money, as we have seen, buys a lot less 'health' in people who already have a great deal of it than in people who do not have as much (Wagstaff and van Doorslaer, 2000).

Take another example. Say there are three countries, each with a population of 100 people, and the total income of each of these populations was exactly £1,000,000. In Country A, 50 people have £7,000 each, 30 people had £10,000 each and 20 had £17,500. In Country B, 10 people have £50,000 each, and the other half-million is shared between all the other 90 people, so that these 90 had around £5,560 each. In Country C, everyone has exactly £10,000. In another country, with the same population size but a total income of only £850,000, it would still be possible for all 100 people to have an income of £8,500 if that income was evenly distributed. So no one would have an income as low as the income of 90/100 of the people in the richer country.

If every pound, dollar or euro bought the same amount of health, what would you expect to see in these three different countries? Let's say people with £8,500 live a healthy 85 years, one year for each £100. This would mean that the people earning £5,560 would live 55.6 years; however, it also means that the people earning £50,000 in that same society would be expected to live 500 years. This is biologically impossible at least at the present time. So whereas in the society of 100 people, where everyone earns £8,500, everyone would live to be 85 and the total years of life in that society would be 8,500, it could not be the case that in the more unequal society the total years of life could equal $(90 \times 55.6) + (10 \times 500) = 10,004$! It would be more like $(90 \times 55.6) + (10 \times 99) = 5,994$. So the more unequal society would produce a lower total number of years of life, and thereby a lower average life expectancy of just under 60 years, as opposed to 85 years in the less equal society. After you have a certain amount of money, having any more is not going to buy you better health or longer life expectancy. To a certain extent, this is not unduly mysterious, but is simply the result of the biological limits on the human lifespan. But its real significance is that it shows that the health of everyone in a population is improved if you take some of the extra money from the very rich and give it to those that are less well off: what is added to health at the bottom will not be subtracted from health at the top. This limit to how much 'health' money can buy makes it fairly easy to see how income redistribution could improve health in a population.

If the income distribution hypothesis was to be supported you would want to see the country with 10 people earning £50,000 each being the least healthy, and possibly the second, poorer country having better health despite their lower average income. Many studies have now replicated these results. Most of those comparing states or cities of the USA (Kaplan et al., 1996; Kennedy, Kawachi and Prothrowstith, 1996; Lynch et al., 1998; Wolfson et al., 1999) do show this kind of relationship, although there are exceptions (Daly et al., 1998). A study of Canadian provinces did not find income inequality to be related to mortality (Ross et al., 2000). Comparisons between OECD countries (the more developed nations that are members of the Organisation for Economic Co-Operation and Development) have caused more controversy and do not all seem to show the same pattern. Wilkinson's original work (Wilkinson, 1986, 1992a, 1992b) compared life expectancy in the developed countries for which it was possible to collect data on both income distribution and life expectancy in the 1970s and 1980s. In other studies using new data from additional countries that only later became available, it did not appear that income distribution was related to health after taking account of differences between countries or areas in average individual income (Judge, 1995; Fiscella and Franks, 1997; Lynch et al., 2000, 2001).

As discussed above, for some commentators the key question is whether there is a specific 'inequality effect', that is, whether individuals earning $33,000 have a longer life expectancy in a country where there are other people who earn $3 million than in countries where no one earns more than perhaps $300,000. The statistician Steven Senn makes an analogy with a field of wheat. If fertilizer is unevenly spread over the field, some patches of wheat will grow faster than others. This is the effect of the uneven muck-spreading. But the social ecology studies suggest, he feels, that there is an additional effect of the taller wheat overshadowing the shorter stems. If less fertilizer had been spread more evenly, none of the wheat would have grown super-tall, but neither would the rest of the wheat-stalks be shut out from the light by their taller neighbours (Senn, 1998). The economist Angus Deaton has expressed the idea of an 'inequality effect' in terms of the 'weight' of money 'pressing down' on top of the average person in a population. The individual's health will be affected by this 'weight', which can be roughly thought of as the number of people who earn more than she does, multiplied by how much each of them earns. So if you earn less than the top earners in your population, how badly this makes you feel depends on both how many people earn more than you *and* how much they earn. If there were only 100 people who earned more than you, this would still be bad news if each of them earned $1 million and you earned $50,000. But if there were even 2,000 people who earned more than you, but each of them only earned $60,000 a year, this would not be nearly so bad. So being in the second-richest 20 per cent of the income distribution of a population of 1,000 people would be 'unhealthier' if there were 10 people at the very top earning $1 million each than being in the middle of a population where, although there were 500 people 'above' you, they all earned a total of less than $10 million. Deaton shows figures from research in the USA which indicate that something like this does seem to happen (Deaton, 2001).

Why Might Income Distribution Be Related to Population Health?

If there is evidence that living in a more unequal social environment is bad for health, why might this be? Can we use explanatory models to approach

Table 8.2   Health inequality and social ecology studies: typology of explanations

Type of explanation	Level of measurement of socio-economic position and circumstances	
	Individual socio-economic position (class, income or status)	**Society (nation, state, province etc.)**
Psycho-social	Low rewards at work (or low status) induce feelings of helplessness and despair, with effects on the endocrine system, HPA activation, lowered immunity.	Where income distribution is unequal, people with relatively lower incomes perceive themselves as of low status in their communities. Resulting low levels of psychological well-being eventually affect the immune and cardiovascular systems. Reduced levels of trust between people damage quality of social relationships.
Behavioural	Healthy behaviours are a way of displaying superior social status. Social disadvantage re-inforces a 'habitus' of low self-care.	In unequal societies people other than the wealthiest feel less valued and are therefore less likely to attempt to improve their own health and life expectancy by healthy behaviours. Poorer quality social relationships increase crime, homicide, suicide.
Material/ 'Neo-material'	Low income influences individuals' home conditions, living environment, neighbourhood access to facilities for health care, exercise, etc.	In countries or areas where there is a lot of income inequality, there may also be lower levels of public and social services such as education, health care, public transport, housing.

this question similar to those we have used in previous chapters on health inequality between social groups within countries? Table 8.2 offers a way of summarizing the different approaches of the 'health inequality' studies versus the 'income distribution and health' studies in a single typology. It shows how the three types of explanation, psycho-social, behavioural and material, might be used to integrate the studies of health inequality with those of income distribution. We need to remember here that social ecology research looks at differences between nations or areas in levels of health and life expectancy for everyone, not just the poorest or least advantaged. There is little evidence of greater health *inequality* in more unequal nations (Kunst, 1997; Mackenbach et al., 1997).

Psycho-social explanation

Even those who agree that there is plenty of evidence for a relationship between income distribution and health differ as to why they believe this might be the case. Several of the leading researchers in this area have adopted a 'psycho-social' explanation. This has been summarized well in a paper by Lynch and colleagues, despite the fact that their intention is to disagree with it. They write:

> Wilkinson has argued that income inequality affects health through perceptions of place in the social hierarchy based on relative position according to income. Such perceptions produce negative emotions such as shame and distrust that are translated 'inside' the body into poorer health via psycho-neuro-endocrine mechanisms and stress induced behaviours such as smoking. . . . Perceptions of relative position and the negative emotions they foster are translated 'outside' the individual into antisocial behaviour, reduced civic participation and less social capital and cohesion within the community. In this way, perceptions of social rank – indexed by relative income – have negative biological consequences for individuals and negative social consequences for how individuals interact. Perceptions of relative income thus link individual and social pathology. (Lynch et al., 2000)

Table 8.2 shows how this kind of explanation for health differences between countries with different income distributions matches up with the psycho-social explanation for health differences between social class, status or income groups. In individual members of less advantaged social groups, the psycho-social conditions in those groups induce 'stress', and this in turn affects the body. In countries or areas with more uneven income distribution, two things seem to be happening (according to this theory at least). First, there are similar effects on people with less than the highest level of income. Because they feel 'relatively deprived', this leads to negative emotions, which in turn set off bodily stress reactions.

Secondly, there are effects on levels of 'social capital' in the more unequal societies. Much of the research puts forward the idea that where people feel very unequal, they are less likely to participate in community organizations (Kaplan et al., 1996; Kawachi et al., 1997). They are less likely to get together to improve their local environment for example. Unequal societies are more competitive and less co-operative in many ways. There is less trust between people and more criminal behaviour (Kawachi and Kennedy, 1997). This has an effect on everyone, not just on those with less money. Everyone becomes more at risk from a less safe environment, with more pollution and traffic hazards, for example, where public participation in pressure groups is lower. Consumers are less able to make sure that the standards of safety in goods are high. And the fear of crime is well known to have a large effect on the quality of life, even when people are not in fact at great risk.

Perhaps one of the most persuasive aspects of the psycho-social explanation for health inequality is that it offers to make sense of both the income inequality work and that on health differences between social groups using the same set of basic ideas. This is because we need to be able to account for the 'social gradient' in health that is so widely observed. The gradient means there is a significant health difference between the most privileged group within a society and the second-most privileged, not just between the poor or deprived and everyone else. If we look at a single country, we do not only find differences between 'the poor' (or the most disadvantaged people in terms of money, status and class position) who are 'sick' while everyone else is 'healthy'. What we find is a 'gradient'. People with two cars live longer than people with only one. Similarly, Wilkinson and his supporters point out that it is only the health of people living in material poverty that is responsible for differences in the overall health of populations: income distribution seems to influence everyone's chances of good health. Therefore, it is argued, there must be something, not just about what you possess but about what you possess *relative to what other people possess*, that affects your health. And the second-richest or second-most privileged group, as well as the 'bottom' group, can feel 'relatively deprived' in relation to the top group.

What is perhaps most controversial about this psycho-social explanation for the ecological health differences between more and less unequal societies is the emphasis that has been placed on people's perceptions of their relative status in a social hierarchy. There is something rather depressing about this idea that not being a 'top dog' in some kind of fixed hierarchy could be so psychologically catastrophic as to have an effect on life expectancy itself. Do people really care so much about not having a bigger car than their neighbours that their immune defence systems collapse in protest? In the research on employment relationships that was described in chapter 5, we saw the evidence for a psycho-social effect resulting from feeling out of control and being subjected to a lot of pressure from superiors. The research on social networks and social support shows that there is some evidence that isolation and loneliness (which are other forms of 'psycho-social risk factor') may also be harmful to health. This does not seem quite so challenging to our images of ourselves as adult human beings as the idea that the mere *perception* of *relative* social status may be a health risk. Do people really die of envy? Or is their position on a ladder of income or status also a measure of other kinds of hazards? This is one reason why, in chapter 6, I tried to show how the material situation, including work hazards such as the asbestos in the example considered there, may vary even between a senior manager and a very senior manager. Not much, but enough to produce significant differences in health between groups where the overall level of risk is very low.

Behavioural explanation

Returning to table 8.2, can we similarly relate the behavioural explanation for health inequality to a behavioural explanation for the effect of income distribution? It is not possible for any relationship of income distribution to population health to be due to selection. It is not very realistic to envisage that health differences between Japan and the USA (which are considerable) could be produced by sick Japanese people migrating to the United States or healthy Americans going in the other direction. This means that the implicit selection model which, we have seen, lies behind the 'behavioural' explanation for health inequality is not plausible when we look at differences between countries. A behavioural explanation for these differences has to hypothesize a pathway from psychological states of mind to health-related behaviours, more in line with the 'social reward/self-regulation theory' described in chapter 4. People who are made to feel inferior may be less motivated to protect their own health, and the stresses on them may induce cravings for unhealthy forms of consumption.

Might income inequality fit in with Bourdieu's theory of lifestyle as a way of expressing social superiority? This is harder to imagine. There does not seem any obvious reason why expressing claims to superiority might be less important in a society where income was more equally distributed. People might just as well put more emphasis on lifestyle where income differences were less, if they were determined to display their status in some way or other. However, we have no systematic studies on whether in fact there are different patterns of health-related behaviours in countries with higher or lower levels of income inequality. Income inequality in 1991 was highest in the United Kingdom and USA, followed by France, Australia and Switzerland, and lowest in Finland, Belgium and Sweden (Lynch et al., 2001). Setting these figures against World Health Organization

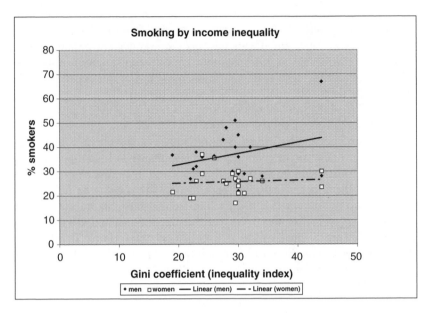

Figure 8.1 Smoking by income inequality

estimates of smoking rates in men and women, we get the pattern seen in figure 8.1. For women (the light squares) income inequality does not seem to be related to smoking rates, but for men (the dark diamond shapes) there is a slight hint that in the more unequal societies smoking rates are higher. A lot of the angle of the gradient, however, depends on one single country, Russia, at the top right hand of the diagram, which has a high inequality index, and a smoking rate higher than any other country.

Material and 'neo-material' explanation

The reason advanced for the relationship between income inequality and population health that has attracted greatest recent attention among researchers and policy-commentators is the so-called 'neo-material' explanation. As we saw in chapter 6, the attraction of a materialist theory is that it pays attention to how social and economic conditions can literally have an impact on the body. Those who put forward a 'neo-material' explanation for the relationship between health and income distribution have written several fairly strongly argued critiques of psycho-social types of explanation (Judge, 1995; Coburn, 2000; Lynch et al., 2000, 2001). They do not agree that health damage takes place as a result of psychological effects of perceived relative deprivation. Rather, they prefer to look for reasons why, in more equal societies, people may have experiences of a kind more favourable to good health across a wide range of situations. The neo-materialists also argue that these more favourable experiences are brought about by different policies towards the provision of public services such as education and health care (Davey Smith, 1996; Kaplan et al., 1996; Coburn, 2000; Lynch et al., 2000).

Lynch and colleagues use the striking image of people on a long-haul flight. In the back are the economy-class passengers with cramped seating and in the front the more luxurious business and first-class passengers. At the end of the trip, the economy passengers will probably be feeling less healthy than the others. Is this, Lynch and colleagues ask, purely because they so resented the relative luxury of the first-class passengers (Lynch et al., 2000)? This is what would be implied by the 'relative deprivation' psycho-social explanation for the relation of health to income inequality. Or is it more plausible to regard the health differences as a result of the greater physical space in first class (we now realize that sitting in cramped conditions can be literally fatal)? Another way to look at this example is to ask whether we would expect the 'average' health of all the passengers to improve if everyone sat in equally cramped conditions? No one would then feel 'relatively deprived', after all. In this example, one's common-sensical reaction would be to say that, of course, it would not help anyone to make all the passengers equally cramped. The health advantage to the first-class passengers would be lost, with no gain to the economy-class passengers. But the example also connects with another important point: the experience of inequality may depend on what else is going on. To extend the image, what would happen if no one on the plane had a cramped position, everyone was comfortable and able to move around easily, but some had still *more* space?

In table 8.2, I have used the example of the effect of income inequalities on housing, because this has a more pervasive effect on more people than the occasional trip in an aeroplane. The example of housing raises another issue that the neo-materialists might like us to consider, which might be described as 'the absolute effect of relative income'. Maybe there really is no such thing as a 'merely relative' income difference. In many areas of life, the cost of things that everyone needs is influenced by the incomes of the wealthiest. The income of a short-order cook in London or Chicago might be a lot more than that of a small farmer in Kerala. But in the rich but unequal cities, that income might only be enough to buy housing of a quality that would harm the health of anyone who had to live in it. High property values could force a person earning around half of the average income for that society into damp, unhygienic conditions in a polluted area where traffic noise made sleep difficult. In a less unequal society or area, a person in the same position in terms of the income distribution might be able to do better in terms of the quality of shelter her money could buy. A recent study has shown no relationship of income inequality to health in different areas of Denmark, where housing policies mean that richer and poorer citizens are far less segregated in terms of where they live than is the case in the USA (Osler et al., 2002).

The relationship of any given amount of money to what the body has to endure is bound to depend on what that money will buy. And where a lot of people have a lot more money than you do, at least some of the things you need tend to be more expensive. We saw in chapter 6 that a large proportion of the cost of the 'healthy life' in Morris and colleagues' study was taken up by rent. Housing is perhaps the most important influence on health to be very greatly affected (or at least potentially affected), by income distribution. This makes it perhaps the best example of the 'neo-material' model for explaining the relationship of income distribution to health. But one could extend the general idea in other directions. If a family on an average income must devote 40 per cent of their income to paying their mortgage, there is that much less money left over to pay for a healthy diet, sufficient heating and maintenance of the home, and health-promoting leisure activities. Where transport is poor, residents in areas with few shops selling fresh food (almost always poor areas) will either eat unhealthy diets or spend a huge proportion of their budget to run a car. In some poor areas of the UK, families need to devote almost 30 per cent of their total income to run a car. High property values often go along with high levels of income inequality because there is a group who have large amounts of money to invest in property which they do not want to live in, purely as a profit-making venture. In countries with low levels of taxation on the wealthy, there may not be much finance available for public transport. Insights of this kind enable us to see that high levels of income inequality have consequences for health without needing to explain the relationship purely in terms of relative deprivation and the emotions that this may arouse (Lynch et al., 2000).

The neo-materialists argue two things. First, that countries or areas with more equal income distributions differ from more unequal ones in all sorts of ways, stemming from their whole economic and political histories. Secondly, the effect of income inequality may itself depend on the availability of publicly provided services and facilities. There are so many of these differences between, for example, Sweden and the United States, that we do not need to focus solely on income, which is an effect rather than a cause. As Daly and colleagues put it: 'an inequitable income distribution may be associated with a set of economic, political, social and institutional processes that reflect a systematic under-investment in human, physical, health and social infrastructure.' (Daly et al., 1998)

The really important differences between countries might therefore be to do with public services, rather than with how people perceive their relative position in some kind of social hierarchy. The most impressive evidence in favour of this position comes from a study of health differences between Canadian provinces (Ross et al., 2000). These researchers found that there was evidence for an effect of income distribution when comparing US states, quite independent of average income. But they did not find the same effect in Canada. They argue that the reason for this is that public services such as health are far more highly developed in Canada, so that receiving such services does not depend on individual income to the same extent. This might indicate that only where income inequality is an indication of poor provision of services will it be related to health.

The implication of the neo-material explanation is that we ought to find health differences between countries with different levels of service provision. It may not surprise you by this time to learn that, once again, we have very few studies that have tried to test out this idea with real data. It is certainly true that, since the end of the Second World War, most industrialized nations have greatly improved the provision of public services and that, during this time, we have also seen very great increases in life expectancy. However, improvements in health have not necessarily been greatest in those nations with better services. In the UK, since 1980, public services have been reduced somewhat, with absolutely no slowing down of the increase in life expectancy overall. There has been some increase in the difference in life expectancy between the most privileged and the most disadvantaged social classes during this time. Although life expectancy of women and men in all classes improved, all lost ground relative to those in the most privileged class (Hattersley, 1999). But, as we saw in chapter 1, this trend is not unique to a time of rising income inequality but seems to have persisted for as long as we can see from the available statistics, at least in Great Britain. This kind of trend produces some difficulties both for the psycho-social version of the income inequality hypothesis, and for the neo-material version. The 1950s and 1960s in Great Britain were times of great expansion of public services and some narrowing of income differences, but health inequality did not decrease.

A 'Life-Course Political Economy' of Health

Readers may have noticed that in the attempt to reconcile the social ecology studies of income inequality and health with the studies of health inequality within populations, the life-course approach described in chapter 7 has been ignored. One reason for this is that there is really no way to bring together the life-course approach with the 'strict' psycho-social explanation for the relationship of income inequality to health. Income inequality is conceptualized and measured as something that exists at a given time-point, and which affects the health of people living at that time regardless of their age. This kind of effect is often called a 'period effect' by epidemiologists or demographers. It is contrasted to a 'cohort effect', which is something that influences the health of a group of people who were all born at the same time, so that at any given time-point, this cohort's health will be different to that of those born before or after them. A realistic example of a cohort effect, which we can see in UK health trend data, is the improvement in nutrition of pregnant women between, for example, 1900 and 1925. As a result, people born after 1925 tended to be less susceptible to illness (Kuh and Davey Smith, 1997).

What if populations passing through periods of increasing (or indeed decreasing) inequality of income (or provision of services) carry with them the 'embodiment' (Fassin, 2000; Krieger, 2000) of earlier experiences? This would mean that, for example, the effect of decreases in income inequality on British citizens in the 1960s would have depended to some extent on what people experienced as children in the recession of the 1930s. Likewise, the effects of increasing inequality in the 1980s would have depended on their experiences as children and young people in the 1950s and 1960s. Anyone aged around 40 or over in the 1980s would have experienced high levels of security of employment, free health care of a high standard, public housing provision of a mixed but often reasonably good standard for most of their adult lives. So the effect of shorter-term social and economic changes in middle-aged and older people (who contribute most to the mortality statistics) might not be expected to be that great. They often had considerable 'reserves of health resources' to fall back on. And not only 'health resources'. For example, many tenants of public housing were enabled to buy their homes at very low prices, and sell them on at a considerable gain. In cities, people who did this and moved away from the more central areas were able to improve their housing, environment and living standards.

If the effects of possibly detrimental economic changes depend on what has happened earlier in the life course of population groups, what would we expect to see? One possible result could be that older groups would be less badly affected, as they had spent more of their life course in the more favourable environment. And in the UK, that is precisely what we do see. Life expectancy in men aged 18–34 actually fell during the 1980s, at the same time as overall life expectancy rose. Because death is a rare event in such young people, their mortality rate has little effect on the overall trends. But the different impact of rising inequality on younger and older men is consistent with what I will call a 'life-course political economy' of health.

Such an approach might lead us to look more closely at the ways in which both income inequality and the sorts of public policies that often accompany such inequality affect the ways in which people are able to build up and protect their health resources, and to deal with such misfortunes as do arise. Education, for example, is regarded by the neo-materialists as an important aspect of social provision. A life-course approach adds to this. It reminds us that education plays at least two roles in building health resources: it enables people to gain access to safer and better-paid and more secure jobs; but it also gives access to cultural resources (Adler, 2002). The level of welfare benefits available to those unable to work is another crucial difference between more and less unequal societies. One of the main sources of income inequality in a population, after all, is the income of those members who are not employed at all. The amount of income that is replaced during periods of unemployment, sickness or parental leave determines to a large extent 'the worst that can happen' and thereby the amount of background anxiety that will be present the rest of the time (Bartley, Blane and Montgomery, 1997).

It may be that there are certain 'critical periods' in the life course, at which having adequate publicly provided support is particularly important. It has been suggested that examples of such critical periods might include the move from home to school, the time of school examinations, the move from school to work, setting up a home of one's own, the transition to parenthood, the onset of physical changes that accompany ageing, and exit from paid work (Bartley, Blane and Montgomery, 1997). At each of these transitions, the quality of services may make a difference between a temporary instability and a long, descending spiral of disadvantage.

An example of this kind of process, in which a small deficit of income at a critical period determines health over the longer term, is the causation of neural tube defects, such as spina bifida, in children. This kind of birth defect has a sharp social gradient. How could a 'life-course political economy' model explain this? The neural tube is formed very early in the development of the embryo, and is detrimentally affected by a lack of vitamin B. Many women will not even be aware that they are pregnant at this time. In households where money for food is short, even for these few weeks, the damage will be done. The only way to be fully protected from the risk of neural tube damage to one's developing baby is to have fully adequate nutrition at all times during the reproductive years. Levels of income provision for unemployed families cannot therefore be set on the basis of allowing enough calories for physical survival, without allowing for food of sufficient quality to ensure adequate intake of vitamin B. Take another example from the classic research on social inequality in mental health of Brown and Harris (Brown and Harris, 1976). It is known that depression in mothers of young children is more likely when there is a less close relationship between the mother and her partner. It is also known that maternal depression is related to children's health and school progress. In families where income is low, employed partners often begin to work longer hours of overtime when children arrive, to cope with the additional costs. This, in turn, makes it more likely that the relationship between parents may become less close and confiding, increasing the risk of maternal depression. The low basic income offered by many jobs thus triggers a sequence of adverse events that may influence the health of at least two generations. Not just health, but also 'health resources', as children who have experienced stress in the household during their early years are then themselves at higher risk of educational failure, unemployment and lower psychological well-being when they become adults. (Montgomery et al., 1996; Wadsworth, 1997; Caspi et al., 1998; Duncan et al., 1998).

Policy Implications

Earlier on in this chapter I mentioned the controversy that has been aroused by the possible policy implications of the ecological income-distribution studies. Chapter 11 will investigate further what health inequality studies may tell us about social and economic policies. But by this point it is probably evident that the type of explanation we accept for the ecological data will influence what kind of changes we might think necessary to improve population health.

Most obviously, the policy lessons of the ecological studies will depend on whether we think that the observed relationships between income distribution and health are due to perceived relative status deprivation, the material effects of relative poverty or 'neo-materialist' factors. Many of the principal objectors to Wilkinson, Kawachi and others who have pursued a psycho-social interpretation of the relationship of income distribution to health do not disagree that there is too much economic and social inequality (Davey Smith, 1996; Muntaner and Lynch, 1999; Lynch, 2000; Coburn, 2000). Rather, they disagree with the 'subjective bias' in the psycho-social interpretation of observed patterns. If, these critics argue, relative income does no more than change people's perceptions of their position in a social hierarchy, policy makers do not really have to worry about money at all. If it were possible (or at least more feasible) to change people's perceptions of their social standing in some other way, then income itself need not be redistributed (by egalitarian but unpopular tax policies, for example). Similarly, if 'social capital', the degree to which people in communities support each other, could be changed by campaigns to change public attitudes, then health might be improved regardless of how much more money some people had than others (Lang and Hornburg, 1998). Neo-materialists attack the psycho-social interpretation of the income distribution studies on the grounds that it saves governments the expense of providing good standards of public services (Muntaner and Lynch, 1999). If all that matters is one's perceived position in a social hierarchy, what is the use of a good health service, education service and public transport?

The criticisms bring us back to the concerns raised in chapter 3 about different meanings of the term 'social inequality', the different ways in which people may be 'unequal' and the different ways in which forms of inequality may affect health. As is the case in studies of health differences between social groups within countries, there are no fixed answers to the question of which types of inequality may be most significant for explaining health differences between countries. What is helpful in the meantime is to try and keep a clear idea of what kind of inequality is being proposed in each study, and what kinds of 'pathways of effect' are being proposed as explanations. In both types of study, the proposed pathways need, in the last analysis, to be 'biologically plausible', that is, to give us a believable account of how social forces get inside the body.

FURTHER READING

I do not intend here to present readings that are biased 'in favour' of Wilkinson's hypothesis. Opponents have written many papers that are cited in the text, but no books.

A very approachable and persuasive account
Wilkinson, R., *Unhealthy Societies: The Afflictions of Inequality*. London: Routledge, 1996.

The most recent collection
Kawachi, I., Kennedy, B., and Wilkinson, R. G. (eds), *Income Inequality and Health: The Society and Population Health Reader*, vol. 1. New York: New Press, 1999.

9

Gender Inequality in Health

This chapter will outline the way in which the approach taken up to now can be used to address two questions. The first of these is: what are the reasons for the health differences between men and women? This question has been very fully researched, and there are many good papers and books dealing with it. (Macintyre et al., 1996; Lahelma et al., 1999; Arber and Cooper, 1999; Manson, 1999; Ladwig et al., 2000; Annandale and Hunt, 2000). Here, therefore, I will only briefly touch on whether gender differences in health could be illuminated further by the explanatory models that have been outlined in previous chapters. Would it help to understand health differences between men and women to distinguish psycho-social, material and life-course theories, for example? What do we know about the effect of income distribution or other 'neo-material' factors, such as the provision of education, on gender differences in health?

The second question is whether health inequalities between social groups are less or greater in women than in men. Because women live longer than men do in industrial societies, relatively less attention has been paid to health differences between women in different socio-economic circumstances. Analysing health inequality in women has also raised many of the problematic issues of theory and method that have been discussed throughout this book. How is the socio-economic position of women best measured? Do women in a given occupation belong in the same social class as, or have similar status to, men in that occupation? Do the stresses of the home affect women in the same way as the stresses of work affect men? Or do domestic responsibilities protect women's health? Only after we have dealt with these issues can we advance further in understanding health inequality in women and the ways in which this differs from that found in men.

Gender 'Inequalities' in Health

Much has been written on why it might be that, in industrial societies, women live longer than men but appear to experience more ill health (Nathanson, 1975; Verbrugge, 1976, 1980a; Waldron, 1976; Verbrugge, 1980b). Higher mortality in men is found in all studies of industrial nations (Blane, Davey Smith and Bartley, 1990; Waldron, 2000). In England and Wales in 2000, women's life expectancy was just over 80 years, compared to men's life expectancy of 75.4 years. In the USA in 1999, the figures were 79.4 years for women and 73.9 years for men, more or less the same. Men have higher mortality from the most common single causes of death. In 1998, men in the USA suffered 254.1 deaths per 100,000 from ischaemic heart disease and 79.9 from lung cancer compared to 155.6 and 41.5 in women (USA, 2002, table 30). In the same year in England and Wales, the male death rates from these causes were 221 per 100,000 from ischaemic heart disease and 64 from lung cancer, while the female rates were 105 and 29 respectively (Office of National Statistics, 2002, table 6.3).

Gender differences in morbidity (illness) have been widely confirmed in representative health surveys in North America and Europe (Verbrugge, 1985; Verbrugge and Wingard, 1987; Popay, Bartley and Owen, 1993; Feeney et al., 1998). In the great majority of these studies, more women than men suffer from somatic complaints such as tiredness, headache, muscular aches and pains. These observations have given rise to the idea that 'men die quicker but women are sicker'. However, questions have also been raised about the validity of studies that show higher illness rates in women (Macintyre, Hunt and Sweeting, 1996). Health outcome variables have taken a wide variety of forms, and not all of these show gender differences of any great importance (Emslie, Hunt and Macintyre, 1999). There seems to be more consistency in studies that examine either minor psychological illness, symptoms of anxiety (Macintyre, Hunt and Sweeting, 1996), sickness absence from work (Feeney et al., 1998), and functional limitation (Arber and Cooper, 1999) or depression, although, even here, higher rates in women disappear after the age of around 55 (Bebbington et al., 1998).

Some have argued that perhaps when we look solely at morbidity rates in 'men' versus 'women' we are not really making a valid comparison. Men and women occupy such different combinations of social roles that gender itself may have little to do with the health differences that are seen. When an effort is made to compare males and females who are in similar social and economic situations, the gender differences in illness become a great deal smaller or even disappear (Emslie, Hunt and Macintyre, 1999). For example, if one compares a group of male and female full-time low-paid clerical workers in equally routine jobs, all without young families at home or other caring responsibility, the men are, if anything, more likely to report mild psychological illness than the women (Jenkins, 1985a, 1985b), although women take more days of sick-leave. The gender difference in illness and need for health care appears to arise as much as anything because many more women work in low-paid routine jobs (Stansfeld et al., 1995) and take major responsibility for caring and domestic work at home (Ladwig et al., 2000). Men in low-paid routine jobs with similar levels of caring work to women suffer similar amounts of illness.

To make this even more confusing (or interesting, perhaps), the more autonomy and responsibility at work a man has, and the higher his pay, the more likely he is to be married with children, whereas the opposite is the case for women. Women in higher-paid professions and managerial positions are in fact more likely than those in low-paid routine work to be unmarried and to have no children (Jenkins and Clare, 1985; Emslie, Hunt and Macintyre, 1999; Khlat, Sermet and Le Pape, 2000).

Table 9.1 shows marriage rates in men and women in different Registrar-General's Social Classes (RGSC) in England in 1998. Whereas almost 77 per cent of men in the most privileged social class were married, this applied to under 64 per cent of the women. By contrast, in social class V, almost 30 per cent of the men had never married while this applied to only 12 per cent of the women. Rates of separation, widowhood and divorce increase slightly with declining levels of social advantage, but this was seen in both men and women. The difference between men and women in how social class was related to their marital status arose from differences in those who had remained single rather than in those who married and subsequently divorced.

Table 9.2 takes a selected group of men and women in similar social class and marital situations. They are all aged 20–60, married and work full time in managerial, clerical or sales-type occupations. I have compared their scores on a measure of psychological health, the General Health Questionnaire (GHQ). The GHQ is designed for use in the community (outside hospitals and clinics) to detect people with minor psychological problems who may be suffering from more serious conditions. In this sub-sample of men and women there is clear evidence that women experienced more minor psychological morbidity, despite the fact that their household and work situations are not very different from those of the men. The table shows a difference of 0.3 points between the 'average' man and woman.

Table 9.1   Registrar-General's Social Class (RGSC) by marital status in men and women in England aged 35–55, 1998

RGSC		Marital status			
		Single (never married)	Married	Separated, widowed or divorced	Number in group
I	Men	13.5	76.6	9.9	222
	Women	20.3	63.8	15.9	69
II	Men	10.1	79.1	10.8	914
	Women	11.1	70.1	18.8	830
IIINM	Men	16.9	67.1	16.0	249
	Women	7.1	74.4	18.5	1,078
IIIM	Men	12.1	73.3	14.6	838
	Women	8.7	66.4	24.9	253
IV	Men	15.0	69.1	15.9	320
	Women	7.8	69.2	23.0	627
V	Men	29.1	55.1	15.8	127
	Women	12.1	65.7	22.2	248

Source: Health Survey for England 1998, author's analysis

Table 9.2   Difference in mean GHQ scores by gender for men and women aged 20–60, in full-time work in Registrar-General's Social Classes (RGSCs) II or IIINM and married

Sex	GHQ score (12-point scale)	
	Mean	N
Men	1.08	1,131
Women	1.38	1,545
Total	1.25	2,676

Source: Health Survey for England 1998, author's analysis

This may not seem very large, but as the average GHQ score for the whole group is only 1.25, women are about 25 per cent worse off in terms of this measure of psychological health than men. This difference is seen even in a group that has been chosen to contain men and women in relatively

Table 9.3 Self-rated health by gender in married, full-time working men and women aged 20–60 in lower managerial or clerical and sales occupations

	General self-rated health		
	Excellent or good	**Fair to very bad**	**Total = 100%**
Men	87.8%	12.2%	1,172
Women	86.9%	13.1%	1,594
Total	2,414	352	2,766
Odds ratio			1.1

Source: Health Survey for England 1998, author's analysis

similar situations. On the other hand, there was no statistically significant difference between the men and the women in terms of how they rated their own 'health in general' (see table 9.3).

Table 9.4 takes the same selected group and looks at gender differences in specific diseases. It is clear that some diseases are more commonly reported by men, some by women, and in some there is no difference. This is as would be expected from the work of Emslie, Macintyre, Hunt and colleagues (Macintyre, Hunt and Sweeting, 1996; Emslie, Hunt and Macintyre, 1999; Hunt and Macintyre, 2000), who have reported in a series of papers that there is 'complexity and subtlety of the pattern of gender differences across different measures of health and across the life course' (Hunt and Macintyre, 2000: 35).

In terms of specific diseases and conditions asked about in the 1998 Health Survey for England, there were few clear differences between men and women, when we compare people of similar age and with similar work and home conditions. Full-time workers in white-collar occupations are, generally speaking, a relatively healthy group of people, and we can see from table 9.4 that rates of illness are not high. Where there are higher rates in women, these are often small differences and not statistically significant. Men have clearly higher rates of heart and circulatory disease, which is exactly what we would expect from looking at the gender differences in mortality. The data in these tables are not altogether consistent with the idea that 'men die quicker but women are sicker'. On the contrary, there are few differences between men and women in most of these diseases, which include the most common and significant causes of illness and mortality. Where there are gender differences in illness these make sense in relation to differences in mortality risk.

From these figures, we might guess that, as the home and work situations of women and men become more similar (as women become more

Table 9.4 Gender differences in rates of illness: married full-time workers aged 20–60 in lower managerial or clerical and sales occupations

Condition	% (number) with condition		
	Men	**Women**	**Significance of difference**
Malignant or benign growth	0.3 (4)	1.3 (21)	women have higher rate
Genito-urinary conditions	1.3 (15)	1.6 (25)	no significant difference
Skin conditions	1.3 (15)	1.6 (25)	no significant difference
Musculo-skeletal conditions	14.2 (166)	11.5 (183)	men have higher rate
Endocrine and metabolic conditions	3.6 (42)	3.1 (50)	no significant difference
Mental disorders	2.1 (25)	3.1 (49)	no significant difference
Diseases of the nervous system	2.1 (25)	3.1 (49)	no significant difference
Eye conditions	0.7 (8)	0.7 (11)	no significant difference
Ear conditions	2.0 (23)	1.0 (16)	men have (just) significantly higher rate
Heart and circulatory system conditions	6.5 (76)	3.8 (60)	men have higher rate
Respiratory conditions	8.7 (102)	7.5 (119)	no significant difference
Digestive system conditions	4.3 (50)	4.1 (65)	no significant difference
Numbers	1,172	1,593	

Source: Health Survey for England, 1998, author's analysis

likely to have full-time jobs of similar status to men, and as work, marriage and children are combined in more similar ways), any remaining health differences between men and women may disappear. There is evidence that the gender gap in mortality has been falling (Charlton, 1997; Waldron, 2000), at least in the USA and other English-speaking developed countries. But research on gender differences in the trends for different forms of illness and disability is rather scarce.

Explaining Gender Differences in Health

It does not look very likely that a psycho-social approach is going to help us to understand gender differences in health. The main reason for women's longer lives has been a relatively low risk of heart disease under the age of 60, the most common cause of death in adults in industrialized nations up to this age. This is despite the fact that, in most studies, women are found to have less autonomy and power at work, and to earn less money than men. One might say the same thing for Effort-Reward Imbalance (ERI). The man who attains success in his job is also likely to be 'rewarded' by having a family, whereas the woman who is similarly successful appears to have far less chance of adding personal 'success' to professional. However, these potential sources of frustration do not seem to result in a higher risk of heart disease. Women are found in some studies to have more close relationships than men, although men have a wider circle of less intimate friendships. Whereas this might appear to be protective, it is also reported that women's close relationships are as much a burden as a help to them (Rael et al., 1995; Stansfeld et al., 1998; Fuhrer et al., 1999). Women do report experiencing stress and frustration more than men. But this does not appear to translate into disease in the same way.

Does health-related behaviour seem a more promising way of explaining health differences between women and men? This is likely to play a major role, not only in the form of smoking and heavy drinking, but other aspects of behaviour, such as taking physical risks and self-harm (Waldron, 2000). Until recently, most 'risky' health behaviours were less frequently seen in women. Smoking in public by women was frowned upon, and many bars did not even admit women. Fewer women drove cars. During the 1970s and 1980s, however, gender differences in smoking and in alcohol consumption (though not 'binge drinking' or 'public drunkenness') decreased (Johansson, 1989). During the 1980s, a series of papers asked whether, as women became more active in the workforce, they would tend to adopt the same types of risky health behaviours as men (Wingard, 1984; Passannante and Nathanson, 1985, 1987; Pugh et al., 1991)? One example of this from the recent past would be the way in which smoking became more acceptable in women during the 'emancipation' of large-scale employment in wartime industries between 1939 and 1945. When, in the 1960s, new research showing the link between smoking and disease became widely known, it was middle-class men who gave up most swiftly. Ironically, as women to some extent gained access to the more powerful and higher-paid jobs previously monopolized by men, smoking rates did not decrease. As a consequence, in some countries at present, smoking is as common in women as it is in men.

These ideas about changes in behaviour as women's roles change have been described as the 'Gender role modernization hypothesis' (Waldron, 2000). In order to evaluate this theory, again, we would not just expect increasing equalization of risk in all major illnesses at the same time. Gender inequalities in different diseases may show different trends. It is likely that the effect of smoking on lung cancer takes place after a person has been smoking for some considerable time, two to three decades (Doll and Peto, 1981), so that we may continue to see the effects of higher rates of smoking in increasing lung cancer mortality in women for some time to come. However, the timing of the effect of smoking on heart attacks is less clear. Tarry substances in cigarettes stimulate tumour production over a long period. But another effect of tobacco smoke is to reduce the ability of red blood cells to carry oxygen around the body. This is why inhaling tobacco smoke can induce a dizzy feeling. This can force the heart to beat harder in an attempt to keep oxygen flowing to the muscles and other body tissues, which, in someone whose heart is already not working at its best, may set off an attack. If this is one of the ways in which smoking increases the risk of heart attacks in women, we should expect to see heart disease rising more quickly after any increase in smoking among women. In the USA at least (Waldron, 2000), the gender difference in heart disease did not change at all during the period when male and female rates of smoking were becoming more similar.

Do materialist factors offer any additional help in explaining gender differences in health? In fact, in some ways, gender differences support a materialist theory of health inequality more strongly than any other form. Higher levels of participation in the labour force in men have exposed them to far higher levels of hazards, such as heavy work, extremes of temperature, chemicals, dust and fumes. Although, like everything else to do with gender relationships, this is now changing, it was for most of the history of industrial production the norm for men to work outside the home from the age at which they were legally permitted to work until death or retirement. In contrast, women in most (though not all) regions of most industrial societies participated only intermittently in paid work outside the home.

During the first half of the twentieth century, increasing numbers of regulations were introduced to protect pregnant women, as a result of the fear that there would be insufficient soldiers for the great wars of that century. These had the effect of excluding women from many of the more hazardous forms of employment. This is not to minimize the hazardous and heavy nature of domestic labour experienced by women as wives, daughters and mothers in working-class households, or as servants in the homes of the rich. However, as contraception became widely understood and available, women effectively gained control of the pace of their own reproductive labour. By the 1970s, women were 'protected' from some of the more hazardous forms of work by legislation and convention, and at the same time able to control the amount of energy they expended in reproduction. Women's life expectancy may also have been more influenced than men's by advances in medical technology, as these resulted in safer confinements and the disappearance of puerperal infection ('childbed fever').

Exclusion from work such as mining, ship building and steel making in the mid-twentieth century meant exclusion from the best-paid jobs available to people who had to leave school early to contribute to the budgets of working-class families, and were unable to gain qualifications. An 'advantage' in terms of certain types of health hazard was combined with a disadvantage in terms of money and living standards. Whereas the majority of women were not dependent solely on their own earning power for their standard of living because they married, the exclusion of working-class women from many higher-paid jobs enforced financial dependency upon them. One result of this may have been the higher rates of anxiety and depression seen in women in many surveys. It may be that financial dependency enforced by law, tradition and lack of child-care has protected women from material hazards at the expense of higher psychological risk.

In this perspective on gender differences in health, it is suggested that these are the outcome of a complex combination of biology, hazard exposures affected by both tradition and legislation, and changes in medical technology. No studies have systematically examined historical trends in gender differences in health in order to test these ideas. If I had to classify this explanation according to the theories of health difference we have worked through up to this point, it seems to come closest to a 'neo-material' form of explanation, although it by no means fits any of them to perfection.

Is Health Inequality Different in Men and Women?

We cannot simply move on from looking at gender differences in *health* to looking at gender differences in health *inequality*. For one thing, there is no great agreement over whether there really are differences between men and women in the extent of health inequality. In 1988, Moser and colleagues reported that 'accurately to reflect the relation between a woman's life circumstances and mortality it is necessary to utilize other measures than those based solely on occupation' (Moser, Pugh and Goldblatt, 1988). In their large longitudinal study, differences between women classified into RGSCs according to their own occupations were not very great among the married women, who were the majority. In non-married women, differences in mortality risk according to social class based on their own occupation were at least as large as those seen in men, but these were the minority. The differences in mortality among married women increased substantially when the researchers included whether the women lived in a household owning one or more cars, and whether the home was owned, rented privately, or rented from the local housing authority (low-income housing scheme).

What this means is that whatever it is that produces a higher risk of early death in people in the less advantaged types of occupations, it has less effect by itself on married women than on men. One reason for this could obviously be that married women are less affected by lower levels of control, autonomy and security at work. Or perhaps occupation is not such a good indicator of a married or co-habiting woman's standard of living as it is for a man or a single woman. This is for two reasons: when a woman is working, her wage may be less than half of the total family income as she will tend to be paid less than her male partner; and when she is out of work she will have access to more money than solely the level of social security benefit. Also, we have already seen that legislation in most industrial nations excludes women from several of the most hazardous occupations. So knowing her social class based on her own occupation will not predict hazard exposure as well in a woman as in a man. Then there is the question of status. A woman married to a doctor who works as his secretary has a different 'standing in the community' from one who is simply a secretary and no more than that. So that, by all of our criteria of how social position may lead to illness, women's own occupations are poorer measures than men's.

These are rather commonsensical ideas, however, and based on what has been observed in the rather few studies of gender differences in health inequality over the past thirty years or so. The ideas need to be checked by looking at more up-to-date studies, and by looking at different countries. Countries vary enormously in the proportion of women who work, the average amount of their lives that women spend in employment, and, to a lesser extent, the sorts of jobs women typically do (Hunt and Macintyre, 2000). Some of the best international comparisons have been done between Great Britain and Finland by Arber, Lahelma, Rahkonen and colleagues (Arber and Lahelma, 1993). These authors point out that in 1996, doing only domestic work in the home was three times more common in Great Britain (22 per cent of women were 'housewives') than in Finland, where only around 7 per cent had no paid employment. Among those women who were employed, four times as many British women were employed part time (45 per cent versus 10 per cent in Finland) (Rahkonen et al., 2000). Do we find, then, that a measure of social class based on occupation is more predictive of health inequality in Finland? Indeed, health differences between social classes defined according to the individual's own job are greater among Finnish women, and more similar to those of men. We do not get larger inequalities in health in Finnish women by adding housing tenure, or marital status to social class (based on occupation) by itself (Arber and Lahelma, 1993). This gives support to the idea that, in the UK, measures of social position based on a woman's own occupation are less good predictors of health because they are less strongly linked to living standards and hazard exposures.

Because of this greater effect of the spouse's or partner's social position on women's health seen in British data, it has been argued that we should routinely analyse health inequality in women using only their partners' social class. However, it has been shown, once again in Finland, where there are different patterns of employment in women, that this would be mistaken. No differences in the degree of health inequality were found, whether the social position of the woman was defined according to her own or her spouse's occupation (Martikainen, 1995b). The same was true for men: the same amount of health inequality was seen whether the man was classified according to his own or his wife's occupation.

So one reason why health inequality might seem to be less in women than in men is that measures of the individual's own social class or prestige may not accurately reflect the risks and advantages experienced by women. The other reason we might find less inequality in mortality risk in women is a more biological one: the main causes of death during working age in women are not the same as those in men. Whereas for men the most common cause is heart disease, which is quite strongly related to socio-economic position, in women one of the most common causes of death in Western nations is breast cancer, which does not have a social gradient. If anything, breast cancer is more common in more privileged women, the complete opposite of the social pattern seen for heart disease and lung cancer. When studies have examined inequality in heart disease mortality in men and women in Finland, where occupational measures of socio-economic position more accurately reflect women's life experiences, the degree of inequality was even greater in women than in men (Pekkanen et al., 1995).

However that may be, in most countries, men and women do relate differently to the world of employment, and health inequality is not the same in the two genders. Which of the aetiological pathways might be involved in different ways in men and women? Differences in health behaviours, as we have seen according to the 'Gender role modernization hypothesis', may be changing. But are social variations in health behaviours different in men and women? Social class differences in smoking in Britain and the USA at present are similar in both genders, while class differences in 'unsafe' levels of alcohol consumption are different. Women in the more advantaged RGSCs are less likely to smoke, but more likely to be high alcohol consumers than their less privileged sisters. If we wanted to test the plausibility of a behavioural explanation for gender differences in health inequality we would have to go through each of the risky behaviours and compare the degree of inequality in each one. And we would have to see whether that degree of inequality was greater or smaller when we classified women according to their own or their partners' occupations. One example of risky behaviour that does seem to have large gender differences is that which leads to accidental and violent injury and death. However, increasingly, unsafe driving (for example) results in the death of pedestrians (who tend to be female, and either children or older people) rather than in the death or injury of the (male) driver. There is little evidence as to whether men in more privileged social groups drive more safely, although they are certain to have newer and safer cars which they can afford to maintain. In the case of diet, there is once again little evidence as to whether inequality in diet quality is greater in men than women. If women tend to cook healthier meals, the higher marriage rates of more privileged men coupled with the fact that it is still the woman in most households who is responsible for cooking makes it possible that diet could create greater health inequalities in men than women.

What of the psycho-social pathway to health inequality? Could this be operating differently in men and women? Or indeed, could such differences vary between nations with higher and lower rates of paid employment for women? If work stress of some kind is one of the causes of health inequality, then we would expect inequality to be greater in men, who are tied to paid employment for more of their lives. But if this is so, we should see less difference in nations where women spend more time in paid employment – which does seem to be the case, if we compare just the Finnish and British studies. Women in Britain and the USA whose occupations would be classified according to the British SEC or the American Wright schemas as having lower levels of power and autonomy have a smaller health disadvantage compared to those in 'better' jobs than men (Sacker et al., 2000b). This is most likely because women spend less of their lives tied to work and thus have less 'exposure' to this kind of risk factor. In Finland, as we have seen, where most women spend most of their working age in paid employment, the differences are far less, and for heart disease in which control at work is likely to be an important risk factor, inequality in women's mortality is greater than it is in men (Pekkanen et al., 1995). This kind of evidence indicates that the effect of psycho-social hazards, such as low control and autonomy at work, are implicated in health inequality in the same way in men and women: it is just that in some countries men get a higher 'dose' over their lifetimes.

How about the psycho-social effects of low status? This is a rather more difficult argument. If we think there is a simple relationship, such as low status in the community leading to poor health, gender differences in health give us a problem. In most countries it would be agreed that, if anything, women are in general accorded lower status than men. As women in industrial nations live considerably longer than men, this does not seem a very promising line of argument (although in some developing nations women's status is even lower and in fact men's life expectancy is higher than that of women). Can we say that there is less status difference between women in more and less advantaged economic or employment circumstances than between men? And we would have to add to this that this 'difference in differences' was itself different in Finland to Britain, for example. Do we really think that men who are consultant surgeons, or earning £50,000 a year are 'further away' in status terms from labourers and bus conductors than are their female equivalents? It is rather hard to think about, and there is little evidence to bring to bear.

If we are going to look at differences in health inequality between men and women, we need to be aware of the problems involved in different definitions of 'inequality'. It may be that health is affected by all three types of inequality: employment relations (class), status and material living standards (Bartley et al., 1999; Sacker et al., 2000a). In men, a single indicator of social position, such as occupational class, gives a fairly good picture of where they stand on all three of these. But in women this is less the case, at least in societies where a lot of women do not spend most of their lives in full-time paid employment. The problems involved in understanding gender differences in health inequality have only begun to be addressed, and seem to be most helpfully analysed by international and comparative studies (Arber and Lahelma, 1993; Martikainen, 1995b; Rahkonen et al., 2000). But these problems also have the advantage of forcing us to think more carefully about what inequality is and about the different ways in which it contributes to ill health.

FURTHER READING

A good general introduction to the topic
Annandale, E., and Hunt, K., *Gender Inequalities in Health*. Buckingham: Open University Press, 2000.

This has a lot to say about women's health generally, not just that of women in poverty
Graham, H., *Hardship and Health in Women's Lives*. London: Harvester Wheatsheaf, 1993.

10

Ethnic Inequalities in Health

Definitions of what is a 'race' or what constitutes 'ethnicity' vary over time and between countries (Jones, 2001; Aspinall, 2002). The term 'race' has been used to refer to groups of people who are thought to differ from each other in some biological way, whereas 'ethnicity' refers to cultural differences, such as language or religion. During the 1970s and 1980s, the term 'race' became discredited as a useful concept for scientific research on human health (Cooper, 1984; Rathwell and Phillips, 1986), as it was realized that there was no scientific basis for the idea that groups of people defined as 'races' shared biological features that had significance for health. 'Race' is now regarded as a socially and politically constructed concept that is used to justify the inferior treatment and greater exploitation of certain groups within a given society (Cooper, 1986). 'Ethnicity' is usually defined in terms of the combination of common geographical origin and linguistic and/or religious differences from the 'majority' or dominant population. So we may think of the Polish communities in England and Scotland as an ethnic group, for example, because they have ancestors from Poland, many still speak Polish and almost all are Catholic.

In many nations, the official statistical organizations have definitions of race and/or ethnicity which are used in censuses and official surveys. These definitions change rapidly and are the subject of so much debate that one could devote an entire book to this topic alone. The US government defines four 'races': White, Black, American Indian/Alaskan Native and Asian or Pacific Islander. Hispanic people are described not as a race but as an ethnic group. Ethnic identification in Great Britain has been classified in many different ways, which differ over time, and between England and Wales, Scotland and Northern Ireland (Aspinall, 2002). In the 2001

Census of England and Wales, respondents were asked how they would choose to classify themselves and given the following choices:

White
  British
  Irish
  Any other White background
Mixed
  White and Black Caribbean
  White and Black African
  White and Asian
  Any other mixed background
Asian or Asian British
  Indian
  Pakistani
  Bangladeshi
  Any other Asian background
Black or Black British
  Caribbean
  African
  Any other Black background
Other ethnic groups
  Chinese
  Any other ethnic groups

Thus the 2001 Census in Great Britain offered quite a large number of possible definitions. Censuses are carried out by separate authorities in England and Wales, in Scotland and in Northern Ireland. In the 2001 Census of Northern Ireland, people were asked,

To which of these ethnic groups do you consider you belong?
  White
  Chinese
  Irish Traveller
  Indian
  Pakistani
  Bangladeshi
  Black Caribbean
  Black African
  Black Other
  Mixed ethnic group, *write in*

What religion, religious denomination or body do you belong to?
Roman Catholic
Presbyterian Church in Ireland
Church of Ireland
Methodist Church in Ireland
Other, *please write in*

(If answer is 'no religion')
What religion, religious denomination or body were you brought up in?
Roman Catholic
Presbyterian Church in Ireland
Church of Ireland
Methodist Church in Ireland
Other, *please write in*

The way in which the questions are posed on the census form shows the great importance given to religious background in Northern Ireland. Even if a person there answered that they had no religious affiliation, they were asked to answer further questions in an attempt to discover the religion in which they were brought up. This ethnic categorization derives its significance, of course, from the specific political situation in Ireland. Other ethnic categories will be similarly affected by the political and economic histories of the regions where they are used, and any relationship of 'ethnicity' with health needs to be interpreted in this light.

The problem with the concept of ethnicity is that the notion of 'ethnic differences in health' was at one time used to imply that health problems in groups of people subjected to discrimination and racial harassment were due to their 'culture' (dietary customs, for example). In many ways this was considered to be just as bad as attributing health differences to biology. It was still an excuse, in the eyes of many, for giving insufficient attention to the position of ethnic or racial minority groups in the social structure, and to the ways in which they have been exploited, often over a long period of history, to the benefit of the majority and more powerful groups. For this reason, most groups who are in any context defined as a racial or ethnic minority support the recording by official surveys of race or ethnicity in one form or another: in order to monitor discrimination and its consequences.

In this chapter, I will use the term 'racial or ethnic minority' to refer to any group of people who are likely to be at risk of unfavourable treatment because of their national origins, shared social histories, or religion. In some contexts, the term 'ethnic group' does not seem suitable. On the other hand, the biological-determinist overtones of the term 'race' are both scientifically incorrect and unattractive. It must also be acknowledged that an ethnic or racial group does not by any means have to be a numerical minority in order to experience forms of discrimination and inequity that might be expected to influence their health. The idea of the 'ethnic majority' is based more importantly on power than on numbers. None of these are fully satisfactory terms. Inequalities between members of different ethnic groups will be situated within a framework of socio-economic inequalities (Nazroo, 2001). It will be argued that ethnic inequality in health can best be understood in terms of where members of different groups are situated within social structures, rather than cultural or biological differences between groups (Cooper, 1986, 1993; Smaje, 1995; Nazroo, 1998) However, differences between people that are defined in terms of race or ethnicity, and that give rise to inequalities in life chances, appear in different places for different reasons in history, reasons which are linked to economic and political forces. For this reason, the experiences of these groups can seldom be entirely captured in terms of their income, social class or living conditions at a single point in time alone (Williams, 1996; Krieger, 1999, 2000).

The largest-scale historical phenomena giving rise to the existence of racial or ethnic minority groups in industrial nations at the present time have been slavery and colonialism. Slavery brought many thousands of people forcibly from Africa to the Americas in the eighteenth and nineteenth centuries. Slavery was enormously important in the development of the economic system we would now call industrial capitalism, the exploitation of African people allowing massive accumulations of wealth that later led to the rise of whole industries in the UK and the USA. British colonialism moved many groups of people round the world in various ways. Three of these streams of migration are most relevant to the present discussion. The first of these was the mass recruitment of Irish workers to build canals and railways in Great Britain in the eighteenth and early nineteenth centuries (Abbotts et al., 1997). Then there was the post-war migration of people from the Caribbean Islands and South Asia (India, Pakistan and Bangladesh), recruited to make up for severe shortages of workers in the UK. In the late 1960s and 1970s, there was also movement of people who had originally migrated from India to Kenya and Uganda when these were all part of the British Empire, who were expelled from the African nations. In 1974, people migrated from Cyprus at the time of the Turkish invasion of the island. However, the Immigration Act of 1962 brought an end to large-scale migration from the 'New Commonwealth' nations to Britain (the 'Old Commonwealth' nations being Australia, Canada and New Zealand) (Smaje, 1995).

What are defined as the characteristic differences in appearance between races or ethnic groups are indefinite and bound to their social and historical context (Williams, 1997; Dyson, 1998; Jones, 2001). Both the definition of a group as ethnically or racially distinct and the expression of discriminatory attitudes and practices are outcomes of economic and social forces. In the 1930s, there were 'race riots' in West London (UK) against Welsh people. They were regarded as unwanted aliens at that time, because people from Wales were brought in to work at lower wages in the new industries that were springing up, displacing the Londoners. In Switzerland in the 1960s and 1970s, myths abounded about the strange cooking and sexual behaviour of Italians. The status of an 'ethnic minority' was in this case due to the position of Italian guest workers, brought in to do unskilled and hazardous jobs at lower wages than Swiss citizens would have accepted. Korean workers in Japan occupy a somewhat similar position. These are examples of the ways in which economic forces produce 'ethnic minority' status. An example of the ways in which political forces do the same thing could be taken from the position of people from Eastern European nations in Western Europe at the present time. These people are at high risk of becoming the target of negative stereotyping, harassment and discrimination. If an outsider were to see an Italian and a Swiss person sitting side by side in a café, it would be impossible to tell which was which. Nor would it be possible for the average British, American or Swiss to tell the difference between a Welsh person and an English person. In the USA, England, Wales and Scotland, studies of health inequality pay no attention to religion itself. But in the Netherlands, it is customary automatically to 'adjust' statistically for Catholic and Protestant religion, because the health differences between these groups are so consistent, in the same way that one takes account of gender. So we can see that the components of 'race/ethnicity' that are seen as important in terms of defining a group that might be at risk of some kind of health disadvantage depend on time and place.

Ethnicity, Biology and Health

In this light, it is no surprise that most researchers now consider it a mistake to explain health differences between races or ethnic groups in terms of biology. Many studies in the past were based on the assumption that there are biological similarities among members of the same racial groups (genetic homogeneity) and differences between groups that might give rise to differences in disease risk. This is very rarely true. Certain genes do influence some of the characteristics that are used in some situations to distinguish racial or ethnic groups, such as hair or skin colour. But these genes do not seem to be very important for the ways in which the body works or responds to disease hazards (Cruickshank and Beevers, 1989;

Cavalli-Sforza, Menozzi and Piazza, 1994; Senior and Bhopal, 1994). In most respects, the genetic differences between groups of people defined in terms of their ethnicity are less than the genetic differences between individuals within any of those groups (Cruickshank and Beevers, 1989). Knowing an individual's racial or ethnic group, for example, is little help in predicting what their blood group will be (Jones, 1981).

It is not particularly surprising that the 'genes' that determine hair, eye or skin colour, for example, do not predict ethnic or racial differences in disease vulnerability. After all, it is not hair, eye or skin colour that create an 'ethnic minority' category. 'Genes' may determine who has auburn hair, green eyes and freckly skin, not the countries in which people with this appearance might or might not be regarded as 'similar' in the sense of constituting a racial or ethnic minority. People of this appearance might be viewed as an ethnic minority in the Spanish Basque country, but not in Italy, for example. However, in David Williams's words, race or ethnicity can, in many places, act as a 'master status': as sex and age do (Williams, 1997). They are one of the first things that people register when they first meet each other. A stream of assumptions follow about what a person is like in many ways (Jones, 2001). Because of this, when discovering pockets of illness in social groups who are regarded as racially or ethnically 'different', doctors have tended to think first of biological or cultural causes. Nazroo (1997) has described this as the 'traditional epidemiological approach'. It focuses on particular diseases and how biological or cultural variations across ethnic groups may be used to provide clues to aetiology. This can lead to 'blaming' members of minority groups for their greater vulnerability to certain diseases. He contrasts to this the 'race relations approach' which 'raises questions about the motives for, and the methods used in, work on ethnicity and health and the implications that this has for the potentially discriminatory conclusions drawn. It focuses on the health disadvantages faced by ethnic minority groups and how the health services ... may be failing to find appropriate ways to meet needs' (Nazroo, 1997: 2–3).

Understanding of disease causation that is sufficient to help in prevention and treatment is more likely to be gained by paying attention to differences in material and psycho-social hazards across the life course (Onwuachi Saunders and Hawkins, 1993; Lillieblanton and Laveist, 1996; Lillieblanton et al., 1996). Dressler (1993) tested three conventional models of health inequalities affecting African-American people in a US study. He terms these the 'racial-genetic model', the 'health behaviour or lifestyle model' and the 'socio-economic status model'. No one model was found to explain the health differences in the study, so he arrived at a fourth, 'social structural model'. Like Williams, Dressler concludes that

Table 10.1 Racial/ethnic disparities in mortality by cause: USA, 2000*

Cause of death	Black	Hispanic	American Indian/Alaskan Native	Asian or Pacific Islander	White
All	1,129.9	596.4	696.8	507.4	852.1
Heart disease	326.5	175.8	165.2	144.9	253.6
All cancers	249.6	123.7	127.3	125.0	198.4
Lung cancer	64.1	22.7	32.7	28.9	56.6
Breast cancer	34.9	16.8	14.7	12.7	26.6
Diabetes	49.7	32.4	41.4	16.6	22.8
Homicide	21.0	8.8	8.1	3.1	3.7

Source: US Centers for Disease Control statistics
<http://www.cdc.gov/nchs/hus.htm> accessed 1 Dec. 2002
*Deaths per 100,000 standard population

skin colour is a kind of 'master status', which serves as a criterion of social class in colour-conscious societies such as that of the United States and most European nations. The reason for differences in health between, in particular, White and Black Americans is the effect that their racial master status has on access to better education, jobs and careers.

There is, however, a considerable debate on the meaning of this kind of exercise. Many studies take two different ethnic or racial groups and adjust for various measures that are plausible explanations for higher ill health or mortality in one of them. If all these adjustments still leave an excess of ill health, how is this to be viewed? In the past, studies concluded that this remaining difference was due to 'racial' genetic differences. This kind of explanation, as we have seen, is now largely discredited.

How Great Are Ethnic or Racial Differences in Health?

What do facts and figures on differences in health between racial or ethnic groups actually reveal? Table 10.1 shows the differences in mortality risk between the racial and ethnic groups defined in US official statistics for some of the most common causes of death in the US population. It uses direct standardization, as described in chapter 3, to give a rate per 100,000 of the population after taking account of any possible age differences between the racial/ethnic groups. In 2000, mortality from all causes was

Table 10.2   Mortality by country of origin: England and Wales, 1989–1992

| | Cause of death | | | | | | |
| | All | | Coronary heart disease | | Lung cancer | | Breast cancer |
	Men	Women	Men	Women	Men	Women	Women
All	100	100	100	100	100	100	100
Scotland	132	136	120	130	149	169	114
Ireland	139	120	124	120	151	147	92
East Africa	110	103	131	105	42	17	84
West Africa	113	126	56	62	62	51	125
Caribbean	77	91	46	71	49	31	75
South Asia	106	100	146	151	45	33	59

Source: Wild and McKeigue (1997: 705)

30 per cent higher for Black Americans (African-American persons) than for White Americans. All the major causes of death were lower in White than in Black Americans: heart disease, lung cancer and even breast cancer (which is often thought to be linked to affluence). Particularly striking is the fact that the risk of death by homicide was over five times greater for Black than for White Americans. The result of all these differences was that life expectancy for Black people was 71.7 years compared to 77.4 years in White people, a difference of 5.7 years. This was a reduction since 1990, when the difference was 7 years (USA, 2002). Hispanic people, in contrast, had more favourable risks in relation to heart disease and cancer, although they were over twice as likely to die from homicide than Whites were. Because homicide is a relatively unusual cause of death, the overall mortality risk for Hispanic Americans was lower than that for Whites.

The US government keeps much more comprehensive statistics on racial or ethnic differences in health (called 'health disparities') than governments of many other nations. This is in sharp contrast to the lack of data on differences between social classes. The opposite is the case in the UK. As we have seen, official government reports on class differences in health in England and Wales go back to 1921, and it has been this unique data series that gave rise to the present-day study of health inequality. However, perhaps in part because there are far fewer people classified as coming from racial or ethnic minorities in the UK than in the USA, data on ethnic differences in health in Great Britain are harder to come by.

Before the Census of 1991, British censuses only collected information on country of birth. Table 10.2 shows the Standardized Mortality Ratios (SMRs) for people aged 20–69, comparing the death rates of people born in various geographical regions. Harding and Maxwell (1997) have examined social class differences in mortality among men and women of different national origins for a similar time period, 1991–3 (see table 10.3).

If we compare the two sets of data summarized in tables 10.2 and 10.3, we see that, as in the United States, the implications of race or ethnicity for health in Britain are very mixed. Table 10.2 uses 'direct standardization', whereas table 10.3 uses 'indirect standardization' and reports relative mortality risk in terms of the SMR. (Chapter 3 explained the difference between the two measures used in tables 10.1 and 10.2–3. Briefly, the directly standardized rates in the first table can be understood just like a percentage, whereas the SMR is a ratio that compares rates of illness to a 'population average'). In tables 10.2–3 the risk for all countries of origin (separately for men and women) is set to be 100, and the figures for each country compare the risk of mortality relative to this 'average' of 100 for everyone. All we can see is the comparison between each ethnic group and the population as a whole. But we can see that both men and women originating in Scotland, Ireland and West Africa have a higher overall relative mortality risk than the rest of the population, while there is a rather high relative risk of heart disease mortality in those from South Asian nations. Because the methods of standardization in the two reports are different, it is not possible to compare the US and British figures directly. We can see, however, that people with Caribbean origins in Britain had a low relative risk for mortality from all causes, including heart disease, compared to the average for the population. People classified as having Asian origins had a rather high relative risk of heart disease mortality but a low relative risk of mortality from lung cancer.

When we combine national origins with social class in the British data we can see that the high relative mortality in the Scottish, Irish and Indian groups is only seen outside of social classes I and II. (This exercise is only possible for men because, as mentioned earlier, social class is not well recorded on women's death certificates.) Looking in even more detail at what causes of death are partly responsible for the ethnic and class inequalities, it is clear that the Scottish and Irish groups have a very high relative risk of lung cancer (and even here, only if they are outside the most privileged social classes I and II). The high relative risks of heart disease mortality in men originating from East Africa (many of whom are descended from earlier migrants from the Indian subcontinent) and the Indian subcontinent are, in contrast, seen among all social classes.

Table 10.3   Mortality by country of origin and Registrar-General's Social Class (RGSC): men, 1991–1993

Country of origin	RGSC			
	I/II	IIINM	IIIM	IV/V
All causes of death				
Scotland	82	121	169	186
Ireland	95	127	166	173
East Africa	104	138	150	120
West/South Africa	136	103	177	112
Caribbean	83	84	105	99
Indian subcontinent	96	112	120	158
Cause of death: coronary heart disease				
Scotland	84	114	157	163
Ireland	92	124	155	148
East Africa	152	195	255	147
West/South Africa	102	22	73	86
Caribbean	51	84	69	69
Indian subcontinent	132	179	183	223
Cause of death: lung cancer				
Scotland	82	114	221	225
Ireland	88	156	216	214
East Africa	–	–	–	–
West/South Africa	–	–	–	–
Caribbean	37	68	66	72
Indian subcontinent	30	51	55	90
Cause of death: accidents and injuries				
Scotland	69	83	233	315
Ireland	79	121	185	280
East Africa	63	63	109	123
West/South Africa	–	–	–	–
Caribbean	91	48	136	123
Indian subcontinent	62	75	99	91

Source: Harding and Maxwell (1997: Tables 9.4, 9.8, 9.10, 9.12)

Here we must remember that ethnic group is only being defined in terms of 'country of origin', which is a very inadequate measure. (We saw in chapter 3 that in most countries ethnic group is not asked about when a death is registered, but in the UK in the 1990s, people were asked where the deceased person had been born.) Many people who would regard themselves as belonging to a minority group were born in the UK. Also, the categories are far too broad. 'South Asia', for example, includes the whole of India, Pakistan and Bangladesh. Within these separate nations, there are three major religious groups: Hindu, Sikh and Muslim. Cutting across these religious groups, in turn, are a far larger number of possible regional and social classifications, such as caste groups (Senior and Bhopal, 1994). All of these mortality statistics need to be read with great caution (Bhopal, 2000). In the first waves of any migration, migrants tend to be fit and healthy people, aiming to face the hazards of going far from home in order to make a better life for themselves. Some migrant groups keep close contact with their home countries, and return there when they become sick or old. There is, for example, a very great difference between being an African-American whose ancestors were brought forcibly to America two hundred years ago, and a Hispanic person whose parents migrated more recently from Latin America. There can be no return to Africa for the former, whereas the latter may well have widespread family ties in their parents' home nation, and will probably still share a common language with them. Similarly, the families of most people from South Asia who were resident in the UK in the 1980s would have arrived relatively recently. In contrast, large-scale migration of people from the Caribbean took place in the 1950s. The great majority of Black British people of Caribbean descent were born in the UK. So the figures in table 10.2 for people of Caribbean descent only apply to rather a unrepresentative group of more recent migrants. They do not necessarily represent the health of all people of Caribbean descent.

Official statistics on the risk of death (mortality statistics) therefore may not give us a very good picture of health differences between races or ethnic groups. Official government mortality statistics depend on having a good system for recording deaths, recording the ethnic group to which a deceased person belonged, and recording the numbers of persons in the ethnic group in the country as a whole. Only in this way is it possible to get an accurate 'rate' (the number of deaths divided by the population and then multiplied by 100 for a percentage, or by whatever other number is required to get rates per 1,000, 100,000 and so on). There are various ways in which inaccuracies can creep into this kind of procedure, most of which can be envisaged by common sense. If members of some ethnic groups are less likely than others to be accurately classified in a national census, but their origins are accurately recorded when they die, then their apparent death rate will be too high. To calculate the rate, the 'correct' number of deaths in this group will have been divided by a population number that is lower than it should be. If, for some reason, ethnicity or race is not correctly classified when a person's death is officially registered, then the death rate will be too low. The same will happen if a large number of people from a certain group return to the country from which they, or their forbears, originated when they become old or ill. So perhaps we should look outside official records at studies specifically designed to investigate health in different races.

Harding and Rosato have looked more closely at cancer incidence (how many people are newly diagnosed each year) among persons born in Scotland, Northern Ireland, the Irish Republic, Caribbean Commonwealth and Indian subcontinent and living in England and Wales. They also found that the incidence of all cancers, including breast cancer, was low among West Indians and South Asians. Looking more carefully at differences between religious groups, they found that, among South Asians, this pattern was consistent for Hindus, Sikhs and Muslims. In contrast, Irish and Scottish women suffered more cancers of the lung, mouth and liver, and men suffered more leukaemia and cancer of the mouth and stomach (Harding and Rosato, 1999). Krieger and colleagues similarly examined ethnic differences in cancer incidence of several common forms of cancer in the San Francisco Bay Area. They found that incidence rates varied as much, if not more, by socio-economic position than by ethnicity. For example, lung cancer incidence was higher in people with less socio-economic advantage, except in Hispanic people: in this group the more affluent had higher incidence. They argue for the use of a social class measure in routine official statistics for cancer in the USA, such as exists in the UK (Krieger et al., 1999).

Ethnicity and Socio-Economic Conditions

Nazroo has reported on a variety of health problems in various groups in the UK, using the first large study designed for this purpose. He is sharply critical of 'lumping' groups together in an unconsidered manner, and of ignoring the importance of socio-economic position and circumstances. For example, within the category of people with Indian family origins, he distinguishes Hindus, Sikhs, Muslims and Christians, and shows that the difference in general health between these groups, as well as between each of these and White people, was considerable. While the general health of Hindu and Christian people from ethnic minorities differed little from Whites, that of Muslims was considerably worse (Nazroo, 1998). Furthermore, within groups classified broadly according to ethnic origins, there were large health differences according to socio-economic circumstances.

When he looked at individual diseases, the importance of socio-economic circumstances was equally striking. In this study, as in others, diabetes was higher in people of Caribbean origins, Indian people who had migrated from both India and Africa, Pakistani and Bangladeshi people than it was in Whites. However, within each of these ethnic groupings, the disease was more prevalent among those in workless households and those engaged in manual occupations (Nazroo, 1997: 103–6). When the excess risk of a number of diseases in ethnic minority groups was adjusted for the average standard of living in each group, this excess was greatly reduced and in many cases disappeared altogether (Nazroo, 1997: 103–7).

The attention paid in this report to the more precise definition of ethnicity enabled it to show that high rates of ill health relative to the White population were a far greater problem for Pakistani and Bangladeshi people than for other groups, such as Indian and Chinese. A more careful definition of socio-economic position and circumstances was the other important innovation. Rather than using social class alone, Nazroo devised an index of social conditions that included household overcrowding, quality of household amenities and ownership of consumer durables. It was this careful attention to defining both the groups involved and the nature of the disadvantages experienced that allowed many of the 'ethnic' differences to be explained (Nazroo, 2001).

Social Ecology of Ethnicity and Health

Residential area is another important variable. People defined as belonging to ethnic or racial minorities do not only tend to find themselves in less advantaged occupations with lower incomes but also in areas that suffer from environmental disadvantage (Acevedo-Garcia et al., 2003; Northridge et al., 2003). In some studies, once account has been taken of income, social class and area of residence, there are no visible 'ethnic effects' at all. In other words, the ethnic 'minority' groups studied were in no poorer health than members of the ethnic 'majority' living in the same conditions in similar areas (Sundquist et al., 1996; Deaton and Lubotsky, 2003; Chandola, 2001).

The economic system that created migration patterns of African people to and within the USA, and of Irish, Indian, Pakistani and Bangladeshi people to and within England and Wales, has not disappeared. In particular, the need for labour power to carry out large-scale agricultural and industrial projects, combined with the problem of what happens to these workers after economic recessions and changes in patterns of employment, still remains. The areas in towns and cities where immigrants have congregated while they worked in these industries often remain polluted, run down and under-developed. When the work is finished, as with the railways, or the industry becomes obsolete, as with the textile and pottery industries, those who worked in them are often forgotten. Hard and hazardous labour is replaced by unemployment. But there is often no good infrastructure of schooling and further education to equip the children of those whose labour has built the old industries to move on and benefit from change.

It is not possible to compare the mortality of first-generation African-American people to that of their descendants born in the USA, as these events took place long before the existence of censuses and health surveys. But we can relate the health disadvantage of African-Americans today to the alarming deterioration in the health experience of the children and grandchildren of Irish people who migrated to England and Wales at the end of the nineteenth century. Whereas first-generation people from the Irish Republic had around 35 per cent higher risk of death between 1971 and 1985, second-generation Irish people had a 54 per cent higher risk (Harding and Balarajan, 1996). The reasons for this persistent and worsening health disadvantage among people of Irish descent is not understood, any more than we clearly understand the reasons for the health disadvantage suffered by African-American people. These questions need to be addressed by consideration of political as well as economic factors. Groups that are discriminated against often find it impossible to break into local power structures that determine which areas will have new schools, better transport and improved health services. The social geography of racism and its implications for health are only just beginning to be understood. For example, Chandola has reported that a combination of social class, a measure of material standard of living and an area-based measure of local deprivation explains away all of the health differences between British South Asians and the White population (Chandola, 2001). Increasing use is now being made of new research methods combined with measures that take account of social and economic conditions, both contemporary and (where relevant) over historical time. These methods may eventually come to be extended beyond the investigation of ethnic or racial differences in health and improve our understanding of differences between social classes and status groups as well.

Explanations for Racial and Ethnic Differences in Health

Overall, these studies from both the UK and the USA seem to support the idea that socio-economic position and circumstances are an important reason for such ethnic or racial differences as we do see in the statistics. Health differences between racial or ethnic groups are nothing like as clear or consistent as socio-economic differences. In many groups defined as racial or ethnic minorities, smoking, alcohol consumption and diet are more favourable to health than those of the 'majority' population, despite the fact that most of the groups studied are subject to various forms of discrimination. When studies attempt to explain the ethnic health inequalities that do exist, however, social class, education and income do not seem to be the whole answer. It seems that we should also take account of the environment in which people live. Areas with very high concentrations of certain ethnic and racial groups seem to experience lower levels of services and worse environmental conditions that add to the disadvantages measured in individual socio-economic terms. This brings us back to the questions concerned with the historical forces that result in any group migrating from their region of origin to a different region. One interesting aspect of the new approach is that it widens out a 'life-course political economy' perspective from concentration on individual nations towards consideration of global forces over long periods of time. This new way of looking at ethnic differences in health is at an early stage of development. It is likely to have important implications for the ways in which we analyse all forms of health inequality.

FURTHER READING

A very useful book covering a wide range of relevant issues
Smaje, C., *Health, 'Race' and Ethnicity*. London: Kings Fund Institute, 1995.

Report of a specific study as well as presenting an account of the author's particular approach to ethnic difference in health
Nazroo, J., *The Health of Britain's Ethnic Minorities*. London: PSI, 1997.

A useful collection addressing many of the difficult questions
Ahmed, W. I. U. (ed.), *Race and Health in Contemporary Britain*. Buckingham: Open University, 1993.

Contains useful papers from the USA
Amick III, B. C., Levine, S., Tarlov, A. R., Chapman Walsh, D., *Society and Health*. Oxford: Oxford University Press, 1995.

11

Health Inequality and Social Policy

One of the most important reasons for carefully reviewing alternative explanations for health inequality in this book has been the need to increase policy relevance. In order to start thinking about policies to reduce health inequality, we first need to be reasonably happy that we have the right explanatory model. Researchers in the 1950s and 1960s were dismayed to find that the inception of the British National Health Service in 1947 had not been followed by a decrease in health inequality. By the 1980s it was clear that health inequality had in fact increased. However, the idea that health care free at the time of use would decrease health inequality was based on a mistaken explanatory model. Not unreasonably, in the period before the Second World War, many commentators assumed that the inequalities in health between richer and poorer areas and social groups were due to the lack of medical care (which had to be paid for). It was thought that everyone was equally likely to get serious diseases, and that the reason for longer life expectancy in richer areas or social groups was that these people could afford medical care.

Although the existence of health inequality had not been an explicit major reason for the setting up of a nationalized health service free at the time of use, it was a shock when it emerged during the 1950s that health inequality had continued to increase (Morris and Heady, 1955). We have seen from the trends shown in chapter 1 that this increase has continued until the present day. Because of this, it was increasingly acknowledged that having access to health services was something that happened 'too late' to protect people against the health consequences of poverty, work hazards, powerlessness or low social status. The diseases that caused most suffering and early mortality in the late twentieth century, and that accounted for most of the inequality in health, were not infections or medical crises that could be dealt with by drugs or surgery. They were chronic conditions, such as heart disease and cancer, which have long, complex and often hidden aetiology. The damp home experienced in childhood, or even the poorly nourished mother-to-be during a person's gestation, could have consequences much later on. Other long-term behavioural patterns, such as smoking and diet, are now also known to play a part in causing the major health problems of modern populations. Health services can do little or nothing about these kinds of risk factors. Even worse, it is possible that a concentration of money and attention on health services perpetuates a mistaken idea of what causes health inequality, and thereby of how to reduce it.

It is now widely acknowledged, certainly in the UK, the Nordic nations and the Netherlands (where most research on health inequality has taken place), as well as increasingly in the USA (Adler et al., 1993), that a so-called 'upstream model' of explanation is needed. An upstream model concentrates on things that happen earlier in the development of diseases, and on prevention rather than cure. The problem once this has been decided upon is to decide which upstream model is closest to reality and will therefore prove the most effective guide to policy. The structure of this book has, accordingly, worked through several alternative (though not necessarily contradictory) explanations. The aim has been to clarify each type of explanation as far as possible, and to help the reader to decide for themselves, in any given case for any particular condition, which is the most accurate.

Do We Need Trials of Policy Options?

It is true that in medicine, for example, finding the right 'cure for the disease' does not always work this way. Often, various drugs or procedures are tried out on the basis of inspired guesses and practitioners' experience. This is why the 'randomized double-blind controlled clinical trial' is such an important part of medicine. It is often not completely understood exactly why drug X improves the state of someone with disease Y. So in order to prove that it does, drug X is given to a randomly selected group of people, and a 'sugar pill' or placebo with no drug in it, is given to another similar group. These trials are described as 'randomized' because those who get the real drug and those who do not are selected completely at random (by the equivalent of tossing a coin), so that any differences between the group who get the medicine and those who do not occur by chance. This was to ensure that there could not be anything about, for example, the motivation of those who take the medicine that might also make them more likely to recover from the disease. The trials are also called 'control' or 'controlled' because of the presence of the group of people who have not been given the drug, called the 'control group' in order to compare the progress of the disease in the two groups. When the patients do not know whether they are receiving a pill that contains the drug or a placebo, trials are called 'single blind'. They are called 'double blind' when neither the patient nor the doctor knows whether the patient is receiving the treatment or the placebo.

After a suitable period of time, statisticians test the difference in health between those who actually received the drug and those who only thought they did. If the drug seems to have made a significant difference to the health of those who received it, it is accepted as effective. The reason why you need a control group of people who are not getting the drug but think they are (and whose doctors think they are) is the power of mind over body. People can show enormous improvement in many health conditions when they think they have good reason to be getting better, even though they may be doing no more than swallowing a sugar pill. Even subtle differences in the behaviour of the doctor who administers the treatment are known to influence the way the patient feels, which is why the doctor as well as the patient must be 'blinded'. This capacity for what we think is happening to us to affect how we feel, and thereby some of the biological processes in the body, is called the 'placebo effect'. (It is, incidentally, one reason to believe that psycho-social factors do form part of the explanation for health inequality.) But it is also one reason why it is very difficult, if not impossible, to apply the test of the randomized double-blind trial to potential 'cures' for health inequality.

One of the great promises of the new knowledge in genetics and molecular biology is that the action of drugs will be understood more fully, in terms of the ways in which their chemical contents interact with the cells in the body to produce effects on disease. With this more detailed understanding of the mechanisms by which drugs act in the body, the clinical trial will become less central. This kind of 'molecular' understanding is closer to what this book has been trying to argue for in the case of health inequality. Of course, health inequality is an enormously complex phenomenon. For one thing, it involves quite a large number of different diseases affecting different bodily systems: it is seen in heart disease, stroke, lung cancer and other lung diseases such as bronchitis and pneumonia. There are also great inequalities in disability and death due to accidents, which have no biological cause in terms of a disease at all. Whatever are the 'causes' of health inequality, they operate at the level of the cell and at the level of the road, home and factory. Suicides, and violent deaths and injuries, also have a strong social gradient, pointing to the importance of the ways in which social inequality deeply influences social relationships and the way people feel about themselves. So it might be argued that if clinical trials are necessary even to discover the effectiveness of a single drug for a single health condition, how much more necessary are 'trial interventions' to discovering whether we can frame effective policies to reduce health inequality.

One virtue of the trial is that it can prevent us from deluding ourselves as to the results of treatments or interventions. Take the recent argument in the UK about whether the combined vaccine for measles, mumps and rubella (MMR vaccine) causes autism in children. If a randomized trial could be done, it would be possible to see whether the non-vaccinated children were less likely to become autistic than the vaccinated ones. If the selection of those to be vaccinated and those not were truly random, there would be no confounding factors, such as the parents' education level or social class, to influence the results. If, even though they had been chosen purely by the 'toss of a coin', more of the vaccinated children became autistic, this would be very damning evidence against MMR. But it would be quite impossible to tell a random group of parents that their children had been put into either of the groups. Most would strongly object to being denied vaccination; others would refuse it because they already believed it to be linked to autism.

The absence of this kind of evidence causes all kinds of problems for basing policy on the kind of research we have on health inequality. There are plenty of examples of policies to improve health generally that may have accidentally increased health inequality. In the USA and increasingly in the UK and other European nations, smoking has been forbidden in more and more workplaces, so that at the present time there are few US or UK offices where it is permitted. One irony of this policy has been the increasing concentration of smoking among people with no paid employment, including mothers of young children (Marsh and McKay, 1994). As smoking is more likely to be forbidden in offices, which are full of white-collar workers, than in factories or building sites, another possible effect of this policy change has been to increase the differences in smoking between the social classes (Jarvis, 1997). Social inequality in smoking (and in health) is much greater in the US and UK than it is in countries such as Spain and Greece where anti-smoking policies are as yet less widespread (Kunst et al., 2000). So there is a good case to be made for the assertion that if we want policies that will reduce health inequality as well as improving health overall, they need to be specially designed for the purpose.

More generally speaking, it is not very easy to meet the criteria needed for the popular and plausible idea that policy should be 'evidence based'. Even when we do have evidence from randomized trials, the results often do not agree. In clinical medicine, databases such as the Cochrane Collaboration collect large numbers of studies (for example, of different types of treatment for complications during the birth of a baby) and use systematic methods to decide which methods (or drugs) are best supported by the evidence. The results of administering different drugs can be collected together and summarized by methods known as 'meta-analysis': sophisticated statistics that show up inconsistencies between trials before deciding what the overall message is for health care. In social policy this type of 'evidence-based' approach has come to be known as a "What works?" approach. But, as discussed above, it is usually not possible in social policy intervention studies to create a similar situation to the double- (or even single-) blind randomized control trial, because people can hardly be given more money, or better services, without being aware of the fact.

Nor is it usually possible to carry out even non-blinded trials where one group is given a service and another is not. This is because in most cases it is so obvious that the 'service' is beneficial in some way or other (even if it may not actually benefit health in the short term) that the ethics of denying it to some people are not acceptable. A good example of this was the development in the UK by Jarman of a computerized system for estimating how much social security benefit the patients of a general medical practice were entitled to. A health worker who was not an expert on welfare rights could sit down with a patient and go through the programme, which would show up any benefits they were not claiming. This could result in the income of some patients rising considerably. How could one carry out a trial of the effects on health of such a service? Even if it had no effect at all on health, there could be no ethical justification for denying a 'control group' of patients the use of the advice service. This would mean they might be denied benefits to which they were entitled by right.

It is for these kinds of reasons that it is very hard to gather much evidence relevant to deciding what might be effective in reducing health inequalities. There have been a few 'intervention studies' dealing with relatively small changes in the social environment. The intervention study is similar to a clinical trial, in that one group of people, or one area, is given a 'dose' of policy (the intervention) and another is not, and results are then compared between the two. Most of these have been based on sensible ideas, which have focused on one particular cause of injury or death. For example, some local authorities in the UK have funded pubs and bars to provide plastic glasses on Friday and Saturday nights when fights often break out during which glass causes injury. Changes in this kind of hazard are relatively easy to monitor, as reductions in injuries would be expected to happen fairly quickly. Another major study is trying out 'peer influence' groups in schools, in which some students are recruited and trained to encourage others not to smoke. Smoking levels amongst the children a year or so later are then compared to those in schools where no peer influence project has been carried out. Because we have no idea whether peer influence will in fact reduce smoking, there is no ethical dilemma (as there would be if we had a strong suspicion that intervention really would achieve lower smoking levels).

However, in general, it is not at all easy to link suggestions for reducing health inequality to 'evidence' in the sense in which it is used in the medical literature. In the *Report of the Independent Inquiry on Inequality in Health* prepared by Acheson for the British government in 1998, an appendix describes how the evidence gathered was evaluated. The 'evaluation group' included the Director of the Cochrane Centre, and the editors of both the *British Medical Journal* and the *Lancet*. In the words of the report, they 'noted that there was a lack of evidence to support many of the suggested policy interventions, and recommended that the Inquiry should make explicit the quality of evidence and argument used to support proposed areas for policy development' (Acheson, 1998: 156–7).

International Comparative Studies

In order to find the kind of evidence about the effect of social and economic policies that is similar to that derived from medical trials, a fruitful avenue is to examine differences between nations. Differences between nations in social policies, economic policies and cultural variables, such as diet, provide a type of 'natural experiment'. This is why the international comparative studies of the team at the Erasmus University in Rotterdam are so important and have been quoted liberally in this book (Kunst and Mackenbach, 1994; Kunst, 1997; Programme Committee on Socio-Economic Inequalities in Health, 2001). In their first study, the Erasmus team came up with some very surprising answers. It seemed that Sweden, with its generous welfare state, high taxes and relatively 'flat' income distribution, had higher levels of health inequality than many other nations (Mackenbach et al., 1997). The nations in the south of Europe around the Mediterranean, such as Spain, France and Italy, had lower levels of health inequality than the Nordic nations (Sweden, Norway, Denmark and Finland) (Cavelaars et al., 1998). Adopting a behavioural rather than an economic model for the causes of health inequality could to some extent explain these results. The particular protective factor in this explanatory model was the Mediterranean diet, which seems to provide some protection to citizens of the Mediterranean nations against social and economic inequalities (Kunst et al., 2000). In countries where smoking was less concentrated among less privileged social groups inequality in health between groups defined according to occupational social class also seemed to be lower. The results caused considerable shock. It had been widely thought that health inequality would be greater in countries where the differences in income between social classes, or between those at the top and bottom of the income range, were greater, rather than in nations such as Sweden where taxation and other social policies limit these differences.

The second Erasmus study used income as its measure of socio-economic position. In this way it included everyone, including people who had not worked for a long period, or ever, or whose only income was from welfare payments. This study compared the degree of health inequality in the mid-1980s with that of the mid-1990s. It was possible to look at how health inequality had changed between the 1980s and 1990s, when economic inequality had risen in most European nations, though not to the same extent in all (Kunst et al., forthcoming). This was a more direct test of the idea that the degree of economic inequality might be important for health inequality. It is more convincing when you see that, as the factor you think is a 'cause' changes, what you think of as the 'effect' also changes in the expected way. So if the actual amount of money earned by those with the highest income increases by more than the income of those with least, we would expect health differences between these two groups to increase as well. In this respect, the Nordic nations did prove different from other less equal nations. In fact they could be regarded as having experienced 'economic crises' similar to those that affected the USA and UK in the 1980s, with rising unemployment, the collapse of traditional heavy industry and the loss of many 'middle-income' jobs. But the proportions of people who saw themselves as having poor or not-so-good health, even in the lowest income groups, did not increase. As a result, health inequality hardly changed. The way this was interpreted by the research group was that there were aspects of social policy in the Nordic nations that 'protected' citizens from the effects of increased income inequality. This conclusion gives us a rather more complex picture than we might have expected. It was not that there was one nation in which neither income inequality nor health inequality increased. No European nation escaped totally the worldwide increase in income inequality that took place during the late 1980s and early 1990s. Rather, it seemed to be that certain institutions in Nordic nations, or aspects of their social policies, were making it easier for people to cope with these changes. It was not within the brief of the Erasmus studies to delve into the detailed causes of their observations. Like a clinical trial, this natural experiment could show that something seemed to work without being able to say exactly why (and if we knew that we would not need the experiment).

Graham interprets the differences in health of vulnerable groups such as single parents between Nordic nations and the UK and USA in terms of the life course (Graham, 2002). She points out that poverty is very common during the early years of child-rearing, which some researchers consider one of the 'critical periods' in the healthy development of the child (Power and Hertzman, 1997). Graham presents evidence about the ways in which policies in Sweden and Finland protect low-income couples with children and single parents from poverty to a far greater degree than those in the UK and the USA, and concludes that in the Nordic nations 'the tax system, the social security system and welfare services combine in ways which temper the life-course effects of social and economic change' (Graham, 2002). These examples show how it is possible to combine international comparative studies with a life-course perspective and an awareness of macro-social policy issues to make sense of health inequalities, how they may arise and what might be done about them.

Admittedly, there are many differences between a comparison of nations, with all the problems of whether answers to questions mean the same thing in different contexts, for example, and the careful design of the clinical trial. But it would be defeatist not to take advantage of what the 'natural experiment' can offer. After all, people do not choose the nation into which they are born – in this sense nationality is 'randomly allocated'. There is no reason to think that there are systematic biological or psychological differences between populations in different countries that would affect the way people reacted to differences in income, working conditions, diet or smoking. It may be remembered that one of the agreed strengths of the studies by Wilkinson and others on income inequality and health in different nations was the impossibility of selection effects. It is not plausible that health differences between Japan and the USA could be due to healthy Japanese people migrating to the States (let alone sick Americans migrating to Japan, which is even more ridiculous). Admittedly, there are migrant populations in all industrialized nations, and the possible effect of these on health inequality measures would need to be examined.

Policy Responses Based on the Behavioural Explanation

As we have seen, differences in health-related behaviours between groups with different levels of income, social status and occupational conditions have emerged from most studies as an important explanation for health inequality. The more recent studies and official recommendations have taken place against the background of many years of individually targeted health education. After many years of advocating non-smoking, exercise and a healthier diet, however, the experiences of the UK (Townsend, Davidson and Whitehead, 1986; Jarvis, 1997), Australia (Bennett, 1995), the USA (Lynch, Kaplan and Salonen, 1997b; Winkleby, 1997) and many European nations (Peltonen et al., 1998; Vartiainen et al., 1998) are that this does not reduce health inequality. As discussed in chapter 4, health differences between social groups are not merely a matter of different access to information: they appear to be grounded in differences in life-histories and culture. The first set of Erasmus studies suggested that behavioural differences between people in different socio-economic positions were the most important causes of health inequality. Countries with less variation in diet and smoking between social classes, or between people with more and less education, had smaller inequalities in mortality and morbidity (up to a point). In contrast, countries with greater inequalities in smoking and in the consumption of high-fat foods seemed to have higher levels of health inequality. Importantly, the countries with high levels of inequality in behavioural risks but lower income inequality – the 'Nordic welfare states', such as Sweden, Norway and Finland – seemed to have at least as much social variation in mortality and morbidity as the UK and the USA where *both* income *and* behavioural inequalities are large. But despite the importance in the Erasmus studies of health behaviours, the Dutch Programme Committee, charged with turning all this information into recommendations for policy, advised the Dutch government that the evidence indicated that 'community level' policies were also needed to change social differences in health behaviours. Merely to offer yet more health education, or even banning smoking in public places, would be targeted too much at the individual level, a strategy now known to fail.

How would one implement such community-level policies? In their Final Report, the Dutch Programme Committee on Socio-Economic Inequalities in Health concluded that 'current knowledge of effective methods to achieve change in behaviour among lower SES groups remains sketchy. New methodologies, such as the community-based approach, have to date only been subject to minimum assessment . . . [there is a] need for . . . further development of methods, and their monitoring using scientific (effect) assessments' (Programme Committee on Socio-Economic Inequalities in Health, 2001: 39).

One approach might be to encourage the conditions under which the 'Mediterranean diet' becomes and remains widespread in a population, regardless of class, status or income (Kunst, 1997). First of all, the cost of 'healthy' food items would need to be addressed, to ensure that eating a healthy diet could not take up more income in the UK, Sweden or Finland (for example) than it does in the nations with less health inequality. Secondly, studies would need to discover the conditions under which the preparation of 'Mediterranean' food by people from all walks of life is feasible.

One complication here could be that more elaborate preparation necessary to produce low-cost healthy meals might be more widely carried out in situations where many women do not have paid employment and therefore have no choice but to spend larger amounts of time in domestic food preparation. In this case, the healthy diet might be regarded as a consequence of inequality in social power between men and women. In fact, it is striking that some of the developed countries with low health inequality are those which have retained more traditional family arrangements, low levels of access to highly paid jobs for women and low divorce rates – such as Japan (and the Mediterranean nations). It is arguable that, in these nations, one reason for lower income inequality is that few women even attempt to live independently, and single motherhood is highly stigmatized. These norms would result both in fewer very poor single-parent families and, because women do not have access to highly skilled, managerial and professional jobs, fewer very-high-income households where both partners have highly paid work. Women living under these conditions might well find themselves spending large amounts of time preparing relatively elaborate, but healthy, foods. In the USA and the UK, where women are increasingly involved in employment with long hours of work, a higher proportion of meals are eaten outside the home. There is also a large market for ready-prepared dishes that require only to be heated in a microwave oven. Presumably, under these social conditions, diet quality will be heavily dependent on women's pay levels. Where the long hours are being spent in a well-paid job, there may be no harm to health, as ready-prepared meals with healthy constituents can be bought, if at rather higher cost. Where they are spent in low-paid 'welfare to work' jobs, the health effects on women and their families could be severe. With no time or energy for elaborate cooking, people on low income are reduced to eating the cheapest, lowest-quality instant foods. No policy-maker would nowadays seriously contemplate relaxing the pressures on single women (including mothers) to seek employment. Although some might think it desirable to somehow reimpose the obligation on men to support sexual partners financially, there is no historical precedent for this: once divorce and separation have become socially acceptable, there is no way to turn the clock back. I know of no research that has looked at any of these issues.

But studies comparing the diet quality of low-income families where the mother works full time with that in families where this is not the case might be instructive. At least, this kind of study would be an alternative to randomizing groups of Swedish or British citizens to receive a Mediterranean diet (without, of course, knowing that they were) and waiting to see which group had a longer life expectancy.

Policy Responses Based on Psycho-Social Explanations

If the best way to change even the behavioural causes of health inequality requires policies at the community level, how would this intervention work in practice? And which of the models of explanation might be most helpful in trying to design a successful intervention? The relationship between social position and circumstances and health behaviours is, I think, best regarded as psycho-social. The idea that we would need to change social relations within communities in order to narrow the social inequalities in health behaviours reflects this. There is nothing about having a low income or status that forces a person to smoke or to take less exercise. Rather, as suggested by the work of Siegrist described in chapter 4 (Siegrist, 1998, 2000), it seems that the individual is affected psychologically by adverse social circumstances in a way that makes it harder to invest in their own health. It is often forgotten that when the US Surgeon-General's report identifying the high health risk of smoking was made widely available to the American public, most middle-class people abandoned the habit before widespread health promotion efforts were in place. Once again, this is an under-researched area. But common sense might indicate that a person whose life is pleasant would place a higher value on a longer life than one whose life is harsh.

Policy Responses Based on Material and Neo-Material Explanations

We have seen already an example of a study which had pointed to important differences in welfare policies between Nordic and other nations, and the extent to which these policies protect families with young children from poverty (Graham, 2002). In combination with the findings of the comparative European study of changes in health inequality, which showed smaller increases in Nordic nations despite rising income inequality, this might indicate support for 'material' or 'neo-material' policy responses. Health may be affected by processes of physical and psychological development over the whole of the life course, perhaps with important 'critical periods' in childhood, so we might expect countries that better protect young families from low income to have more favourable trends in health inequality.

Official studies commissioned by governments that have decided to tackle health inequalities have also focused on material factors: for instance, the ways in which social and economic arrangements affect the access of individuals and families to safe and well-paid employment, good quality housing, safe and clean environments. Suggested policy responses have acknowledged the difficulty of bringing about large-scale changes in income inequality, and attempted to suggest interim measures of various kinds.

The UK Acheson Report had no reservations whatever about recommending an increase in the levels of benefits paid to people with no work, or with low-paid work, to a level which brought incomes in those groups closer to 'average living standards' (Acheson, 1998: 36). It also recommended co-operation between labour unions, management and other relevant agencies to improve working conditions, increase autonomy and variety at work and the development and use of skills (1998: 50). The Dutch Programme Committee saw itself as faced with a slightly different task, in that

> in the Netherlands, the welfare state is characterised by a relatively strong redistribution of income, and thus a relatively small income inequality . . . We have therefore already utilised a considerable portion of the potential possibilities in this policy area. Although in the Netherlands the income differences can theoretically be further reduced [for example, to the level of Sweden and Norway], which would in principle be expected to yield a . . . reduction in inequalities in health, both political and social support would currently appear to be lacking for such a measure. (Programme Committee on Socio-Economic Inequalities in Health, 2001: 23)

A more important task, as they saw it, was to stop present trends towards the 'globalization' of increases in inequality from taking away the policy gains that had already been won by previous measures. Rather than attempting further redistribution of income, a sustained attempt to raise the incomes of the poorest 10 per cent of Dutch citizens was recommended in this report.

Recent Dutch and Swedish research, some of it undertaken with British collaboration, has also turned towards policies to try and reduce the impact of disease, however caused, on people's lives. Nations other than Sweden (which already has such policies) are now considering giving more help to people who develop long-term illness to retrain for jobs they are still able to do, thus continuing to earn a wage or salary. In many cases, this last objective would depend on a general improvement in working conditions, thus meeting one of the objectives set out by the Acheson Report. This, in turn, could have a positive impact on health throughout an organization. If people have more autonomy over their working lives and are able to vary arrival and departure, and the pace of work, not only will some with illnesses be able to remain productive but others may, the evidence suggests, avoid developing illness. Such changes would also improve the 'work–life balance', with benefit to family life and the development of children. This kind of policy change gives a good example of a 'neo-material' explanation for the relationship between income inequalities and health. In a country with policies favouring flexible work times and greater autonomy for the individual worker, income inequality might well be reduced, as more people would be able to avoid poverty by remaining in paid jobs. In this case, there would have been no particular attempt to reduce income inequality, for example, by taxation. Rather, a policy aimed at improving the general well-being of working people would have the effect of reducing income inequality.

Another 'neo-material' policy advocated by the Dutch Programme Committee is education. As with income redistribution, social policy in the Netherlands is felt to have gone a long way towards 'reducing the correlation between [social] background and probability of a successful school career' (Programme Committee on Socio-Economic Inequalities in Health, 2001: 23). The Acheson Report was obliged to be more critical of the links between social disadvantage and educational achievement in the UK. It pointed out that

> those living in disadvantaged circumstances, who are most in need of the benefits of education, may be least able to gain access to them. Analysis suggests that inequalities in resource allocation [by government] to schools ... have widened over the last two decades. Schools in disadvantaged areas are more likely to be restricted in space and have the environment degraded ... Logic and equity argue that children most in need should receive increased resources for their education. (Acheson, 1998: 38–9)

One way of breaking the cycle of poverty and low educational attainment that has been given a trial in practice is pre-school education. In the USA, the Perry/High Scope studies showed that a planned programme of pre-school education continued to have effects many years later in the life course of poor children. Those allocated to the special-education group, in a 'trial' type of design, not only did better in secondary school, but earned more, were less likely to commit crimes, and had more stable marriages as young adults. There is little information on any health effects. But the Perry study gives us a good example of what policies based on a 'life-course' model might look like. The advantages in terms of social conditions that followed from the pre-school experiment would, on all available evidence, be expected to produce better health as the cohort entered the ages where the major causes of ill health in the populations of developed nations begin to arise.

What this kind of policy can do nothing about, however, is any kind of health risk that arises from relative social position or income. If a good pre-school scheme enables a group of children to compete more successfully for good jobs, this merely displaces the problem as other young people lose out. Whether we think that the main cause of health inequality is to do with envy of others' relative advantage, or due to the effects of income inequality on things like house prices and rents, no amount of education can serve as a remedy. As with so much of what we need to know about the causes of health inequality (and therefore the policy answers), there is not a great deal of relevant research. For example, if there were still a great deal of income inequality but people moved up and down between more and less privileged social classes more rapidly, would this decrease health differences between income groups or social classes? We actually have no idea. Or if income differences were less closely related to differences in employment relations? What if there were a set of occupations with low income but high levels of job security and work autonomy? One might say that teachers are at present an experiment in this combination, because they have experienced both a decline in their relative income and a decrease in work autonomy as the number of regulations governing their work has grown. Buddhist monks are a group who deliberately eschew possessions of all material kinds and yet enjoy very high status in some societies – unfortunately these are not societies with large health studies that would enable us to compare the health of the monks with that of materially richer groups of equal status.

The policy implications of research on health inequality are therefore extremely difficult to state with clarity. And it would be rash to claim that they can at present even be stated with any great confidence based on existing evidence. Directions can, however, be discerned, which enable us perhaps to point the way to those areas of research that need to be prioritized. As in the past, it may well be that policies we later discover to be effective against health inequality will have been adopted for quite different reasons to do with people's needs for freedom, security and quality of life.

FURTHER READING

The most important British policy document in this area since the Black Report
Acheson, D., *Independent Inquiry into Inequalities in Health: Report.* London: HMSO, 1998.

The first serious attempt to apply the results of a programme of research to change policy
Programme Committee on Socio-Economic Inequalities in Health (SEGV-II), *Reducing Socio-Economic Inequalities in Health.* The Hague: Ministry of Health, Welfare and Sports, 2001.

Just as useful for the policy debate as the scientific one, a more international perspective
Keating, D. P., and Hertzman, C., *Developmental Health and the Wealth of Nations.* New York: The Guilford Press, 1999.

References

ABBREVIATIONS USED

Acta Paediatr	*Acta Paediatrica*
Acta Physiol Scand	*Acta Physiologica Scandinavica*
Am Heart J	*The American Heart Journal*
Am J Public Health	*American Journal of Public Health*
Am Sociol Review	*American Sociological Review*
Ann Epidemiol	*Annals of Epidemiology*
Annu Rev Sociol	*Annual Review of Sociology*
Arterioscler Thromb Vasc Biol	*Arteriosclerosis, Thrombosis and Vascular Biology*
Blood Press Suppl	*Blood Pressure Supplement*
BMJ	*British Medical Journal*
Br J Gen Pract	*The British Journal of General Practice*
Br J Ind Med	*British Journal of Industrial Medicine*
Br J Sociol	*The British Journal of Sociology*
Br Med Bull	*British Medical Bulletin*
Community Med	*Community Medicine*
Eur Heart J	*European Heart Journal*
Health Psychol	*Health Psychology Update*
Int J Epidemiol	*International Journal of Epidemiology*
Int J Health Serv	*International Journal of Health Services*
Int J Psychophysiol	*International Journal of Psychophysiology*
Isr J Med Sci	*Israel Journal of Medical Sciences*
J Aging Health	*Journal of Aging Health*
J Cardiovasc Risk	*Journal of Cardiovascular Risk*
J Epidemiol Community Health	*Journal of Epidemiology and Community Health*
J Gerontol	*Journal of Gerontology*

J Health Soc Behav	*Journal of Health and Social Behavior*
J Hypertens	*Journal of Hypertension*
J Natl Cancer Inst	*Journal of the National Cancer Institute*
J Occup Med	*Journal of Occupational Medicine*
J Psychosom Res	*Journal of Psychosomatic Research*
J Public Health Med	*Journal of Public Health Medicine*
JAMA	*Journal of the American Medical Association*
Med Anthropol Q	*Medical Anthropology Quarterly*
Milbank Mem Fund Q	*The Milbank Memorial Fund Quarterly*
Milbank Q	*The Milbank Quarterly*
N Eng J Med	*The New England Journal of Medicine*
Occup Environ Med	*Occupational and Environmental Medicine*
Patient Educ Couns	*Patient Education and Counseling*
Prev Med	*Preventive Medicine*
Psychol Med	*Psychological Medicine*
Psychosom Med	*Psychosomatic Medicine*
Scand J Soc Med	*Scandinavian Journal of Social Medicine*
Scand J Work Environ Health	*Scandinavian Journal of Work, Environment and Health*
Scott Med J	*Scottish Medical Journal*
Soc Biol	*Social Biology*
Soc Forces	*Social Forces*
Soc Sci Med	*Social Science and Medicine*
Sociol Health Illn	*Sociology of Health and Illness*

Abbotts, J., Williams, R., Ford, G., Hunt, K., and West, P. (1997), Morbidity and Irish Catholic descent in Britain: an ethnic and religious minority 150 years on. *Soc Sci Med* 45, 3–14.

Acevedo-Garcia, D., Lochner, K. A., Osypuk, T. L., and Subramanian, S. V. (2003), Future directions on residential segregation and health research: a multilevel approach. *Am J Public Health* 93, 215–21.

Acheson, D. (1998), *Independent Inquiry into Inequalities in Health: Report*. London: HMSO.

Adler, N. (2002), Socioeconomic disparities in health: identifying the ways education plays a role. *Facts of Life* 7, 2–9.

Adler, N. E., Boyce, W. T., Chesney, M. A., Folkman, S., and Syme, S. L. (1993), Socioeconomic inequalities in health: no easy solution. *JAMA* 269, 3140–5.

Anderson, R. T., Sorlie, P., Backlund, E., Johnson, N., and Kaplan, G. A. (1997), Mortality effects of community socioeconomic status. *Epidemiology* 8, 42–7.

Annandale, E., and Hunt, K. (2000), Gender inequalities in health: research at the crossroads. In E. Annandale and K. Hunt (eds), *Gender Inequalities in Health*, 1–35. Buckingham: Open University Press.

Arber, S., and Cooper, H. (1999), Gender differences in health in later life: the new paradox? *Soc Sci Med* 48, 61–76.

Arber, S., and Lahelma, E. (1993), Inequalities in women's and men's ill-health: Britain and Finland compared. *Soc Sci Med* 37, 1055–68.

Aspinall, P. J. (2002), Collective terminology to describe the minority ethnic population. *Sociology* 36, 803–16.

Barker, D. J. P. (1992), *Fetal and Infant Origins of Adult Disease.* London: BMJ Publishing Group.

Barker, D. J., and Clark, P. M. (1997), Fetal undernutrition and disease in later life. *Reviews of Reproduction* 2, 105–12.

Bartley, M., Blane, D., and Montgomery, S. (1997), Health and the life course: why safety nets matter. *BMJ* 314, 1194–6.

Bartley, M., and Plewis, I. (2002), Accumulated labour market disadvantage and limiting long-term illness: data from the 1971–1991 Office for National Statistics' Longitudinal Study. *Int J Epidemiol* 31, 336–41.

Bartley, M., Sacker, A., Firth, D., and Fitzpatrick, R. (1999), Understanding social variation in cardiovascular risk factors in women and men: the advantage of theoretically based measures. *Soc Sci Med* 49, 831–45.

Bebbington, P. E., Dunn, G., Jenkins, R., Lewis, G., Brugha, T., Farrell, M., and Meltzer, H. (1998), The influence of age and sex on the prevalence of depressive conditions: report from the National Survey of Psychiatric Morbidity. *Psychol Med* 28, 9–19.

Beck, U. (1992), *Risk Society.* London: Sage.

Ben-Shlomo, Y., White, I. R., and Marmot, M. (1996), Does the variation in the socioeconomic characteristics of an area affect mortality? *BMJ* 312, 1013–14.

Bennett, S. (1995), Cardiovascular risk factors in Australia: trends in socioeconomic inequalities. *J Epidemiol Community Health* 49, 363–72.

Berney, L. R., and Blane, D. B. (1997), Collecting retrospective data: accuracy of recall after 50 years judged against historical records. *Soc Sci Med* 45, 1519–25.

Berry, J. W., Poortinga, Y. H., Segall, M. H., and Dasen, P. R. (1992), *Cross-Cultural Psychology.* Cambridge: Cambridge University Press.

Beteille, A. (1992), Caste in a south Indian village. In D. Gupta (ed.), *Social Stratification,* 142–62. Delhi: Oxford University Press.

Bhopal, R. (2000), What is the risk of coronary heart disease in South Asians? A review of UK research. *J Public Health Med* 22, 375–85.

Black, D., Morris, J. N., and Townsend, P. (1982), Inequalities in health: The Black Report. In P. Townsend and N. Davidson (eds), *The Black Report and the Health Divide,* 39–233. Harmondsworth: Penguin.

Blane, D. (1985), An assessment of the Black Report's explanations of health inequalities. *Sociol Health Illn* 7, 231–64.

Blane, D., Davey Smith, G., and Bartley, M. (1990), Social class differences in years of potential life lost: size, trends, and principal causes. *BMJ* 301, 429–32.

Blane, D., Davey Smith, G., and Bartley, M. (1993), Social selection: what does it contribute to social-class differences in health? *Social Health Illn* 15, 2–15.

Blane, D., Bartley, M., and Davey Smith, G. (1998), Disease aetiology and materialist explanations of socioeconomic mortality differentials. *European Journal of Public Health* 7, 385–91.

Blane, D., Berney, L., Davey Smith, G., Gunnell, D. J., and Holland, P. (1999), Reconstructing the life course: health during early old age in a follow-up study based on the Boyd Orr cohort. *Public Health* 113, 117–24.

Blane, D., Mitchell, R., and Bartley, M. (2000), The 'inverse housing law' and respiratory health. *J Epidemiol Community Health* 54, 745–9.

Blane, D., Berney, L., and Montgomery, S. (2001), Domestic labour, paid employment and women's health: analysis of life course data. *Soc Sci Med* 52, 959–65.

Blaxter, M. (1990), *Health and Lifestyles*. London: Tavistock.

Bond, R., and Saunders, P. (1999), Routes to success: influences on occupational attainment of young British males. *Br J Sociol* 50, 217–49.

Bosma, H., Marmot, M. G., Hemingway, H., Nicholson, A. C., Brunner, E., and Stansfeld, S. (1997), Low job control and risk of coronary heart disease in Whitehall II (prospective cohort), study. *BMJ* 314, 555–65.

Bosma, H., Peter, R., Siegrist, J., and Marmot, M. (1998), Two alternative job stress models and the risk of coronary heart disease. *Am J Public Health* 88, 68–74.

Bosma, H., van de Mheen, H. D., and Mackenbach, J. (1999), Social class in childhood and general health in adulthood: questionnaire study of contribution of psychological attributes. *BMJ* 318, 18–22.

Bourdieu, P. (1984), *Distinction*. London: Routledge.

Breen, R., and Rottman, D. (1995), Class analyses and class theory. *Sociology* 29, 453–75.

Brown, G., and Harris, T. (1976), *Social Origins of Depression*. London: Tavistock.

Brunner, E. (1997), Socioeconomic determinants of health: stress and the biology of inequality. *BMJ* 314, 1472–6.

Brunner, E. (2000), Toward a new social biology. In L. F. Berkman and I. Kawachi (eds), *Social Epidemiology*, 306–31. Oxford: Oxford University Press.

Brunner, E. J., Marmot, M. G., White, I. R., O'Brien, J. R., Etherington, M. D., Slavin, B. M., Kearney, E. M., and Davey Smith, G. (1993), Gender and employment grade differences in blood cholesterol, apolipoproteins and haemostatic factors in the Whitehall II study. *Atherosclerosis* 102, 195–207.

Bucher, H. C., and Ragland, D. R. (1995), Socioeconomic indicators and mortality from coronary heart disease and cancer: a 22-year follow-up of middle-aged men. *Am J Public Health* 85, 1231–6.

Bunton, R., and Burrows, R. (1995), Consumption and health in the 'epidemiological' clinic of late modern medicine. In R. Bunton, S. Nettleton and R. Burrows (eds), *The Sociology of Health Promotion*, 206–22. London: Routledge.

Bynner, J., Ferri, E., and Shepherd, P. (1997), *Twenty-Something in the 1990s: Getting on, Getting by, Getting Nowhere*. Aldershot: Ashgate.

Cable, T. A., Meland, E., Soberg, T., and Slagsvold, S. (1999), Lessons from the Oslo Study Diet and Anti-Smoking Trial: a qualitative study of long-term behaviour change. *Scandinavian Journal of Public Health* 27, 206–12.

Cameron, D., and Jones, I. G. (1985), An epidemiological and sociological analysis of the use of alcohol, tobacco and other drugs of solace. *Community Med* 7, 18–29.

Carroll, D., Davey Smith, G., Sheffield, D., Shipley, M. J., and Marmot, M. G. (1997), The relationship between socioeconomic status, hostility, and blood pressure reactions to mental stress in men: data from the Whitehall II study. *Health Psychol* 16, 131–6.

Caspi, A., Wright, B. R. E., Moffitt, T. E., and Silva, P. A. (1998), Early failure in the labor market: childhood and adolescent predictors of unemployment in the transition to adulthood. *Am Sociol Rev* 63, 424–51.

Cavalli-Sforza, L. L., Menozzi, P., and Piazza, A. (1994), *The History and Geography of Human Genes*. Princeton: Princeton University Press.

Cavelaars, A. E. J. M., Kunst, A. E., Geurts, J. J. M., Crialesi, R., and Grotvedt, L. (1998), Differences in self reported morbidity by educational level: a comparison of 11 Western European countries. *J Epidemiol Community Health* 52, 219–27.

Chandola, T. (1998), Social inequality in coronary heart disease: a comparison of occupational classifications. *Soc Sci Med* 47, 525–33.

Chandola, T. (2001), Ethnic and class differences in health in relation to British South Asians: using the new National Statistics Socio-Economic Classification. *Soc Sci Med* 52, 1285–96.

Charlton, J. (1997), Trends in all-cause mortality: 1841–1994. In J. Charlton and M. Murphy (eds), *The health of adult Britain, 1841–1994*, 17–29. London: HMSO.

Coburn, D. (2000), Income inequality, social cohesion and the health status of populations: the role of neo-liberalism. *Soc Sci Med* 51, 135–46.

Cochrane, A. L., and Moore, F. (1981), Death certification from the epidemiological point of view. *Lancet* 2, 742–3.

Colgrove, J. (2002), The McKeown thesis: a historical controversy and its enduring influence. *Am J Public Health* 92, 725–9.

Colley, J. R. T., Douglas, J. W. B., and Reid, D. D. (1973), Respiratory disease in young adults: influences on early childhood lower respiratory tract illness, social class, air pollution and smoking. *BMJ* 2, 195–8.

Cooper, R. (1984), A note on the biological concept of race and its application in epidemiological research. *Am Heart J* 108, 715–23.

Cooper, R. (1986), Race, disease and health. In T. Rathwell and D. Phillips (eds), *Health, Race and Ethnicity*, 21–79. London: Croom Helm.

Cooper, R. S. (1993), Health and the social status of blacks in the United States. *Ann Epidemiol* 3, 137–44.

Coxon, A. P. M., and Fisher, K. (1999), Criterion Validation and Occupational Classification: The Seven Economic Relations and the NS-SEC. Mimeograph, Institute for Social and Economic Research, University of Essex.

Cruickshank, J., and Beevers, D. (1989), *Ethnic Factors in Health and Disease*. Sevenoaks: Wright.

Daly, M. C., Duncan, G. J., Kaplan, G. A., and Lynch, J. W. (1998), Macro to micro links in the relation between income inequality and mortality. *Milbank Mem Fund Q* 76, 315–39.

Davey Smith, G. (1996), Income inequality and mortality: why are they related? Income inequality goes hand in hand with underinvestment in human resources. *BMJ* 312, 987–8.

Davey Smith, G., Bartley, M., and Blane, D. (1990), The Black Report on socioeconomic inequalities in health 10 years on. *BMJ* 301, 373–7.

Davey Smith, G., Blane, D., and Bartley, M. (1994), Explanations for socioeconomic differentials in mortality: evidence from Britain and elsewhere. *European Journal of Public Health* 4, 131–44.

Davey Smith, G., Neaton, J. D., Wentworth, D., Stamler, R., and Stamler, J. (1996*a*), Socioeconomic differentials in mortality risk among men screened for the Multiple Risk Factor Intervention Trial, I: White men. *Am J Public Health* 86, 486–96.

Davey Smith, G., Wentworth, D., Neaton, J. D., Stamler, R., and Stamler, J. (1996*b*), Socioeconomic differentials in mortality risk among men screened for the Multiple Risk Factor Intervention Trial, II: Black men. *Am J Public Health* 86, 497–504.

Davey Smith, G., Hart, C., Blane, D., Gillis, C., and Hawthorne, V. (1997), Lifetime socioeconomic position and mortality: prospective observational study. *BMJ* 314, 547–52.

Davey Smith, G., Neaton, J. D., Wentworth, D., Stamler. R., and Stamler, J. (1998), Mortality differences between Black and White men in the USA: contribution of income and other risk factors among men screened for the MRFIT. *Lancet* 351, 934–9.

Davey Smith, G., Ben-Shlomo,Y., and Lynch, J. (2002), Life course approaches to inequalities in coronary heart disease risk. In S. Stansfeld and M. Marmot (eds), *Stress and the Heart*, 20–49. London: BMJ Books.

Deaton, A. (2001), Relative Deprivation, Inequality and Mortality (Working Paper, Research Program in Development Studies). Center for Health and Wellbeing, Princeton: Princeton University. <http://www.wws.princeton.edu/~chw/papersf.html>

Deaton, A., and Lubotsky, D. (2003), Mortality, inequality and race in American cities. *Soc Sci Med* 56, 1139–53.

Department of Health and Social Security (1980), *Inequalities in Health: Report of a Working Group*. London: DHSS. [The Black Report]

Doll, R., and Peto, R. (1981), The causes of cancer: appendix E. *J Natl Cancer Inst* 66, 1291–305.

Dollamore, G. (1999), Examining adult and infant mortality rates using the NS-SEC. *Health Statistics Quarterly* 2, 33–40.

Doniach, I., Swettenham, K. V., and Hawthorn, M. K. S. (1975), Prevalence of asbestos bodies in a necropsy series in East London: association with disease, occupation, and domiciliary address. *Br J Ind Med* 32, 16–30.

Dressler, W. W. (1993), Health in the African-American community: accounting for health inequalities. *Med Anthropol Q* 7, 325–45.

Drever, F., and Whitehead, M. (1997), *Health Inequalities*. London: HMSO.

Drever, F., Bunting, J., and Harding, D. (1997), Male mortality from major causes of death. In F. Drever and M. Whitehead (eds), *Health Inequalities*, 122–42. London: HMSO.

Duncan, G. J., Daly, M. C., McDonough, P., and Williams, D. R. (2002), Optimal indicators of socioeconomic status for health research. *Am J Public Health* 92, 1151–7.

Duncan, G. J., Yeung, W. J., Brooks-Gunn, J., and Smith, J. R. (1998), How much does childhood poverty affect the life chances of children? *Am Sociol Rev* 63, 406–23.

Duncan, O. D. (1961), A socioeconomic index for all occupations. In A. J. Reiss Jr. (ed.), *Occupations and Social Status*, 109–38. New York: Free Press.

Dyson, S. M. (1998), 'Race', ethnicity and haemoglobin disorders. *Soc Sci Med* 47, 121–31.

Elder, G. H. (1985), *Life course dynamics*. Ithaca, NY: Cornell University Press.

Elstad, J. I. (1998), The psycho-social perspective on social inequalities in health. In M. Bartley, D. Blane, and G. Davey Smith (eds), *The Sociology of Health Inequalities*, 39–58. Oxford: Blackwell.

Emslie, C., Hunt, K., and Macintyre, S. (1999), Problematizing gender, work and health: the relationship between gender, occupational grade, working conditions and minor morbidity in full-time bank employees. *Soc Sci Med* 48, 33–48.

Eng, H., and Mercer, J. B. (1998), Seasonal variations in mortality caused by cardiovascular diseases in Norway and Ireland. *J Cardiovasc Risk* 5, 89–95.

Eng, H., and Mercer, J. B. (2000), The relationship between mortality caused by cardiovascular disease and two climatic factors in densely populated areas in Norway and Ireland. *J Cardiovasc Risk* 7, 369–75.

Erikson, R., and Goldthorpe, J. H. (1992), *The Constant Flux*. Oxford: Clarendon Press.

Evans, G. (1992), Testing the validity of the Goldthorpe class schema. *European Sociological Review* 8, 211–32.

Fassin, D. (2000), Qualifier les inégalités. In A. Leclerc, D. Fassin, H. Grandjean, M. Kaminski, and T. Lang (eds), *Les Inégalités sociales de santé*, 124–44. Paris: INSERM/La Découverte.

Featherman, D. L., and Hauser, R. M. (1976), Prestige of socioeconomic scales in the study of occupational achievement? *Sociological Methods and Research* 4, 403–22.

Feeney, A., North, F., Head, J., Canner, R., and Marmot, M. (1998), Socioeconomic and sex differentials in reason for sickness absence from the Whitehall II study. *Occup Environ Med* 55, 91–8.

Ferrie, J. E., Shipley, M. J., Marmot, M. G., Stansfeld, S., and Davey Smith, G. (1995), Health effects of anticipation of job change and non-employment: longitudinal data from the Whitehall II study. *BMJ* 311, 1264–9.

Fiscella, K., and Franks, P. (1997), Poverty or income inequality as predictor of mortality: longitudinal cohort study. *BMJ* 314, 1724–8.

Ford, D. E., Mead, L. A., Chang, P. P., Cooper P. L., Wang, N. Y., and Klag, M. J. (1998), Depression is a risk factor for coronary artery disease in men: the precursors study. *Arch Intern Med* 158, 1422–6.

Fox, A. J., and Goldblatt, P. O. (1982), *Longitudinal Study: Socio-demographic mortality differentials*. London: HMSO.

Fox, A. J., Goldblatt, P. O., and Adelstein, A. M. (1982), Selection and mortality differentials. *J Epidemiol Community Health* 36, 151.

Fox, A. J., Goldblatt, P. O., and Jones, D. R. (1985), Social-class mortality differentials: artifact, selection or life circumstances. *J Epidemiol Community Health* 39, 1–8.

Friedman, M., Rosenman, R. H., and Carrol, V. (1958), Changes in the serum cholesterol and blood clotting time in men subjected to cyclic variation of occupational stress. *Circulation* 17, 852–61.

Fuhrer, R., Stansfeld, S. A., Chemali, J., and Shipley, M. J. (1999), Gender, social relations and mental health: prospective findings from an occupational cohort (Whitehall II study). *Soc Sci Med* 48, 77–87.

Gardner, M. J., Winter, P. D., and Acheson, E. D. (1982), Variations in cancer mortality among local authority areas in England and Wales: relations with environmental factors and search for causes. *BMJ* 284, 784–7.

Giddens, A. (1991), *Modernity and Self-Identity*. Cambridge: Polity Press.

Giele, J. Z., and Elder, G. H. (1998), Life course research: development of a field. In J. Z. Giele and G. H. Elder Jr. (eds), *Methods of Life Course Research: Qualitative and Quantitative Approaches*, 5–27. New York: Sage.

Goldblatt, P. O. (1990*a*), Mortality and alternative social classifications. In P. O. Goldblatt (ed.), *Longitudinal Study: Mortality and Social Organization*, 163–92. London: HMSO.

Goldblatt, P. O. (ed.), (1990*b*), *Longitudinal Study: Mortality and Social Organization*. London: HMSO.

Goldthorpe, J. H., Llewellyn, C., and Payne, C. (1980), *Social Mobility and Class Structure in Modern Britain*. Oxford: Clarendon Press.

Gorey, K. M., and Vena, J. E. (1995), The association of near poverty status with cancer incidence among Black and White adults. *J Community Health* 20, 359–66.

Graham, H. (1998), Promoting health against inequality. *Health Education Journal* 57, 292–302.

Graham, H. (2002), Building an inter-disciplinary science of health inequalities: the example of lifecourse research. *Soc Sci Med* 55, 2005–16.

Gran, B. (1995), Major differences in cardiovascular risk indicators by educational status. *Scand J Soc Med* 23, 9–16.

Greenwood, D. C., Muir, K. R., Packham, C. J., and Madeley, R. J. (1996), Coronary heart disease: a review of the role of psychosocial stress and social support. *J Public Health Med* 18, 221–31.

Gunnell, D. J., Frankel, S., Nanchahal, K., Braddon, F. E., and Davey Smith, G. (1996), Lifecourse exposure and later disease: a follow-up study based on a survey of family diet and health in pre-war Britain (1937–1939). *Public Health* 110, 85–94.

Hammond, E. C., Selikoff, I. J., and Seidmann, H. (1979), Asbestos exposure, cigarette smoking and death rates. *Ann N Y Acad Sci* 330, 473–90.

Harding, S., and Balarajan, R. (1996), Patterns of mortality in second generation Irish living in England and Wales: longitudinal study. *BMJ* 312, 1389–92.

Harding, S., and Maxwell, R. (1997), Differences in mortality of migrants. In F. Drever and M. Whitehead (eds), *Health Inequalities*, 108–21. London: HMSO.

Harding, S., and Rosato, M. (1999), Cancer incidence among first generation Scottish, Irish, West Indian and South Asian migrants living in England and Wales. *Ethnicity and Health* 4, 83–92.

Harding, S., Brown, J., Rosato, M., and Hattersley, L. (1999), Socio-economic differentials in health: illustrations from the Office for National Statistics' Longitudinal Study. *Health Statistics Quarterly* 1, 5–15.

Hart, C. L., Davey Smith, G., and Blane, D. (1998*a*), Inequalities in mortality by social class measured at 3 stages of the lifecourse. *Am J Public Health* 88, 471–4.

Hart, C. L., Davey Smith, G., and Blane, D. (1998*b*), Social mobility and 21 year mortality in a cohort of Scottish men. *Soc Sci Med* 47, 1121–30.

Hattersley, L. (1999), Trends in life expectancy by social class: an update. *Health Statistics Quarterly* 2, 16–24.

Hauser, R. M., and Warren, J. R. (1996), *Socioeconomic Indexes for Occupations: A Review, Update and Critique*. Madison: Center for Demography and Ecology, University of Wisconsin-Madison.

Heck, K. E., and Pamuk, E. R. (1997), Explaining the relation between education and postmenopausal breast cancer. *Am J Epidemiol* 145, 366–72.

Hoeymans, N., Smit, H. A., Verkleij, H., and Kromhout, D. (1996), Cardiovascular risk-factors in relation to educational-level in 36,000 men and women in the Netherlands. *Eur Heart J* 17, 518–25.

Holland, P., Berney, L., Blane, D., Davey Smith, G., Gunnell, D. J., and Montgomery, S. M. (2000), Life course accumulation of disadvantage: childhood health and hazard exposure during adulthood. *Soc Sci Med* 50, 1285–95.

Hollingshead, A. B. (1971), Commentary of 'the indiscriminate state of social class measurement'. *Soc Forces* 49, 563–7.

Holtzman, N. A. (2002), Genetics and social class. *J Epidemiol Community Health* 56, 529–35.

Howard, J. A. (2000), Social psychology of identities. *Annu Rev Sociol* 26, 367–93.

Hunt, K., and Macintyre, S. (2000), Gendre et inégalités de santé [Gender and health inequality]. In A. Leclerc, D. Fassin, H. Grandjean, M. Kaminski, and T. Lang (eds), *Les Inégalités sociales de santé*, 364–75. Paris: INSERM/ La Découverte.

Iribarren, C., Luepker, R. V., McGovern, P. G., Arnett, D. K., and Blackburn, H. (1997), Twelve-year trends in cardiovascular disease risk factors in the Minnesota Heart Survey: are socioeconomic differences widening? *Arch Intern Med* 157, 873–81.

Jarvis, M. (1997), Patterns and predictors of smoking cessation in the general population. In C. Bolliger and K. Fagerstrom (eds), *Progress in Respiratory Research: The Tobacco Epidemic*, 151–64. Basel: S. Karger.

Jenkins, R. (1985a), Minor psychiatric morbidity and labour turnover. *Br J Ind Med* 42, 534–9.

Jenkins, R. (1985b), Sex differences in minor psychiatric morbidity. *Psychol Med* (Monogr Suppl.), 53–71.

Jenkins, R., and Clare, A. W. (1985), Women and mental illness. *BMJ (Clin Res Ed)* 291, 1521–2.

Johansson, S. (1989), Longevity in women. *Cardiovasc Clin* 19, 3–16.

Johnson, J. V., Stewart, W., Hall, E. M., Fredlund, P., and Theorell, T. (1996), Long-term psycho-social work-environment and cardiovascular mortality among Swedish men. *Am J Public Health* 86, 324–31.

Jones, C. P. (2001), Invited commentary: 'Race', racism and the practice of epidemiology. *Am J Epidemiol* 154, 299–304.

Jones, J. (1981), How different are human races? *Nature* 293, 188–90.

Jonsson, D., Rosengren, A., Dotevall, A., Laas, G., and Wilhelmsen, L. (1999), Job control, job demands and social support at work in relation to cardiovascular risk factors in MONICA 1995, Goteborg. *J Cardiovasc Risk* 6, 379–85.

Judge, K. (1995), Income-distribution and life expectancy: a critical appraisal. *BMJ* 311, 1282–5.

Kaplan, G. A., Pamuk, E. R., Lynch, J. W., Cohen, R. D., and Balfour, J. L. (1996), Inequality in income and mortality in the United States: analysis of mortality and potential pathways. *BMJ* 312, 999–1003.

Kaprio, J., Sarna, S., Fogelholm, M., and Koskenvuo, M. (1996), Total and occupationally active life expectancies in relation to social class and marital status in men classified as healthy at 20 in Finland. *J Epidemiol Community Health* 50, 653–60.

Karasek, R. (1996), Job strain and the prevalence and outcome of coronary-artery disease. *Circulation* 94, 1140–1.

Kaufman, J. S., Long, A. E., Liao, Y., Cooper, R. S., and McGee, D. L. (1998), The relation between income and mortality in U.S. blacks and whites. *Epidemiology* 9, 147–55.

Kauhanen, J., Kaplan, G. A., Cohen, R. D., Julkunen, J., and Salonen, J. T. (1996), Alexithymia and risk of death in middle-aged men. *J Psychosom Res* 41, 541–9.

Kawachi, I., and Kennedy, B. P. (1997), Socioeconomic determinants of health, 2: Health and social cohesion: why care about income inequality? *BMJ* 314, 1037–40.

Kawachi, I., Kennedy, B. P., Lochner, K., and Prothrowstith, D. (1997), Social capital, income inequality, and mortality. *Am J Public Health* 87, 1491–8.

Kennedy, B. P., Kawachi, I., and Prothrowstith, D. (1996), Income distribution and mortality: cross-sectional ecological study of the Robin Hood index in the United States. *BMJ* 312, 1004–7.

Khlat, M., Sermet, C., and Le Pape, A. (2000), Women's health in relation with their family and work roles: France in the early 1990s. *Soc Sci Med* 50, 1807–25.

Kitagawa, E. M., and Hauser, P. M. (1973), *Differential Mortality in the United States: A Study in Socioeconomic Epidemiology*. Cambridge, Mass.: Harvard University Press.

Kivimaki, M., Leino-Arjas, P., Luukkonen, R., Riihimaki, H., Vahtera, J., and Kirjonen, J. (2002), Work stress and risk of cardiovascular mortality: prospective cohort study of industrial employees. *BMJ* 325, 857–62.

Krieger, N. (1999), Embodying inequality: a review of concepts, measures, and methods for studying health consequences of discrimination. *Int J Health Serv* 29, 295–352.

Krieger, N. (2000), Refiguring 'race': epidemiology, racialized biology, and biological expressions of race relations. *Int J Health Serv* 30, 211–16.

Krieger, N. (2001), Theories for social epidemiology. *Int J Epidemiol* 30, 668–77.

Krieger, N., Quesenberry, C., Peng, T., Horn Ross, P., Stewart, S., and Brown, S. (1999), Social class, race/ethnicity, and incidence of breast, cervix, colon, lung, and prostate cancer among Asian, black, Hispanic, and white residents of the San Francisco Bay Area, 1988–92 (United States). *Cancer Causes Control* 10, 525–37.

Kroeber, A. L., and Kluckhohn, C. (1952), *Culture: A Critical Review of Concepts and Definitions*. Cambridge, Mass.: Peabody Museum.

Kuh, D., and Ben-Shlomo, Y. (eds) (1997), *A Life Course Approach to Chronic Disease Epidemiology*. Oxford: Oxford University Press.

Kuh, D., and Davey Smith, G. (1997), The life course and adult chronic disease. In D. Kuh and Y. Ben-Shlomo (eds), *A Life Course Approach to Chronic Disease Epidemiology*, 169–200. Oxford: Oxford University Press.

Kunst, A. (1997), *Cross-National Comparisons of Socio-Economic Differences in Mortality*. The Hague: CIP-Gegevens Koninklijke Bibliotheek.

Kunst, A. E., and Mackenbach, J. P. (1994), *Measuring Socio-Economic Inequalities in Health*. Copenhagen: WHO.

Kunst, A., Groenhof, F., Mackenbach, J. P. (2000), Inégalités sociales de mortalité prématurée: la France comparée aux autres pays européens. In A. Leclerc, D. Fassin, H. Grandjean, M. Kaminski, and T. Lang (eds), *Les Inégalités sociales de santé*, 54–68. Paris: INSERM/La Découverte.

Kunst, A., Bos, V., Lahelma, E., Bartley, M., Lissau, I., Regidor, E., Mielck, A., Cardano, M., Costa, G., Dalstra, J. A. A., Geurts, J. J. M., Helmert, U., Lennartsson, C., Ramm, J., Stronegger, W. J., and Mackenbach, J. P. (forthcoming), Trends in socio-economic inequalities in self assessed health in 10 European countries. *Int J Epidemiol*.

Ladwig, K. H., Marten Mittag, B., Formanek, B., and Dammann, G. (2000), Gender differences of symptom reporting and medical health care utilization in the German population. *Eur J Epidemiol* 16, 511–18.

Lahelma, E., Martikainen, P., Rahkonen, O., and Silventoinen, K. (1999), Gender differences in illhealth in Finland: patterns, magnitude and change. *Soc Sci Med* 48, 7–19.

Landsbergis, P. A., Schnall, P. L., Warren, K., Pickering, T. G., and Schwartz, J. E. (1994), Association between ambulatory blood-pressure and alternative formulations of job strain. *Scand J Work Environ Health* 20, 349–63.

Lang, R. E., and Hornburg, S. P. (1998), What is social capital and why is it important to public policy? *Housing Policy Debate* 9, 1–16.

Langman, L. (1998), Identity, hegemony, and social reproduction. *Current Perspectives on Social Theory* 18, 185–226.

Lantz, P. M., Lynch, J. W., House, J. S., Lepkowski, J. M., Mero, R. P., Musick, M. A., and Williams, D. R. (2001), Socioeconomic disparities in health change in a longitudinal study of US adults: the role of health risk behaviours. *Soc Sci Med* 53, 29–40.

Lillard, L. A., and Panis, C. W. A. (1996), Marital status and mortality: the role of health. *Demography* 33, 313–27.

Lillieblanton, M., and Laveist, T. (1996), Race/ethnicity, the social-environment, and health. *Soc Sci Med* 43, 83–91.

Lillieblanton, M., Parsons, P. E., Gayle, H., and Dievler, A. (1996), Racial-differences in health – not just black and white, but shades of gray. *Annu Rev Public Health* 17, 411–48.

Link, B. (2002), McKeown and the idea that social conditions are fundamental causes of disease. *Am J Public Health* 92, 730–2.

Lithell, H. O., McKeigue, P. M., Berglund, L., Mohsen, R., Lithell, U.-B., and Leon, D. A. (1996), Relation of size at birth to non-insulin dependent diabetes and insulin concentrations in men aged 50–60 years. *BMJ* 312, 406–10.

Lloyd, E. L. (1991), The role of cold in ischaemic heart disease: a review. *Public Health* 105, 205–15.

Lloyd, O. L. (1978), Respiratory cancer clustering associated with localised air pollution. *Lancet* 1, 318–20.

Lynch, J. (2000), Income inequality and health: expanding the debate. *Soc Sci Med* 51, 1001–5.

Lynch, J. W., Kaplan, G. A., Cohen, R. D., Kauhanen, J., Wilson, T. W., Smith, N. L., and Salonen, J. T. (1994), Childhood and adult socioeconomic status as predictors of mortality in Finland. *Lancet* 343, 524–7.

Lynch, J. W., Kaplan, G. A., Cohen, R. D., Tuomilehto, J., and Salonen, J. T. (1996), Do cardiovascular risk-factors explain the relation between socio-economic-status, risk of all-cause mortality, cardiovascular mortality, and acute myocardial-infarction? *Am J Epidemiol* 144, 934–42.

Lynch, J., Krause, N., Kaplan, G. A., Tuomilehto, J., and Salonen, J. T. (1997*a*), Workplace conditions, socioeconomic status, and the risk of mortality and acute myocardial infarction: The Kuopio Ischemic Heart Disease Risk Factor Study. *Am J Public Health* 87, 617–22.

Lynch, J. W., Kaplan, G. A., and Salonen, J. T. (1997*b*), Why do poor people behave poorly? Variation in adult health behaviours and psycho-social characteristics by stages of the socioeconomic lifecourse. *Soc Sci Med* 44, 809–19.

Lynch, J. W., Kaplan, G. A., Pamuk, E. R., Cohen, R. D., Heck, K. E., Balfour, J. L., and Yen, I. H. (1998), Income inequality and mortality in metropolitan areas of the United States. *Am J Public Health* 88, 1074–80.

Lynch, J. W., Davey Smith, G., Kaplan, G. A., and House, J. S. (2000), Income inequality and mortality: importance to health of individual income, psycho-social environment, or material conditions. *BMJ* 320, 1200–4.

Lynch, J., Davey Smith, G., Hillemeier, M., Raghunathan, T., and Kaplan, G. (2001), Income inequality, the psycho-social environment, and health: comparisons of wealthy nations. *Lancet* 358, 194–200.

McDonough, P., and Amick III, B. C. (2001), The social context of health selection: a longitudinal study of health and employment. *Soc Sci Med* 53, 135–45.

McEwen, B. S. (1998), Protective and damaging effects of stress mediators. *N Engl J Med* 338, 171–9.

McIsaac, S. J., and Wilkinson, R. G. (1997), Income distribution and cause-specific mortality. *European Journal of Public Health* 7, 45–53.

McKeown, T. (1966), *The Role of Medicine*. Oxford: Blackwell.

Macintyre, S. (1997), The Black Report and beyond: what are the issues? *Soc Sci Med* 44, 723–45.

Macintyre, S., Hunt, K., and Sweeting, H. (1996), Gender differences in health: are things really as simple as they seem? *Soc Sci Med* 42, 617–24.

Mackenbach, J. P., Looman, C. W., and Kunst, A. E. (1993), Air pollution, lagged effects of temperature, and mortality: The Netherlands, 1979–87. *J Epidemiol Community Health* 47, 121–6.

Mackenbach, J. P., Kunst, A. E., Cavelaars, A. E. J. M., Groenhof, F., and Geurts, J. J. M. (1997), Socioeconomic inequalities in morbidity and mortality in western Europe. *Lancet* 349, 1655–9.

Malmstrom, M., Sundquist, J., Bajekal, M., and Johansson, S. E. (1999), Ten-year trends in all-cause mortality and coronary heart disease mortality in socio-economically diverse neighbourhoods. *Public Health* 113, 279–84.

Mann, S. L., Wadsworth, M. E. J., and Colley, J. R. T. (1992), Accumulation of factors influencing respiratory illness in members of a national birth cohort and their offspring. *J Epidemiol Community Health* 46, 286–92.

Manson, J. E. (1999), Gender differences and risk factors for cardiovascular disease. *Journal of Women's Health* 8, 697.

Marmot, M. (1989), Socioeconomic determinants of CHD mortality. *Int J Epidemiol* 18, 196–202.

Marmot, M. (1993), Epidemiological approach to the explanation of social differentiation in mortality: the Whitehall studies. *Soz Praventivmed* 38, 271–9.

Marmot, M. G., Rose, G., Shipley, M., and Hamilton, P. J. S. (1978), Employment grade and coronary heart disease in British civil servants. *Journal of Epidemiology and Community Health* 32, 244–9.

Marmot, M. G., Davey Smith, G., Stansfeld, S., Patel, C., North, F., Head, J., White, I., Brunner, E., and Feeney, A. (1991), Health inequalities among British civil servants: the Whitehall II study. *Lancet* 337, 1387–93.

Marmot, M., Ryff, C. D., Bumpass, L. L., Shipley, M., and Marks, N. F. (1997), Social inequalities in health: next questions and converging evidence. *Soc Sci Med* 44, 901–10.

Marsh, A., and McKay, S. (1994), *Poor Smokers*. London: Policy Studies Institute.

Marsh, C., and Blackburn, R. M. (1992), Class differences in access to higher education in Britain. In R. Burrows and C. Marsh (eds), *Consumption and Class: Divisions and Change*, 184–211. London: Macmillan.

Marshall, G. (1997), *Repositioning Class: Social Inequality in Industrial Societies*. London: Sage.

Marshall, G., Rose, D., Newby, H., and Vogler, C. (1988), *Social Class in Modern Britain*. London: Hutchinson.

Martikainen, P. (1995a), Women's employment, marriage, motherhood and mortality: a test of the multiple role and role accumulation hypotheses. *Soc Sci Med* 40, 199–212.

Martikainen, P. (1995b), Socioeconomic mortality differentials in men and women according to own and spouse's characteristics in Finland. *Sociol Health Illn* 17, 353–75.

Martikainen, P., Ishizaki, M., Marmot, M., Nakagawa, H., and Kaganmimori, S. (2001), Socioeconomic differences in behavioural and biological risk factors: a comparison of a Japanese and an English cohort of employed men. *Int J Epidemiol* 30, 833–8.

Martin, C. J., Platt, S. D., and Hunt, S. (1987), Housing conditions and health. *BMJ* 294, 1125–7.

Matthews, S., Stansfeld, S., and Power, C. (1999), Social support at age 33: the influence of gender, employment status and social class. *Soc Sci Med* 49, 133–42.

Mitchell, R., Blane, D., and Bartley, M. (2002), Elevated risk of high blood pressure: climate and the inverse housing law. *Int J Epidemiol* 31, 831–8.

Moan, A., Eide, I. K., and Kjeldsen, S. E. (1996), Metabolic and adrenergic characteristics of young men with insulin resistance. *Blood Press Suppl* 1, 30–7.

Moller, L., Kristensen, T. S., and Hollnagel, H. (1991), Social class and cardiovascular risk factors in Danish men. *Scand J Soc Med* 19, 116–26.

Montgomery, S. M., Bartley, M. J., Cook, D. G., and Wadsworth, M. E. J. (1996), Health and social precursors of unemployment in young men in Great Britain. *J Epidemiol Community Health* 50, 415–22.

Morris, J. N., and Heady, J. A. (1955), Social and biological factors in infant mortality, V: mortality in relation to father's occupation. *Lancet* 1, 554–9.

Morris, J. N., Donkin, A. J. M., Wonderling, D., Wilkinson, P., and Dowler, E. A. (2002), A minimum income for healthy living. *J Epidemiol Community Health* 54, 885–9.

Moser, K. A., Pugh, H. S., and Goldblatt, P. O. (1988), Inequalities in women's health: looking at mortality differentials using an alternative approach. *BMJ* 296, 1221–4.

Muntaner, C., and Lynch, J. (1999), Income inequality, social cohesion, and class relations: a critique of Wilkinson's neo-Durkheimian research program. *Int J Health Serv* 29, 59–81.

Mustard, C. A., Derksen, S., Berthelot, J. M., Wolfson, M., and Roos, L. L. (1997), Age-specific education and income gradients in morbidity and mortality in a Canadian province. *Soc Sci Med* 45, 383–97.

Myllykangas, M., Pekkanen, J., Rasi, V., Haukkala, A., Vahtera, E., and Salomaa, V. (1995), Hemostatic and other cardiovascular risk factors, and socio-economic status among middle-aged Finnish men and women. *Int J Epidemiol* 24, 1110–16.

Nam, C. B., and Terrie, W. E. (1982), Measurement of socioeconomic status from United States Census data. In P. H. Rosse and S. L. Nock (eds), *Measuring Social Judgements: The Factorial Survey Approach*, 95–118. Beverley Hills: Sage.

Nathanson, C. (1975), Illness and the feminine role: a theoretical review. *Soc Sci Med* 9, 57–62.

Nazroo, J. Y. (1997), *The Health of Britain's Ethnic Minorities*. London: PSI.

Nazroo, J. (1998), Genetic, cultural or socio-economic vulnerability? Explaining ethnic inequalities in health. *Sociol Health Illn* 20, 710–30.

Nazroo, J. Y. (2001), South Asian people and heart disease: an assessment of the importance of socioeconomic position. *Ethn Dis* 11, 401–11.

Netterstrom, B., Kristensen, T. S., Moller, L., Jensen, G., and Schnohr, P. (1998), Angina pectoris, job strain, and social status: a cross-sectional study of employed urban citizens. *International Journal of Behavioral Medicine* 5, 312–22.

Newhouse, M. L., and Wagner, J. C. (1969), Validation of death certificates in asbestos workers. *Br J Ind Med* 26, 302–7.

Northridge, M. E., Stover, G. N., Rosenthal, J. E., and Sgerard, D. (2003), Environmental equity and health: understanding complexity and moving forward. *Am J Public Health* 93, 209–14.

Office of National Statistics (2002), Death, selected causes and sex. *HSQ* 16, 58–9.

Office of Population Censuses and Surveys (1978), *Occupational Mortality: The*

Registrar-General's Decennial Supplement for England and Wales, 1970–1972. London: HMSO.

Office of Population Censuses and Surveys (1980), *Classification of Occupations.* London: HMSO.

Onwuachi Saunders, C., and Hawkins, D. F. (1993), Black-white differences in injury: race or social class? *Ann Epidemiol* 3, 150–3.

Osler, M., Gerdes, L. U., Davidsen, M., Bronnum-Hansen, H., Madsen, M., Jorgensen, T., and Schroll, M. (2000), Socioeconomic status and trends in risk factors for cardiovascular diseases in the Danish MONICA population, 1982–1992. *J Epidemiol Community Health* 54, 108–13.

Osler, M., Prescott, E., Gronbeck, M., Christensen, U., Due, P., and Engholm, G. (2002), Income inequality, individual income, and mortality in Danish adults: analysis of pooled data from two cohort studies. *BMJ* 324, 1–4.

Ostergren, P. O., Lindbladh, E., Isacsson, S. O., Odeberg, H., and Svensson, S. E. (1995), Social network, social support and the concept of control: a qualitative study concerning the validity of certain stressor measures used in quantitative social epidemiology. *Scand J Soc Med* 23, 95–102.

Pappas, G., Queen, S., Hadden, W., and Fisher, G. (1993), The increasing disparity in mortality between socioeconomic groups in the United States, 1960 and 1986. *N Engl J Med* 329, 103–9.

Passannante, M. R., and Nathanson, C. A. (1985), Female labor force participation and female mortality in Wisconsin, 1974–1978. *Soc Sci Med* 21, 655–65.

Passannante, M. R., and Nathanson, C. A. (1987), Women in the labor force: are sex mortality differentials changing? *J Occup Med* 29, 21–8.

Pekkanen, J., Tuomilehto, J., Uutela, A., Vartiainen, E., and Nissinen, A. (1995), Social class, health behaviour, and mortality among men and women in eastern Finland. *BMJ* 311, 589–93.

Peltonen, M., Huhtasaari, F., Stegmayr, B., Lundberg, V., and Asplund, K. (1998), Secular trends in social patterning of cardiovascular risk factor levels in Sweden: the Northern Sweden MONICA Study, 1986–1994. *J Intern Med* 244, 1–9.

Pensola, T. H., and Valkonen, T. (2000), Mortality differences by parental social class from childhood to adulthood. *J Epidemiol Community Health* 54, 525–9.

Peter, R., and Siegrist, J. (1997), Chronic work stress, sickness absence, and hypertension in middle managers: general or specific sociological explanations? *Soc Sci Med* 45, 1111–20.

Peter, R., Alfredsson, L., Hammar, N., Siegrist, J., Theorell, T., and Westerholm, L. (1998), High effort, low reward, and cardiovascular risk factors in employed Swedish men and women: baseline results from the WOLF Study. *J Epidemiol Community Health* 52, 540–7.

Pickering, T. G., Devereux, R. B., James, G. D., Gerin, W., Landsbergis, P., and Schnall, P. L. (1996), Environmental influences on blood pressure and the role of job strain. *J Hypertens* 14, 179–85.

Platt, S. D., Martin, C. J., Hunt, S., and Lewis, C. W. (1989), Damp housing, mould growth and symptomatic health state. *BMJ* 298, 1673–8.

Pocock, S. J., Shaper, A. G., Cook, D. G., Phillips, A. N., and Walker, M. (1987),

Social class differences in ischaemic heart disease in British men. *Lancet* 2, 197–201.

Popay, J., Bartley, M., and Owen, C. (1993), Gender inequalities in health: social position, affective-disorders and minor physical morbidity. *Soc Sci Med* 36, 21–32.

Power, C., and Hertzman, C. (1997), Social and biological pathways linking early life and adult disease. *Br Med Bull* 53, 210–21.

Power, C., Manor, O., Fox, A. J., and Fogelman, K. (1990), Health in childhood and social inequalities in health in young adults. *Journal of the Royal Statistical Society, Series A: Statistics in Society* 153, 17–28.

Power, C., Manor, O., and Fox, J. (1991), *Health and Class: The Early Years.* London: Chapman and Hall.

Power, C., and Matthews, S. (1997), Origins of health inequalities in a national population sample. *Lancet* 350, 1584–9.

Power, C., Matthews, S., and Manor, O. (1998), Inequalities in self-rated health: explanations from different stages of life. *Lancet* 351, 1009–14.

Prandy, K. (1986), Similarities of life-style and the occupations of women. In R. Crompton and M. Mann (eds), *Gender and Stratification*, 137–53. Cambridge: Polity Press.

Prandy, K., and Bottero, W. (1998), The social analysis of stratification and mobility (SRG Working Paper 18). Cambridge: Social Research Group.

Programme Committee on Socio-Economic Inequalities in Health (2001), *Reducing Socio-Economic Inequalities in Health.* The Hague: Ministry of Health, Welfare and Sports.

Pugh, H., Power, C., Goldblatt, P., and Arber, S. (1991), Women's lung cancer mortality, socio-economic status and changing smoking patterns. *Soc Sci Med* 32, 1105–10.

Rael, E. G., Stansfeld, S. A., Shipley, M., Head, J., Feeney, A., and Marmot, M. (1995), Sickness absence in the Whitehall II study, London: the role of social support and material problems. *J Epidemiol Community Health* 49, 474–81.

Rahkonen, O., Arber, S., Lahelma, E., Martikainen, P., and Silentoinen, K. (2000), Understanding income inequalities in health among men and women in Britain and Finland. *Int J Health Serv* 30, 27–47.

Rathwell, T., and Phillips, D. (1986), *Health, Race and Ethnicity.* London: Croom Helm.

Reijneveld, S. A. (1995), Causes of death contributing to urban socioeconomic mortality differences in Amsterdam. *Int J Epidemiol* 24, 740–9.

Robert, S., and House, J. S. (1996), SES differentials in health by age and alternative indicators of SES. *J Aging Health* 8, 359–88.

Roos, N. P., and Mustard, C. A. (1997), Variation in health and health care use by socioeconomic status in Winnipeg, Canada: does the system work well? Yes and no. *Milbank Q* 75, 89.

Rose, D., and O'Reilly, K. (1998), *Final Report of the ESRC Review of Government Social Classifications.* Swindon: ESRC/ONS.

Rosengren, A., Orth-Gomer, K., Wedel, H., and Wilhelmsen, L. (1993), Stressful life events, social support, and mortality in men born in 1933. *BMJ* 307, 1102–5.

Ross, N. A., Wolfson, M. C., Dunn, J. R., Berthelot, J. M., Kaplan, G. A., and

Lynch, J. W. (2000), Relation between income inequality and mortality in Canada and in the United States: cross sectional assessment using census data and vital statistics. *BMJ* 320, 898–902.

Sacker, A., Bartley, M., Firth, D., and Fitzpatrick, R., (2000*a*), Social inequalities in the health of women in England: occupational, material and behavioural pathways. *Soc Sci Med* 52, 763–81.

Sacker, A., Firth, D., Fitzpatrick, R., Lynch, K., and Bartley, M. (2000*b*), Comparing health inequality in men and women: prospective study of mortality, 1986–1996. *BMJ* 320, 1303–7.

Schnall, P. L., Landsbergis, P. A., and Baker, D. (1994), Job strain and cardiovascular-disease. *Annu Rev Public Health* 15, 381–411.

Schnall, P. L., Pieper, C., Schwartz, J. E., Karasek, R. A., Schlussel, Y., and Devereux, R. B. (1990), The relationship between job strain, workplace diastolic blood-pressure, and left-ventricular mass index: results of a case-control study. *JAMA* 263, 1929–35.

Schnall, P. L., Schwartz, J. E., Landsbergis, P. A., Warren, K., and Pickering, T. G. (1998), A longitudinal study of job strain and ambulatory blood pressure: results from a three-year follow-up. *Psychosom Med* 60, 697–706.

Sen, A. (1992), *Inequality Explained*. Cambridge, Mass.: Harvard University Press.

Senior, P. A., and Bhopal, R. (1994), Ethnicity as a variable in epidemiological research. *BMJ* 309, 327–30.

Senn, S. (1998), Mortality and distribution of income. *BMJ* 316, 1611–12.

Shatenstein, B., and Ghadirian, P. (1998), Influences on diet, health behaviours and their outcome in select ethnocultural and religious groups. *Nutrition* 14, 223–30.

Shewry, M. C., Smith, W. C. S., Woodward, M., and Tunstallpedoe, H. (1992), Variation in coronary risk-factors by social-status: results from the Scottish Heart Health Study. *Br J Gen Pract* 42, 406–10.

Shively, C. A., Clarkson, T. B., and Kaplan, J. R. (1989), Social deprivation and coronary artery atherosclerosis in the female cynomolgus monkey. *Atherosclerosis* 77, 69–76.

Siegrist, J. (n.d.), Stressful work, self-experience and cardiovascular disease prevention. Institute of Medical Sociology, University of Düsseldorf. TS.

Siegrist, J. (1995), Emotions and health in occupational life: new scientific findings and policy implications. *Patient Educ Couns* 25, 227–36.

Siegrist, J. (1998), Reciprocity in basic social exchange and health: can we reconcile person-based with population-based psychosomatic research? *J Psychosom Res* 45, 99–105.

Siegrist, J. (2000), Place, social exchange and health: proposed sociological framework. *Soc Sci Med* 51, 1283–93.

Siegrist, J., and Peter, R. (1996), Threat to occupational status control and cardiovascular risk. *Isr J Med Sci* 32, 179–84.

Siegrist, J., Peter, R., Junge, A., Cremer, P., and Seidel, D. (1990), Low status control, high effort at work and ischemic heart disease: prospective evidence from blue-collar men. *Soc Sci Med* 31, 1127–34.

Siegrist, J., Peter, R., Motz, W., and Strauer, B. E. (1992), The role of hypertension, left ventricular hypertrophy and psycho-social risks in cardiovascular disease: prospective evidence from blue-collar men. *Eur Heart J* 13 (Suppl. D), 89–95.

Siegrist, J., Klein, D., and Voigt, K. H. (1997), Linking sociological with physiological data: the model of effort-reward imbalance at work. *Acta Physiol Scand* 161, 112–16.

Simon, P. A., Hu, D. J., Diaz, T., and Kerndt, P. R. (1995), Income and AIDS rates in Los Angeles county. *AIDS* 9, 281–4.

Sloggett, A., and Joshi, H. (1998), Deprivation indicators as predictors of life events 1981–1992 based on the UK ONS longitudinal study. *J Epidemiol Community Health* 52, 228–33.

Smaje, C. (1995), *Health, 'Race' and Ethnicity*. London: Kings Fund Institute.

Stansfeld, S., Feeney, A., Head, J., Canner., R., North, F., and Marmot, M. (1995), Sickness absence for psychiatric illness: the Whitehall II Study. *Soc Sci Med* 40, 189–97.

Stansfeld, S. A., Fuhrer, R., and Shipley, M. J. (1998), Types of social support as predictors of psychiatric morbidity in a cohort of British Civil Servants (Whitehall II study). *Psychol Med* 28, 881–92.

Steptoe, A. (2000), Stress, social support and cardiovascular activity over the working day. *Int J Psychophysiol* 37, 299–308.

Steptoe, A., and Willemsen, G. (2002), Psychophysiological responsivity in coronary heart disease. In S. Stansfeld and M. Marmot (eds), *Stress and the Heart*, 168–80. London: BMJ Books.

Steptoe, A., Roy, M. P., Evans, O., and Snashall, D. (1995), Cardiovascular stress reactivity and job strain as determinants of ambulatory blood pressure at work. *J Hypertens* 13, 201–10.

Stewart, A., Prandy, K., and Blackburn, R. M. (1973), Measuring the class structure. *Nature* 245, 415–17.

Stewart, A., Prandy, K., and Blackburn, R. M. (1980), The measurement of stratification. In A. Stewart, K. Prandy, and R. M. Blackburn (eds), *Social Stratification and Occupations*, 17–70. London: Macmillan.

Stockwell, E. G., Goza, F. W., Jiang, Y., and Luse, V. O. (1994), Trends in the relationship between socioeconomic-status and infant-mortality in metropolitan Ohio, 1960–1990. *Popul Res Policy Rev* 13, 399–410.

Stockwell, E. G., Goza, F. W., and Roach, J. L. (1995), The relationship between socioeconomic-status and infant-mortality in a metropolitan aggregate, 1989–1991. *Sociological Forum* 10, 297–308.

Stockwell, E. G., Goza, F. W., and Luse, V. O. (1997), Infectious disease mortality among adults by race and socioeconomic status: Metropolitan Ohio, 1989–1991. *Soc Biol* 44, 148–52.

Stronks, K., van de Mheen, H., Looman, C. W. N., and Mackenbach, J. P. (1997), Cultural, material, and psychosocial correlates of the socioeconomic gradient in smoking behavior among adults. *Prev Med* 26, 754–66.

Sundquist, J., Bajekal, M., Jarman, B., and Johansson, S. E. (1996), Underprivileged area score, ethnicity, social-factors and general mortality in district health authorities in England and Wales. *Scand J Prim Health Care* 14, 79–85.

Theorell, T. (2000), Working conditions and health. In L. F. Berkman and I. Kawachi (eds), *Social Epidemiology*, 118–36. Oxford: Oxford University Press.

Theorell, T., Tsutsumi, A., Hallquist, J., Reuterwall, C., Hogstedt, C., Fredlund, P., Emlund, N., Johnson, J. V., and the SHEEP Study Group (1998), Decision latitude, job strain and myocardial infarction: a study of working men in Stockholm. *Am J Public Health* 88, 382–8.

Townsend, P., Davidson, N., and Whitehead, M. (1986), *The Black Report and the Health Divide*. Harmondsworth: Penguin.

Tunstall Pedoe, H., Woodward, M., Tavendale, R., A'Brook, R., and McCluskey, M. K. (1997), Comparison of the prediction by 27 different factors of coronary heart disease and death in men and women of the Scottish Heart Health Study: cohort study. *BMJ* 315, 722–9.

Tylor, E. B. (1871), *Primitive Culture*. London: Murray.

Tyroler, H. A. (1989), Socioeconomic status in the epidemiology and treatment of hypertension. *Hypertension* 13, 194–7.

US Department of Health and Human Services (2002), *Health, United States, 2002*. Washington, DC: USDoHH.

Vagero, D., Koupilova, I., Leon, D. A., and Lithell, U. B. (1999), Social determinants of birthweight, ponderal index and gestational age in Sweden in the 1920s and the 1980s. *Acta Paediatr* 88, 445–53.

Vahtera, J., Kivimaki, M., Pentti, J., and Theorell, T. (2000), Effect of change in the psychosocial work environment on sickness absence: a seven year follow up of initially healthy employees. *J Epidemiol Community Health* 54, 484–93.

van de Mheen, H. (1998), Is There Indirect Selection? Determinants of Intergenerational Social Mobility: Findings from the Dutch GLOBE Study. Ph.D. thesis, Erasmus University, Rotterdam.

van de Mheen, H., Stronks, K., van den Bos, J., and Mackenbach, J. P. (1997), The contribution of childhood environment to the explanation of socioeconomic inequalities in health in adult life: a retrospective study. *Soc Sci Med* 44, 13–24.

van de Mheen, H., Stronks, K., Looman, C. W., and Mackenbach, J. P. (1998), Does childhood socioeconomic status influence adult health through behavioural factors? *Int J Epidemiol* 27, 431–7.

van de Mheen, H., Stronks, K., Looman, C. W. N., and Mackenbach, J. P. (1998), Role of childhood health in the explanation of socioeconomic inequalities in early adult health. *J Epidemiol Community Health* 52, 15–19.

Vartiainen, E., Pekkanen., J., Koskinen, S., Jousilhati, P., Salomaa, V., and Puska, P. (1998), Do changes in cardiovascular risk factors explain the increasing economic difference in mortality from ischaemic heart disease in Finland? *J Epidemiol Community Health* 52, 416–19.

Verbrugge, L. M. (1976), Females and illness: recent trends in sex differences in the United States. *J Health Soc Behav* 17, 387–403.

Verbrugge, L. M. (1980a), Sex differences in complaints and diagnoses. *J Behav Med* 3, 327–55.

Verbrugge, L. M. (1980b), Recent trends in sex mortality differentials in the United States. *Women's Health* 5, 17–37.

Verbrugge, L. M. (1985), Gender and health: an update on hypotheses and evidence. *J Health Soc Behav* 26, 156–82.

Verbrugge, L. M., and Wingard, D. L. (1987), Sex differentials in health and mortality. *Women's Health* 12, 103-45.

Vrijkotte, T. G. M., van Doornen, L. J. P., and De Geus, E. J. C. (1999), Work stress and metabolic and hemostatic risk factors. *Psychosom Med* 61, 796–805.

Wadsworth, M. E. J. (1986), Serious illness in childhood and its association with later life achievements. In R. G. Wilkinson (ed.), *Class and Health*, 50–74. London: Tavistock.

Wadsworth, M. E. J. (1991), *The Imprint of Time*. Oxford: Oxford University Press.

Wadsworth, M. E. J. (1997), Health inequalities in a life course perspective. *Soc Sci Med* 44, 859–70.

Wagstaff, A., and van Doorslaer, E. (2000), Income inequality and health: what does the literature tell us? *Annu Rev Public Health* 21, 543–67.

Waldron, I. (1976), Why do women live longer than men? *Soc Sci Med* 10, 349–62.

Waldron, I. (2000), Trends in gender differences in mortality: relationships to changing gender differences in behaviour and other causal factors. In E. Annandale and K. Hunt (eds), *Gender Inequalities in Health*, 151–81. Buckingham: Open University Press.

Wamala, S. P., Murray, M. A., Horsten, M., Eriksson, M., Schenck Gustafsson, K., Hamsten, A., Silveira, A., and Orth Gomer, K. (1999), Socioeconomic status and determinants of hemostatic function in healthy women. *Arterioscler Thromb Vasc Biol* 19, 485–92.

Wannamethee, G., and Shaper, A. G. (1994), The association between heart rate and blood pressure, blood lipids and other cardiovascular risk factors. *J Cardiovasc Risk* 1, 223–30.

Wannamethee, G., and Shaper, A. G. (1997), Socioeconomic status within social class and mortality: a prospective study in middle-aged British men. *Int J Epidemiol* 26, 532–41.

Warren, J. R., Sheridan, J. T., and Hauser, R. M. (1998), Choosing a measure of occupational standing: how useful are composite measures in analyses of gender inequality in occupational attainment? *Sociological Methods and Research* 27, 3–76.

Wild, S., and McKeigue, P. (1997), Cross sectional analysis of mortality by country of birth in England and Wales. *BMJ* 314, 705.

Wilkinson, R. G. (1986), Income and mortality. In R. G. Wilkinson (ed.), *Class and Health: Research and Longitudinal Data*. London: Tavistock.

Wilkinson, R. G. (1992*a*), National mortality-rates: the impact of inequality. *Am J Public Health* 82, 1082–4.

Wilkinson, R. G. (1992*b*), For debate: income-distribution and life expectancy. *BMJ* 304, 165–8.

Wilkinson, R. G. (1996), *Unhealthy Societies: The Afflictions of Inequality*. London: Routledge.

Williams, D. R. (1996), Race/ethnicity and socioeconomic-status: measurement and methodological issues. *Int J Health Serv* 26, 483–505.

Williams, D. R. (1997), Race and health: basic questions, emerging directions. *Ann Epidemiol* 7, 322–33.

Williams, F. L., and Lloyd, O. (1991), Trends in lung cancer mortality in Scotland and their relation to cigarette smoking and social class. *Scott Med J* 36, 175–8.

Wilson, T. W., Kaplan, G. A., Kauhanen, J., Cohen, R. D., Wu, M., Salonen, R., and Salonen, J. T. (1993), Association between plasma fibrinogen concentration and five socioeconomic indices in the Kuopio ischemic heart disease risk factor study. *Am J Epidemiol* 137, 292–300.

Wingard, D. L. (1984), The sex differential in morbidity, mortality, and lifestyle. *Annu Rev Public Health* 5, 433–58.

Winkleby, M. A. (1997), Accelerating cardiovascular risk factor change in ethnic minority and low socioeconomic groups. *Annals of Epidemiology* 7, 96–103.

Wolfson, M., Rowe, G., Gentleman, J. F., and Tomiak, M. (1993), Career earnings and death: a longitudinal analysis of older Canadian men. *J Gerontol* 48, 167–79.

Wolfson, M., Kaplan, G., Lynch, J., Ross, N., and Backlund, E. (1999), Relative income inequality and mortality: empirical demonstration. *BMJ* 319, 953–7.

Wong, M. D., Shapiro, M. F., Boscardin, W. J., and Ettner, S. L. (2002), Contribution of major diseases to disparities in mortality. *N Engl J Med* 347, 1585–92.

Woodward, M., Shewry, M. C., Smith, W. C. S., and Tunstall-Pedoe, H. (1992), Social status and coronary heart disease: results from the Scottish Heart Health Study. *Preventive Medicine* 21, 136–48.

World Health Organization (2001), *World Health Chart, 2001*. Geneva: WHO.

Wright, E. O. (1985), *Classes*. London: Verso.

Wright, E. O. (1997), *Class Counts*. Cambridge: Cambridge University Press.

Index

absolute difference 40
absolute risk 40–1
accidents 94, 95, 103, 112, 146, 166
Acheson Report (1998) 169, 175, 176
addiction 80
adjustment 47, 48, 50–2, 57
African-Americans 154–5, 156, 159,
    161, 162
Africans, migration patterns and
    health equality 152, 157, 158, 161
age factor 4–7, 46
AIDS 91, 93
alcohol 20, 75–6, 112, 141, 146, 163
Annandale, E. 135
Arber, S. 135, 144–5, 147
asbestosis 95
assets *see* income and wealth
asthma 95
Australia 1, 126, 172

behaviour 18, 78, 163, 165
    see also cultural-behavioural model;
    psycho-social model
Belgium 126
Ben-Shlomo, Y. 116
Berney, L. R. 96, 105
birth cohort studies 13–14, 105, 106,
    115
Black Report 1, 2–4, 8–10, 13, 14, 15,
    64, 65, 66, 68, 90, 91, 101

Blackburn, R. M. 30, 34
Blane, D. B. 96, 105, 115
Blaxter, M. 69–70, 71, 72
blood pressure 76, 81, 82–3, 84, 87,
    88, 95
Bosma, H. 113
Bourdieu, P. 69, 70, 72–3, 126
Boyd-Orr cohort study 105, 115
breast cancer 11, 105, 145, 155, 156,
    160
Breen, R. 22
bronchitis 4, 94, 95, 166
Brown, G. 133
Bynner, J. 105

calories, regression models of
    relationship to weight 53–7
Cambridge scale 30–1, 34, 72, 73
Cameron, D. 20
Canada 1, 90, 91, 116, 121, 130
cancer 4, 95, 140, 155, 160, 165, 166
    see also breast cancer; lung cancer
car ownership 91, 125, 129, 144
Caribbean immigrants 152, 157, 158,
    159, 160, 161
caste system 29, 33, 73, 159
census data 5–6, 23, 27, 39, 91, 149,
    150–1, 157
Chandola, T. 73, 162
cholesterol 83, 95

climate 14
clinical methods 37, 165–9
Coburn, D. 127, 128, 133
Cochrane Centre 169
Cochrane Collaboration 168
coefficient of variation 118–19
colonialism 152
comfort behaviour 20, 34, 71
community level policies 172, 174
'confounding' 37–8, 48, 58, 112
  smoking as example of 50–2
Cooper, H. 135
coping skills 38, 66, 111
coronary disease *see* heart disease
cultural-behavioural model 9, 10, 16,
    17, 33, 64–77, 95, 111, 117
  cultural explanations 68–76, 80
  'direct' behavioural explanations
    65–8
  and gender differences in health
    141–2, 146
  psychological factors 66–8, 70–2,
    73, 80, 126
  social ecology 123–4, 126–7
  social policy responses 171–4
culture 149, 151, 169
  see also cultural-behavioural
    model
Cushing's syndrome 82

Daly, M. C. 121, 129–30
Darwinian natural selection 9
Davey Smith, G. 115, 128, 133
Davidson, N. 64
death rates *see* mortality rates
Deaton, A. 122
Denmark 129
denominators 38–9
Department of Health and Social
    Security *see* Black Report
depression 47–8, 82, 133, 143
diabetes 4, 155, 161
diet 34
  cultural-behavioural model 9, 64,
    65, 70, 72, 73, 74, 75–6
  and ethnicity 163

and gender 146
materialist model 92, 94, 99
social ecology 129
and social policy 165, 169–70,
    172–4
direct selection 9, 111
direct standardization 42–6, 48, 157
diseases of affluence 3
Dressler, W. W. 154–5
drugs 20

Eastern Europe 153
economic policy 17, 102, 115, 133–4,
    169
education
  cultural-behavioural model 70–1,
    73–4, 76
  and ethnicity 155, 162, 163
  life-course model 105, 111, 114
  as measure of health inequality 6
  as measure of socio-economic
    position 23, 29–30
  neo-materialist model 117
  research methods 36–7
  social ecology 123, 128, 132, 133,
    134
  and social policy 172, 176–7
effort-reward imbalance (ERI) 79,
    88–9, 141
emphysema 95
employment relations and conditions
    17, 19
  and gender difference in health 141,
    144, 146–7
  psycho-social model 12–13, 79, 83,
    86–9, 123
  social ecology 131
  and social policy 175, 176, 177
  and social position 24–8, 33, 34
  see also occupation; unemployment
Emslie, C. 139
environment
  and ethnicity 161, 162, 163
  material model 92, 94, 95, 96, 123
  research methods 41
  and social policy 168, 175

Erasmus University, Rotterdam
    112–13, 169–71, 172
ERI *see* effort-reward imbalance
Erikson-Goldthorpe class schema
    26–7, 31, 32, 33, 88, 89
ethnicity 6, 33, 39, 149–63
    biology and health 153–5
    definitions 149–53
    explanations for differences in
        health 162–3
    mortality risks 155–60
    research methods 39
    social ecology 161–2
    socio-economic conditions 160–1
exercise
    cultural-behavioural model 9, 33,
        64, 65, 69, 70
    materialist and neo-materialist
        model 15, 99
    and social policy 172

family, traditional 173–4
Fassin, D. 69
Ferri, E. 105
Finland
    cultural-behavioural model 75
    gender 144–6, 146–7
    health inequality 79
    life-course model 112, 113
    social ecology 126
    social policy 171, 172, 173
Fiscella, K. 122
Fox, J. 105
France 75, 101, 126, 169–70
Franks, P. 122
friendship, as measure of social status
    30–1, 72, 73

gender 135–48
    cultural-behavioural model 65
    differences in health 136–40
    differences in health inequality
        143–7
    explanations of differences in health
        141–3
    and social policy 173–4

statistical research methods 36–7,
    47–8
gender role modernization hypothesis
    142, 146
General Health Questionnaire (GHQ)
    137–8
genetics
    and ethnicity 153–5
    explanations of health inequality
        10–12
geopolitical units
    cultural-behavioural model 74–6
    and gender inequalities in health
        144–5, 146–7
    life-course model 105–6
    materialist and neo-materialist
        model 14–15, 90–1, 101
    measures in official statistics 1, 6;
        see also mortality rates
    psycho-social model 13
    social policy 169–71
    see also social ecology
Gini coefficient 118, 127
Goldblatt, P. O. 144
Goldthorpe, J. H. 25–6, 96
    Erikson-Goldthorpe class schema
        26–7, 31, 32, 33, 88, 89
Graham, H. 114–15, 171
Greece 15, 75, 76, 101, 167
growth models 59

habitus 69, 70, 72, 123
Harding, S. 157–8, 160
Harris, T. 133
health disparity 6, 156
health education 169, 172
health gradient 33, 79, 87, 91, 97–8,
    99, 103, 125, 132, 166–7
health inequality 1–21
    explanations 8–18, 165
    identity and 18–21
    research methods 35–63
    size of social differences in health 2–7
    statistical models 46–57
health services 8, 14–15, 117, 162,
    164–5

social ecology 123, 128, 130, 131, 134
Health Survey for England (1998) 65, 138, 139, 140
heart disease 3–4, 79
  cultural-behavioural model 75, 76
  and ethnicity 155, 156, 157, 158
  and gender 136, 139, 140, 141, 142, 145–6, 147
  materialist model 93, 95
  psycho-social model 82, 83, 84, 85, 86, 87
  research methods 40, 42
  and social policy 165, 166
Hindu culture 29, 73
Hispanic people 149, 156, 159, 160
HIV 93
Holocaust 10
Holtzman, N. A. 11
homicide 75, 155, 156
housing
  and gender 144
  life-course model 114
  materialist and neo-materialist model 15, 91, 92, 94, 96, 99, 100, 102, 117, 123
  research methods 58
  social ecology 123, 128–9, 131
  and social policy 175, 177
human capital 111
Hunt, K. 135, 139

identity 18–21
income and wealth 8, 17, 19
  cultural-behavioural model 9, 65, 68, 69
  and ethnicity 163
  and gender differences in health 141
  materialist and neo-materialist model 9, 90–102 *passim*
  as measure of socio-economic position 23–30 *passim*, 33
  psycho-social model 13, 79, 83–4
  research methods 36–7, 39
  social ecology 116–34

and social policy 169, 170, 171, 175, 177
India 116
indirect selection 9–10, 14, 104, 111–13
indirect standardization *see* SMRs
industrial capitalism 152
infectious diseases 8, 48, 49, 93–4
influenza 4
intelligence 38, 47, 66, 111
international comparative research 74–6, 144–5, 146–7, 169–71
Ireland 74
  health inequality of people originating in 152, 157, 158, 160, 162
Italy, Italians 15, 74, 75, 101, 153, 169–70

Japan 76, 153, 173
job strain 86–8
Jones, I. G. 20
Judge, K. 122, 127

Kaplan, G. A. 13, 66, 121, 124, 128
Karasek, R. 86
Kawachi, I. 13, 121, 124, 133
Kennedy, B. P. 121
Kluckhohn, C. 69
Krieger, N. 160
Kroeber, A. L. 69
Kunst, A. E. 74, 169, 170

Ladwig, K. H. 135
Lahelma, E. 135, 144–5, 147
Lancet 169
life chances concept 96, 97
life course, life-course model 13–14, 16, 17, 19–21, 73, 96, 97, 103–15, 117
  analytical methods 107–11
  and ethnicity 154
  information sources 105–6
  research approaches 104–5
  risk accumulation 103, 104, 113, 114–15

life course, life-course model (cont'd)
  selection 111–13
  and social policy 165, 171, 172,
    175, 177
life-course political economy 15, 17,
  115, 130–3, 163
life expectancy
  and ethnicity 156
  and gender 136, 143
  neo-materialist model 101
  social ecology 116, 118, 120–2, 130,
    131
  social gradient 79, 97, 99
  see also mortality rates
life-grids 105
lifestyle *see* cultural-behavioural model
linear regression 53–6, 58, 107
linked method 39
locus of control 66–8, 111
logistic models *see* odds ratio
logistic regression 56–7, 58, 107
Longitudinal Study of England and
  Wales 39
lung cancer 40
  and ethnicity 155, 156, 157, 158,
    160
  and gender 136, 142, 145–6
  life-course model 103
  materialist model 93, 94
  and social policy 166
lung disease 4, 75, 94, 95, 166
Lynch, J. W. 66, 79, 113, 116, 121,
  122, 124, 127, 128, 133, 134

Macintyre, S. 135, 139
McIsaac, S. J. 116
Mackenbach, J. P. 74, 101, 113, 169
McKeown, T. 14
Manor, O. 105
Manson, J. E. 135
Marmot, M. 116
Marshall 96
Martikainen, P. 76, 147
Marx, Karl 24
materialist model 9, 12, 16, 17, 68,
  90–100

cost of health 98–100
  and ethnicity 154, 162
  and gender differences in health
    142–3, 147
  measurement of risk 92–6
  social ecology 123, 124, 126,
    127–30, 133
  social gradient 97–8
  social policy responses 174–7
  see also neo-materialist model
Maxwell, R. 157–8
Mediterranean lifestyle 15, 74, 75,
  169–70, 172–4
men 2–7, 97, 131–2
  see also gender
mental health 133
mesothelioma 95
middle class 75
migration 152, 157–62, 163, 171
minimum wage 69
Montgomery, S. 96
Morris, J. N. 90, 99–100, 102, 129
  see also Black Report
mortality rates 1, 2–7
  cultural shift 74–6
  and ethnicity 155–60
  and gender 140, 144
  health behaviour 78
  material risk 92–6
  research methods 38–9, 41–6, 59–63
Moser, K. A. 143–4
mumps 104
Muntaner, C. 133, 134

Nathanson, C. A. 141
National Statistics Socio-Economic
  Classification (NS-SEC) 27–8, 32,
    33, 72, 88, 89, 146
Nature 30
Nazroo, J. Y. 154, 160–1
neo-materialist model 14–15, 101–2,
  117
  and gender 143
  social ecology 123, 127–30, 132,
    133, 134
  social policy responses 174–7

Netherlands
  health inequality research 68,
    105–6, 112–13, 165, 169–71,
    172
  religion and ethnicity 153
  social policy 172, 175, 176
neural tube defects 132–3
NHS 8, 14, 164
Nordic nations
  cultural-behavioural model 74, 75
  life-course model 105–6, 113
  neo-materialist model 101
  research methods 39
  social policy 165, 169–70, 171, 172,
    174
  see also Denmark; Finland; Sweden
Northern Ireland, ethnicity 150–1,
    160
Norway 74, 75, 172
NS-SEC *see* National Statistics Socio-
    Economic Classification
numerators 38–9

occupation
  cultural-behavioural model 72, 76,
    78
  and ethnicity 152, 153, 155
  and gender 135, 137, 139, 140,
    141–3, 144–5, 146, 147
  life-course model 105, 114
  materialist model and neo-
    materialist model 92, 94, 95, 96,
    101–2, 126
  as measure of socio-economic
    position 1, 5, 23–33 *passim*
  psycho-social model 12–13, 89
  research methods 36–7, 39
  social ecology 131
  and social policy 173–4, 175–6
  see also employment relations;
    unemployment
odds ratio (OR) 40–1, 47–8, 49, 51–2,
    53, 57
  life-course model 108–10
OECD 121
Osler, M. 66

Panel Study of Income Dynamics 39,
    106
Passannante, N. R. 141
path models 59
pathways approach 57–9, 104–5, 134
pensions 14
Perry/High-Scope studies 176–7
Peter, R. 88
pneumoconiosis 95
pneumonia 4, 166
political economy explanation 16
  see also life-course political
    economy
Portugal 74
power 19, 97–8, 146–7, 162, 173
Power, C. 105
Prandy, K. 30, 34
prestige *see* social status
prevention 15, 165
psycho-social model 12–13, 16, 17, 18,
    78–89, 95, 117
  and ethnicity 154
  fight or flight response 80–3, 85, 86
  and gender differences in health
    141, 146–7
  social ecology 123–6, 127–8, 130,
    131, 133–4
  social policy responses 174
  social support as factor 79, 85–6
  work hazards as factor 79, 86–9
psychology
  as confounder 38
  cultural-behavioural model 66–8,
    70–2, 73, 80, 126
  and gender 137–8
  life-course model 111, 112–13
  and social policy 177
  see also psycho-social model
public health 8, 40
public services
  and ethnicity 163
  neo-materialist model 14, 101–2,
    117
  social ecology 123, 128, 130, 134
public transport 15, 123, 129, 134,
    162

qualitative methods 37

race 6, 149
racism 162
Rahkonen, O. 144–5, 147
randomized clinical trials 165–8
Registrar-General's Social Classes
  (RGSC) 2–3, 5, 6, 31–2, 42
regression models 53–7
relative deprivation 100, 133, 177
  psycho-social model 79, 83–4, 128
relative difference 40
relative risk 40–1
religion, and ethnicity 149, 151, 153,
  159, 160
RGSC *see* Registrar-General's Social
  Classes
Rosato, M. 160
Rottman, D. 22
Russia 127

Sacker, A. 73
Salonen, J. T. 66
Sanitary Reports 8
Sanskritisation 73
Scottish people, migration patterns
  and health inequality 157, 158,
  160
Second World War 10
selection 9–10, 12, 68, 111–13, 126,
  171
Sen, A. 100
Senn, S. 122
Shepherd, P. 105
Siegrist, J. 71, 80, 88–9, 174
Singh-Manoux, A. 69, 73
single parents 171, 173
slavery 152
smoking 9, 20, 79
  cultural-behavioural model 9, 33,
    64, 65, 69–70, 72, 75, 76
  and ethnicity 163
  and gender 141–2, 146
  life-course model 114–15
  materialist model 93
  research methodology 50–2, 57–8

social ecology 127
  and social policy 165, 167, 169,
    170, 172, 174
  and social position 33, 34
SMRs 2–3, 4, 41–6, 48, 157
  calculation example 59–63
social capital 72, 124, 134
social class 78–9, 117
  cultural-behavioural model 9, 64–5,
    66–7, 72, 75
  ethnicity 155, 157–8, 160, 162,
    163
  and gender 135, 137–8, 144, 145,
    146, 147
  life-course model 107–11
  materialist model 90, 91, 92, 93, 96,
    97
  as measurement of social position
    22, 23, 24–8, 31–2, 33
  psycho-social model 83–4, 88, 89
  relationship to mortality risk 1, 2–7
  research methodology 42–7, 50–2,
    57
  social ecology 118
  and social policy 167, 172, 177
social ecology 116–34
  controversies about income
    distribution and health 119–22
  and ethnicity 161–2
  explanations for relation of income
    distribution to population health
    122–30
  life-course political economy of
    health 130–3
  policy implications 133–4
  relation of income distribution to
    population health 117–19
social gradient *see* health gradient
social inclusion/exclusion 20, 98, 99,
  100
social norms and values 17, 69, 71,
  76, 173
social policy 17, 102, 115, 133–4,
  164–78
  international comparative studies
    169–71

possibility of trials of options
165–9
responses based on cultural-
behavioural model 69, 171–4
responses based on materialist and
neo-materialist model 174–7
responses based on psycho-social
model 174
social security *see* welfare benefits
social status 17, 19, 117
cultural-behavioural model 65,
72–4, 75, 76, 123, 126
and gender 144, 145, 147
life-course model 104, 115
materialist model 96
as measurement of socio-economic
position 22, 23, 28–31, 32, 33–4
psycho-social model 12, 13, 83–4,
89, 123
social ecology 118, 123, 126
and social policy 177
social support 79, 85–6, 92–3
socio-economic position 17, 22–34
cultural-behavioural model 64–5,
72–5, 76, 80
and ethnicity 160–1, 162–3
and gender 135, 136–40
life-course model 104, 114–15
psycho-social model 79–80, 83–4,
174
research methods 57–9
and social policy 174, 177
see also income and wealth; social
class; social status
South Asians, migration patterns and
health inequality 152, 157, 158,
159, 160, 161, 162
Spain 15, 75, 76, 167, 169–70
'spuriousness' 37–8, 48, 112
standardization 41–6, 48
Standardized Mortality Ratios *see*
SMRs
statistical explanation 36–7
statistical methods 35–63
absolute/relative 39–41
analysing pathways 57–9

basic concepts 35–8
calculation example of SMR 59–63
life-course model 107–11
models 46–57
numerators/denominators 38–9
standardization 41–6
Stewart, A. 30, 34
stress
cultural-behavioural model 126
and gender 135, 141, 146
materialist model 92–3
psycho-social model 12, 13, 80–4,
85, 117, 124
stroke 88, 166
Stronks, K. 68
suicide 166
Sweden
cultural-behavioural model 74, 75,
76
neo-materialist model 101
social ecology approach 126, 129
social policy 169, 170, 171, 172,
173, 175
Switzerland 75, 101, 126, 153

TB 4, 14
Theorell, T. 87
Townsend, P. 64, 90, 91
see also Black Report
triglycerides 83
Tylor, E. B. 69
typhus 14

ulcers 4
understanding (*verstehen*) 36
unemployment 101, 132–3, 162
United Kingdom
cultural-behavioural model 75, 76
ethnicity 149–51, 152, 153, 156–61,
162
gender inequality in health 136,
137–40, 144–5, 146–7
health inequality 1, 2–7, 8–10, 13,
14, 78–9
life-course model 13, 105, 106,
115

United Kingdom (cont'd)
materialist and neo-materialist
model 14, 90, 91, 93, 94, 97,
101
measurement of socio-economic
position 23, 27–8
research methods 39
social ecology 116, 126, 129, 130,
131
social policy 164, 165, 167, 168–9,
170, 171, 172, 173, 175, 176
United States
cultural-behavioural model 74, 75
ethnicity 149, 153, 154–6, 160, 161,
162
gender inequality in health 136,
140, 142, 146
life-course model 106
materialist model 90, 91
measurement of health inequality
6
measurement of socio-economic
status 1, 29–30
social ecology 116, 121, 126, 129
social policy 165, 167, 170, 171,
172, 173, 174, 176–7
unlinked method 39
unobserved heterogeneity 112

Van de Mheen, H. D. 105, 112,
113
verstehen (understanding) 36

Wadsworth, M. E. J. 105
Waldron, I. 142
Weber, M. 24, 25, 36, 96
weight, regression models of
relationship to calories 53–7
welfare benefits 14, 15, 69, 101, 115,
117, 132–3, 168, 170, 174, 175
Welsh 153
White, I. R. 116
Whitehall Studies 78, 87, 90
Whitehead, M. 64
Wilkinson, R. G. 13, 116, 117, 121,
124, 125, 133, 171
Williams, D. 154
Wingard, D. L. 141
Wolfson, M. 116, 121
women
cultural-behavioural model 65
genetic explanations of health
inequality 11
health inequality 5, 33, 97
life-course model 105
role in identity maintenance 19
social ecology 131, 132–3
social policy 173–4
socio-economic position 5, 33, 97
see also gender
Woodward, M. 66
World Health Organization 42, 126
Wright, E. O. 96, 97
class schema 24–5, 26, 27, 28, 31,
32, 33, 88, 146

4-29-04